Noël 1982
de Louis.

Also by Thomas C. Renner

MAFIA PRINCESS (with Antoinette Giancana)
MY LIFE IN THE MAFIA (with Vincent Teresa)
VINCENT TERESA'S MAFIA (with Vincent Teresa)
WALL STREET SWINDLER (with Michael Hellerman)

CECIL KIRBY and THOMAS C. RENNER

MAFIA ASSASSIN

The Inside Story
of a Canadian
Biker, Hitman,
and Police Informer

 METHUEN

Toronto New York London Sydney Auckland

Canadian Cataloguing in Publication Data

Kirby, Cecil.
  Mafia assassin

Includes index.
ISBN 0-458-80440-1

1. Kirby, Cecil. 2. Crime and criminals—
Canada—Biography. 3. Mafia—Canada.
4. Organized crime—Canada. 5. Motorcycle
gangs—Canada. I. Renner, Thomas C.
II. Title.

HV6248.K57A3 1986   364.1
  C86-094188-4

Printed and bound in Canada

1 2 3 4 86 90 89 88 87

To Mark, Ted, and Lyle, who did so much.
C.K.

To my wife, Nancy, and to my daughters,
Elaine, Dawn, Sandra, and Jacqueline,
without whose understanding and
support this book would never have been
possible.
T. C. R.

CONTENTS

FOREWORD

To former Ontario Attorney General Roy McMurtry, contract killer Cecil Kirby represented "the first real breakthrough in penetrating the conspiracy of silence" that shrouds the Calabrian Mafia and other organized crime groups.

To veteran FBI agent John Schiman, Kirby was the "best double agent I have met in my ten years as an FBI agent. He is sauve, self-assured, and knows how to handle underworld figures."

And to the leadership of the Calabrian Mafia in Italy, Canada, and the United States, Kirby remains a dangerous threat, so dangerous that this secret society's killers have been promised $100,000 if they can find and kill the protected Kirby.

Today Kirby is one of the most sought-after witnesses since Vincent Teresa and Jimmy (The Last Mafioso) Fratianno. He lives under a controversial immunity agreement that protects him from prosecution for former crimes to which he has admitted, including murder. And he is judiciously protected by police in Canada and the United States.

The Canadian government wanted him because he exposed, for the first time, the inner structure of the Calabrian Mafia, a crime organization that operates in Ontario, Quebec, and British Columbia and engages in crimes ranging from extortion and bribery to murder and the smuggling of heroin and other narcotics. His testimony was destined to put more than twenty men in prison, including three Calabrian Mafia crime bosses.

The FBI wanted him because he held the key to unravelling the secrets of the Calabrian Mafia in the United States, where it spans New York, Connecticut, and New Jersey and has connections as far west as California. The key that Kirby held was his testimony in a bizarre murder plot in which he was hired by Calabrian mafiosi in Toronto to murder the girlfriend of a mafioso in Connecticut.

But Cecil Kirby is far more important than being instrumental in so many trials, indictments, and convictions. Kirby is not just another Mafia witness who has broken the code of silence. He is also the only member of a violent motorcycle gang, Satan's

Choice, to have actually become the chief enforcer for a Mafia-type crime family and the first high-ranking member to directly link the crimes of the Calabrian Mafia with those of the motor-cycle bandits.

Cecil Kirby is the most disarming professional criminal I have ever met — and I have met hundreds during my thirty-two years as a journalist-author, twenty-five of them as an investigative reporter of organized crime. He is also one of the first criminals to break with Canadian organized crime's code of silence and provide evidence that has resulted in the jailing of Calabrian Mafia bosses.

Curly, reddish-blond hair frames an impish, almost boyish face that often breaks into an infectious smile. Sky-blue eyes twinkle with devilish delight as he engages interviewers in word duels, smiling broadly when he knows he has disarmed or shocked them. Yet the infectious smile and musical laugh can change suddenly to a deadly scowl while the eyes harden to steely coolness in unexpected moments of anger. In those moments the taut, muscular chest and arms of the avid weight lifter flex, the mouth hardens, and language that only moments before suggested the character of a mild-mannered businessman suddenly becomes the gutter vocabulary of a vicious enforcer and assassin, reflecting the criminal underworld he lived in and often dominated in Toronto for nearly fifteen years.

I first met Kirby on September 13, 1983, in an office provided by television journalist James Dubro, who was trying to convince Kirby to appear with him on the CBC's "the fifth estate." Kirby's interest lay in having a book written about his exploits, while mine at that time centred on the growth and danger of new and emerging organized-crime groups that were proliferating in awesome numbers and sophistication in Canada and the United States. As a writer, I felt that interviewing Kirby would provide a unique opportunity for me to acquire graphic insight into the criminal activities of two of these rapidly growing and dangerous new groups.

The only thing resolved at that meeting was that Kirby would consider the television show, I would think about a book, and Kirby and I would meet again before I left Toronto. As a sign of good faith, Kirby agreed to permit me to use a stack of documents and news clippings, which he had brought with him in a brown leather briefcase, as well as whatever information we taped in a subsequent meeting for news articles I hoped to write about how these new criminal groups were growing and threatening the very fabric of Canadian and American societies.

There was no advance notice for our second meeting two days later — only a ring on the telephone, Kirby's voice on the other end, and, within what seemed like seconds, a pounding on the door of my room at the Royal York Hotel. As I peered out from behind the door, I could see two burly plain-clothes men, members of a three-man team from the RCMP Special Enforcement Unit, standing at my door.

"You Tom Renner?" one of them asked.

I nodded, noticing a walkie-talkie he held in one hand and the high-powered pistol under his coat. "That's right," I said. "Who are you?"

He flashed a police identity card and asked me for some identification, but said nothing more. I ushered the detectives into my room, and while I showed my questioner my New York driver's licence and police press pass, his partner checked out every nook and cranny of the room, including the door to the adjoining room, the closets, and under the bed.

Once the room and all the hallway and stairway exits of the hotel floor had been thoroughly checked out, the first detective spoke into his walkie-talkie and told Kirby it was safe for him to come up. Within a minute he and two other men appeared. The two men stationed themselves at either end of the hallway, and the detectives left Kirby in my room, making sure the door was locked. Kirby sat down, a walkie-talkie at his side, and we began the first of what was to become a series of interview sessions spanning a period of two years.

It was during that first four-hour interview at the Royal York Hotel that I fully realized Kirby's importance in showing the links that have been forged between outlaw motorcycle gangs and so-called Mafia groups. While law enforcement agencies had up to then talked about criminal links and business ties between cycle gangs and Mafia groups, no gang member had ever surfaced as an informer-witness to talk publicly about his role with both criminal groups. In fact, Kirby is still the only one to do this.

Disclosures of business ties were, however, surfacing. In Philadelphia members of the Pagans outlaw motorcycle gang were engaged in drug trafficking with members of the Angelo Bruno crime family. They were also recruited for hits on Bruno crime family members by rebellious Bruno family members. In Chicago a special report prepared by the office of U.S. attorney Dan K. Webb found that there was a "sinister criminal association" and a "loose alliance" between gangster flunkies of Chicago mob boss Anthony (Big Tuna) Accardo and the Outlaws, a motorcycle club that resorted to extortion, kidnapping, and murder to supply for profit nude dancers and prostitutes to Chicago mob clubs and massage parlours.

By 1985 both the Federal Bureau of Investigation (FBI) in the United States and the Criminal Intelligence Service of Canada (CISC) agreed on one thing: outlaw motorcycle gangs represented major organized crime threats to both countries. This belief was supported by a growing number of disclosures in testimony before U.S. Senate committees and during federal trials in Philadelphia and Chicago. These disclosures detailed extortions, kidnappings, murder, narcotics trafficking, counterfeiting, white slavery, and a general brutality that was difficult for even the most hardened observer to comprehend.

There was also evidence of a new sophistication among outlaw bikers. From behind the stereotyped image of the hairy, ape-like biker who took over towns to rape and pillage has emerged the computer-age criminal with international connections who uses electronic listening devices, computers, and the world of high finance to thwart law enforcement and the courts and invest in real estate, bars, restaurants, motorcycle shops, and other business ventures.

The bikers' reputation for brawn and unbridled violence and their ability to generate fear have enabled them to obtain contracts to act as strikebreakers for an international oil company, provide drugs and bodyguards for an internationally famous country singer, muscle in on rock concerts and rock groups, and engage in multi-million-dollar narcotics-smuggling enterprises.

Other witnesses had testified in Chicago, Philadelphia, Arizona, and California about outlaw biker gangs, but they could testify only about their particular gangs, so the scope of their knowledge was generally regional. Their gangs, however — the

Hell's Angels, the Outlaws—were international, with branches in Australia, Austria, Brazil, Denmark, England, France, Holland, Switzerland, and West Germany, as well as Canada and the United States.

Cecil Kirby was able to provide information on the international activities of these motorcycle gangs, because he became an upper-echelon member (chapter vice-president) of the Satan's Choice, once the most vicious and powerful motorcycle gang in Canada. He knew and travelled with members of other outlaw cycle gangs, including the Stateside Outlaws. He also possessed accurate, documented information about outlaw biker crimes such as murder, extortion, and narcotics trafficking. However, Kirby could go beyond painting a portrait of the international outlaw biker. After leaving Satan's Choice, he became the only non-Italian to be taken into the inner circles of the Honoured Society as the trusted chief enforcer and hired assassin of a *locale*'s (crime family branch) boss.

While Canadian law enforcement agencies had credible evidence of the existence and operation of this Calabrian crime organization and had even made some arrests, they had, during over a decade of investigation, been unable to penetrate its inner structure. American authorities had had far less success, depending almost entirely on the tidbits of intelligence provided them by their Canadian counterparts.

That set the stage for Kirby, the outlaw biker who had become the trusted Calabrian enforcer and who wanted forgiveness for crimes past in return for his testimony and an eventual agreement to carry a body mike. With that body mike he recorded Honoured Society bosses and others ordering him to commit extortion, arson, assault, and murder. The body mike helped police at least temporarily prevent the planned murder of Toronto mob boss Paul Volpe.

On the witness stand Kirby was extremely poised. As a result of his testimony, at least eighteen criminals, many of them major Honoured Society mafiosi, have been put behind bars for a total of more than 100 years. Another has been sentenced to life imprisonment for murder, arson, assault, and extortion. Because of Kirby, scores of major crimes have been solved, resulting in close to 100 arrests on charges ranging from murder and arson to narcotics trafficking and robbery. His information tipped off a plot to take over the small Caribbean nation of Dominica and foiled plans to blow up nightclubs. And he saved the life of a Connecticut woman by convincing mob bosses he'd carried out a contract to kill her while FBI agents kept her in hiding.

Few law enforcement agencies in Canada or the United States are equipped to deal with either the astonishing growth of outlaw biker gangs or the Calabrian Honoured Society. Many barely know of the existence of the Honoured Society or understand what it represents, and no agency in the United States is actively investigating its operations unless they are related to specific crimes. Since Kirby's emergence as a witness, there has been no attempt to penetrate or publicly expose the criminal operations of the Honoured Society on either side of the border.

Because of budgetary and staff constraints as well as political pressure, agencies have instead concentrated on Cosa Nostra, Colombian cocaine rings, some cycle gangs, and Asian crime groups. Narcotics trafficking by scores of organized groups from Asia to Colombia to Sicily, and especially by Cosa Nostra, is necessarily the top target, and the deeply entrenched Cosa Nostra must be considered the most powerful criminal organization in both Canada and the United States.

This situation makes Kirby's story all the more important. Neglect of the criminal organizations he operated with and talks about constitutes a significant threat to the societies of both countries. Had there been Cecil Kirbys around ninety years ago to tell their tales of violence about Cosa Nostra, just possibly the public might have been sufficiently aroused and motivated to fund law enforcement and demand the tough laws necessary to impede the growth of this secret society.

There is nothing heroic about Cecil Kirby. He has lived a violent, often brutal life and hurt a great many people. He has killed; he has lived off the proceeds of prostitution; he has blown up restaurants, intimidated contractors, plotted murders, and stalked his victims like a hunter tracks animals. When he faced the likelihood that his own life might be terminated by the very bosses who hired him to kill, he took the route of the informer to survive.

The deal he cut with then Ontario Attorney General Roy McMurtry has been a source of controversy for many years. In return for his testimony against Honoured Society crime leaders and other criminals, Kirby was given immunity from prosecution for past crimes, including what he claims was the accidental murder of a cook who was killed in a restaurant he had been hired to blow up. He was also guaranteed subsistence and protection for a period of five years or until he was through testifying.

McMurtry acknowledged while in office that without Kirby, there would probably have been no penetration of the Honoured Society and no conviction of its bosses. And many more Calabrian-ordered murders, extortions, arsons, and other crimes, including the planned murder of Helen Nafpliotis, formerly of Connecticut, would have been carried out.

Because of his long life of violent crime, Kirby has been reviled and cursed for eluding jail, for receiving subsistence from Canadian authorities for himself and his family, and for being allowed to work on this book for his own profit. In 1984 and 1985 there were attempts to introduce legislation in Parliament to prohibit him from receiving money from any book or media show based on his criminal life. Crown prosecutors who had extolled Kirby's worth as a witness and arranged for his immunity and subsistence waffled under the media heat, claiming they didn't know he was writing a book and that he shouldn't profit from past crimes. There were even cheap attempts to cut his subsistence and change the rules of past agreements.

Through it all, Kirby has kept his word. He has been brutally frank about his criminal life and has made no apology for being what he is. He has fought openly and publicly with prosecutors over subsistence agreements, and he has broken away from the protection he was once provided by Canadian law enforcement to survive by his own wits somewhere in Canada, even though assassins still hunt him.

What unfolds in the pages that follow is a fascinating personal account of underworld crime, one that for the first time gives insight into the brutal, violent, and hitherto secret worlds of the outlaw bikers and the Honoured Society.

Thomas C. Renner

CHAPTER

1

NO HONOUR
AMONG THIEVES

It was May 1979 when I first began to suspect that my safety as the personal enforcer and hit man for Honoured Society crime boss Cosimo Commisso might be in jeopardy. My suspicions were aroused as we sat eating at the Casa Commisso, his banquet hall and the meeting place for the Calabrian Mafia that he and his brothers, Remo and Michele, operated and worked out of not far from Toronto's Little Italy.

There were no threats, no special events occurred, nothing unusual was said—I just got a sort of eerie feeling in my gut as I listened to him talk about murders and vendettas and the traditions of Calabria. I knew he was talking about the Calabrian Mafia, or the Honoured Society, as it's generally called, but these words were never mentioned. When he or his brothers said anything, it was usually about "our people" or "our family," not "the Mafia."

Cosimo and his brothers were born in a small southern Italian town called Marina di Gioiosa. It was a town of about 25,000, on the water and very close to Siderno Marina, which is considered to be the birthplace of the Calabrian Mafia or Sidernese mob of Canada and the United States. Cosimo was just sixteen when he came to Canada with his mother, Emilia, in 1961. His father, Giralomo, had been killed in a Calabrian Mafia shootout

1

in Siderno in 1949. Cosimo didn't grow up on the streets as a fighter and hustler like me, but he did grow up with a tradition that had its roots in Calabria and in the family. His family knew Mike Racco, the old Siderno mafioso who was the "godfather" of all the Calabrian hoods in Ontario until his death in 1980.

From the time he and Remo were kids in this country, all they could think about was avenging their dad's murder. Remo was always telephoning people in the old country, mafiosi and relatives, and sometimes travelling there to handle contracts — or what Cosimo would call "affairs of honour." It was, I suppose, because of this tradition and because they knew Racco that Cosimo and his brothers became big shots in Toronto and headed their own crime family. By the time I met Cosimo in 1976, he had become what they call the *Capo Bastone*, or "crime boss," of one of several Calabrian crime families.

He was only thirty-four in 1979 when we sat together in the Casa Commisso, but he was a crime boss in every sense of the word. He weighed about 180 pounds and had a heavy Italian accent that was so thick that at times I could hardly understand what he was saying. He was married and had two kids. Strangely, his wife was Jewish. She was quiet and you never heard from her, and he treated her with respect whenever I saw them together at home. But when he stepped out the door to meet me or some of his Calabrian Mafia friends at the Casa Commisso or at poolhalls, he became a different man. Cosimo wasn't tough — he was homicidal. He'd kill you as soon as look at you if he thought you were crossing him, if he thought it was good for business, or if he thought you had insulted him or his family. The lives of other people meant nothing to him.

Cosimo had fire in his eyes as he pushed himself back from the kitchen table at the Casa Commisso. He belched contentedly as he wiped tomato sauce from his mouth and brush-like mustache and picked at the last remnants of flesh stuck in the crevices of the lobster tail shell on the plate in front of him. He gulped down some red wine, then belched again, rubbing his bloated belly. A peculiar smile crossed his face as he watched me toy with the small plate of spaghetti and lobster in front of me.

"It's good, no?" Cosimo asked.

I nodded. "It's good, yes," I answered and continued eating. Cosimo kept talking, but the conversation wasn't about food. It was about murder.

"You know, it's not too long ago when one of my uncles, he's involved in a war between our family and another family back in Italy," Cosimo said softly, glancing around the kitchen to make certain we were alone and no one was listening.

"We went after that other fuckin' family," he said with a glint of satisfaction on his face. "They had this big house in this village near Siderno. It took a while, but we got into this house when the whole family was there, and we shot and killed everybody in the place — even the little bambino in the crib."

For a split second I thought he was bullshitting me. Then I looked up from my food at that round, moon-like face and wild, unbrushed, scraggly hair of his. His sleepy, dark brown eyes danced with a hidden deadliness I'd come to know over the years. I knew this was no tall mob tale. It was a matter-of-fact, you-kill-everyone-opposed-to-you true story told without emotion, but with obvious relish.

He was giving me a little historical lesson in the ways of the Calabrian Mafia in Italy, particularly his family's home area of Siderno. But there was more to it than just a little history and a tale of vengeance. Cosimo was working his way up to something that he wanted me to handle, and there was something about the way he was doing it that bothered me. I wasn't squeamish about the murders. What the hell — I'd been around murder and violence for a long time as a biker and as Cosimo's enforcer, but I've got antennae around me that sense things that are wrong for me, and those antennae were vibrating like mad and sending off warning signals.

The bottom line to the stories was a rather wild murder plot Cosimo wanted me to carry out — not in Canada or the United States, but in Calabria. And his target wasn't just any Italian or Canadian hood, it was Girolomo (Momo) Piromalli, the most powerful Calabrian boss in southern Italy.

"Cec," he said, "we got this job for you, and it's important — very important!"

Now when Cosimo said a job was important, it was *important*. Usually jobs were just jobs, nothing special. I'd handled extortions, bombings, beatings, card game rip-offs, plotted murders — you name it. For me the bottom line was always money. For Cosimo the bottom line was always results. But up until May 1979 he had never said that anything was as important as this was supposed to be.

"What's the job," I asked, "and how much are we talking about?"

"It's worth ten thousand dollars, and we pay all your expenses. We arrange everything for you," he answered.

"What's the job?" I pressed.

"We want you to do this person," he said. "We get you to Italy. We arrange for all your travel there and back. We set things up —boom, boom—it's over. You got the money, and we get rid of this pig."

The "pig," Piromalli, lived on a big estate in Gioia Tauro, a steel-making town in southern Italy. Cosimo said the estate had guards all around it, but they had a way of taking them out.

"Why not use someone over there to kill this guy?" I asked.

"No, no, no," he said. "It must be kept a big secret. We can't use anybody from there to do this job. We need you."

Now my father didn't raise a stupid son. Curly-haired, blondish, blue-eyed Canadians who don't speak Italian don't exactly blend into the scenery of the mountain country of Reggio Calabria. It's a place where the mob runs everything from shops and hotels to politicians and cops.

"Hey, Cosimo—I'll stand out like an Arab sheik in a Dublin pub," I said. "They'll spot me in a second, and even if I could do the job, I'd have less chance of surviving than a snowball in hell."

Cosimo waved his hands excitedly in the air, shaking his head vigorously. "Don't you worry," he said. "We got this plan."

He emphasized over and over the importance of maintaining the secrecy of the plot—that absolutely no one must know about it. I couldn't talk to anybody about it, not even his brothers.

He told me that Piromalli was the mafioso who bossed a big kidnapping ring in Calabria, the one that in July 1973 had kidnapped J. Paul Getty III, then the sixteen-year-old grandson of the oil billionaire, John Paul Getty. For his safe return, Cosimo said, Piromalli's people had demanded a $2.9-million ransom. The kid was finally released after being held for five months, but not before Piromalli's men cut off one of his ears and sent it to the Getty family to force them to pay the ransom. Piromalli was arrested with six others but then acquitted because the cops couldn't come up with enough evidence.

Cosimo said that there were fifteen or twenty people in the kidnapping group who had collected nearly $200 million in ransoms in less than five years. The racket had been booming until 1978, when the Italian police arrested fifteen more Calabrians, including Piromalli's brother, Giuseppe. Until those arrests Piromalli and his Honoured Society had kidnapped more than 100 rich people, including industrialists and heirs to big fortunes, and had collected some really big ransoms, like $600,000 for the release of an Italian businessman named Giovanni Fagioli.

I knew this couldn't be a scheme that Cosimo had hatched all by himself. Remo and others in Calabria had to be involved too, and in my gut I just knew that I wasn't supposed to come out alive — that maybe this was their way of getting rid of a non-Italian hit man who knew too much about their affairs.

"I don't know, Cosimo," I said, rubbing my chin and looking as deep into his eyes as I could to see if there was something he was hiding from me, something else I should know. "I'll have to think about it and let you know."

"Okay, Cec," he said. "You think. Guaranteed — it's ten thousand dollars, and it's safe."

Cecil Kirby in Calabria — it didn't make sense. I had a nagging feeling that it was a set-up, that I was going to be taken there to hit this Piromalli fellow, and then they were going to do me on one of those back roads of theirs or leave me by Piromalli's body. My sixth sense told me no, but the money made it interesting, and there was a sense of intrigue and excitement about it that I liked. It was something to think about — carefully.

The Piromalli murder scheme, I learned later, was all part of a mob struggle for leadership in Calabria that had gone on since the 1949 murder of the Commisso brothers' father, Giralomo. He had been killed as part of the struggle for power among the bosses, although he was never higher than what they call a *Sgarrista* or *Cammista*, the same thing as a soldier in Cosa Nostra. He was the kind of guy who approached businesses to extort money, and he could give orders to members of his group, associates who are called *Picciotti*, people like me who place the bombs, beat up the victims, apply the muscle, and collect the loan-shark debts or other fees.

Cosimo said that mob control in Calabria was so absolute that even international industrial companies knuckled under to their demands. In the early seventies a big hotel chain came to Siderno to buy property and build a big hotel. About halfway through construction it was bombed. The Calabrian Mafia didn't want outsiders in their waterfront town. If there were going to be any hotels, they themselves would build them and own them.

The big Honoured Society boss before Piromalli was Antonio Macri. He controlled all the Calabrian families like a Cosa Nostra boss of bosses, but he didn't like change. Most Calabrians don't. They stick to the old ways of making money. New ways, like narcotics trafficking, were not allowed. But the money was too big, Piromalli was too ambitious, and in 1975 Macri was set up and gunned down when his chauffeur-driven car stopped at a main intersection in Siderno. Five or six men jumped from nowhere and shot everyone in the car except Macri's right-hand man, a guy named Frank Commisso, a distant cousin of Cosimo's.

Piromalli tried, but he could never get the power that Macri had. He remained a local boss, not a boss of bosses, and rivals hated him for killing Macri. The Commisso brothers had sided with factions that opposed Piromalli. That's why, I supposed, they had turned to me to handle his killing.

I bought a pass on the plan to kill Piromalli because Cosimo kept putting it off. Then Piromalli died anyway from natural causes. But I had begun to think seriously about ending my association with the Commissos.

Finding a way out of an organization that sometimes kills just because it's insulted isn't the easiest thing to do. But between Cosimo's stories about Calabria and the scheme to kill Piromalli, I was beginning to feel uneasy about some of the things the Commissos wanted me to handle. I knew that there was only one way it would end. I'd be lured to some place by Cosimo or his brothers to collect some money or plot some job, and I'd be killed.

In October 1980 I was facing trial for break and entry as well as extortion and assault. They were the latest in a series of criminal charges acquired since my youth that numbered more than sixty. I was certain I would be convicted on one, probably the break and entry, and if I was, I'd do big time.

My choice was to either do a long stretch in jail and probably be killed in prison by one of the Commissos' people or be done by the Commissos outside prison walls. I was between a rock and a hard place. The trouble was, I didn't know who the hell to talk to. I had never found a cop I could trust.

I had tried trusting a cop named Terry Hall of the Ontario Provincial Police (OPP). Hall was a particularly tough cop who had become a thorn in the ass of the Vagabonds, one of Toronto's worst motorcycle gangs. He had become their shadow — turn around in a bar, and he was there. Step out of the house, and there he was on the street. He was always hounding them, breaking their balls, making their lives miserable. He had put the fear of God into them. He was a tough cop and an honest cop, and they were afraid of him. I couldn't understand why all these big, rough bikers were so afraid of just one big, tough cop.

One night in 1978 I heard from a biker friend of mine, Armand Sanguigni, that the Vagabonds had put out a contract to kill Hall. "They're desperate to get rid of this copper," he said.

I figured I'd do myself and Hall a favour by tipping him off about what was happening. I called him, met him, and told him about the murder plot. I figured I'd get some consideration from him down the road if I was charged with something. Well, I was charged later on, but I got no consideration from him at all — not even a thank-you for saving his fuckin' life. I shoulda let them do him. Anyhow, I knew I couldn't turn to him to get any consideration on this case.

On October 11, 1980, I took a chance and called the Toronto Royal Canadian Mounted Police National Crime Intelligence Section and asked to talk to someone. I got a break that day — I got to talk to Cpl. Mark Murphy.

I didn't identify myself to him that first day. I simply told him I was a former member of the Satan's Choice motorcycle gang and that I could provide him with a lot of good information if he could help me with some charges I had pending. He didn't promise me anything, but we talked regularly, and I gave him information that he found was accurate.

At first he wasn't impressed. He still didn't know my name and referred to me only as "Joe." Still no promises. Then I began feeding him information on narcotics dealers, prison beatings and murders, robberies, and other crimes, and I dangled promises that I could deliver much, much more, including information on everything from arsons and murder to the Commissos and their organization.

Up to that time I had no intention of becoming a witness or doing anything except provide tips to Murphy. All I wanted in return was a light sentence. Murphy was willing to talk to Crown prosecutors for me, but he was opposed by biker cops from the Metropolitan Toronto Police and the OPP, including Hall.

That really jammed me. If I didn't keep co-operating, one of those cops could put the word out on the street that I was an informer, and I'd have bikers and Rounders — along with the Commissos — out to kill me. If I did, I'd still go to jail for a long term because of the cops who wouldn't listen to Murphy.

It was the Commissos who gave me the bargaining chip I needed. They handed me a $20,000 contract to kill a good-looking broad in Stamford, Connecticut. Her name was Helen Nafpliotis, and she was the girlfriend of Nick Melia, a convicted receiver of stolen goods whose brother was a high-ranking member of the Connecticut branch of the Calabrian Mafia.

I was certain that this hit contract was really part of a plan to take me out. They wanted this Nafpliotis woman killed because she was costing them money — money they were losing because Melia wasn't paying attention to business. I knew that if I took the contract, chances were they'd do me after I'd done her. But if I didn't handle it, they'd have her killed anyhow, their suspicions about me would be raised another notch, and I'd probably be hit anyhow.

It was now February 1981, the Commissos were pressing, and I hadn't told Murphy about the contract. As I tried to make up my mind about what to do, I found myself wondering where it had all begun, how the hell I had gotten myself into this mess where my future — my life — rested on the whims of some cops and some crazy Calabrians . . .

CHAPTER

2

BORN TO VIOLENCE

I was born in 1950 in Weston, a suburb of Toronto, and from
the time I was in kindergarten, I was fighting with kids around
me, fighting to survive. My parents weren't rich — they had to
work like hell to make enough money to support the family —
but we weren't poor either. I never wanted for food or clothes. I
may have had to use an outhouse for a bathroom at the cottages
we lived in, or I might have had to walk a mile or more to get
water for the house, but there was always good, wholesome food
on the table and plenty of it, and there were always enough decent
clothes for everyone.

We lived in a tough neighbourhood. There were Irish and
English, Jews and Poles, Italians and Greeks, but there weren't
any Spics or Blacks or any Orientals that I can remember. An
Irish kid like myself had to stand his ground and fight his way
against kids of other nationalities who fought to establish their
reputations and uphold their origins.

I didn't go looking for fights, but there were kids in school
who would try to push me around, and I wasn't one to be pushed.
Someone would give me a shove, and bang! — that was it. I'd
lose my cool and start fighting. Many was the night I'd come
home bruised and bloodied. My dad would give me hell and then
ask, "You whip him?" and I'd nod my head and say, "Yeah, I beat
him." He'd say, "Good — go get cleaned up." Sometimes it was a
draw, and sometimes I got the hell kicked outta me, but as far as
I was concerned I was a winner because I didn't knuckle under

to anyone. I never told Dad I lost. He wouldn't have wanted to hear that anyhow, and I didn't need sympathy.

When I was ten, my parents moved to Wasaga Beach, a small resort community about eighty miles north of Toronto on Georgian Bay, off Lake Huron. My mother, Muriel, wanted to change my environment, hoping the fights would stop and I'd do better in school. It didn't do any good. The fights went on, and I missed as many as 100 days of school in a year. I just didn't like school, and I was always getting into trouble for playing hooky.

During the summers I played baseball for a team in Stayner, about four miles from where we lived, and it was there that I began hanging around with other kids in the area who broke into cottages with me. The break-ins were mainly for excitement. We never got much money or valuables. We weren't really looking for them as much as we were looking for some thrills. The idea was to fool the coppers, watch 'em scramble. The satisfaction was in never getting caught.

Within three years my parents were divorced. They just stopped getting along. They were always fighting. My dad, Kitchener Kirby, moved back to Weston. He had never liked Wasaga Beach, and he had trouble earning a living there. My mother stayed, and after a few months I told her I wanted to go live with my dad in Weston. There was a hellavan argument, but finally she agreed to let me go.

My dad and I were pretty close. I guess I've always admired him. He's got a lot of courage, and he's an extraordinarily agile man for his age. During the war Dad was a motorcycle dispatch rider in Europe with the Canadian army. When he came back from the war, he became a trick bike rider in the circus. He used to ride the barrel, take the bike through hoops of fire, and do other tricks like that. I can't remember when he didn't have at least a couple of bikes around the yard.

When I was quite young, about nine years old, he would ride around with me sitting on the gas tank in front of him. Then one day, as we were riding like the wind, he shouted in my ear, "Cecil, you want to hold the handlebars?" I nodded excitedly, and he added, "We'll go down the street. Now hold the handlebars and keep the bike up." I was excited, steering the bike for the first time, sure that the whole of Weston was watching me. They weren't. I turned my head to look behind, and there was Dad, standing on his head on the rear of the seat while I was steering! There wasn't much he couldn't do with a bike, and a lot of the bike-riding skills that helped me become a top biker with the outlaw biker gangs were developed through him.

Dad was also a regular playboy. He'd been married three times, and when he wasn't married, he had all kinds of girlfriends. For twenty or twenty-five years he was a waiter in hotels. He was also a hotel bouncer. He could always handle himself and still can, even now that he's in his seventies. He still goes ice-skating, and until a short time ago he could still ride a motorcycle with the best of them.

Dad had remarried by the time I moved in with him, and at first I resented my stepmother. But after I got to know her, I found she really wasn't a bad person. Dad tried his damnedest to reform me, but there was no way. We'd argue a lot, but even with the arguments we still got along, and my stepmother, Mary, was good to me. She stuck up for me, and both of them were always bailing me out of jail. Mary died in 1979. She'd been an invalid for almost a year, but she didn't complain. Neither did my dad. No matter what happened, they both stood behind me.

After I moved in with my dad, it wasn't long before I got into trouble again and was kicked out of Weston Public School for fighting. I moved on from Weston to Roseland Public School in the Mount Dennis area of Toronto. In the first month I must have gotten into ten fights, all of which I won. My reputation as a tough kid was following me, and every so-called tough in the school wanted to take me on and beat me. It was sorta like being the fastest gun in the west — there was always some wise guy who thought he was faster and would try to draw on the guy with the reputation.

I got thrown out of Roseland by the summer, but not before I had met and either fought or become associated with a number of students who, like me, later became members of motorcycle gangs. Some of them fought with me, others against me as members of rival gangs. But our lives would never be the same. I can't say there was anything about our environment or our economic stature or our ethnic backgrounds that made us that way. It just happened. We just drifted into the gangs and got into trouble. The only thing we had in common was that we played hooky a lot, and we bumped around on the streets and hung out in garages because we wanted to become auto mechanics. It seemed everyone in school wanted to be an auto mechanic then.

I was supposed to go on to George Harvey Secondary School as a ninth grader, but the summer break came, and I never went back to school. Instead I went to work driving a truck for a Ford dealership on Dufferin Street. I had turned sixteen by then and had started buying old cars, 1956 Fords and Chevrolets, reconditioning them and selling them. I enjoyed that. But I got into fights even then, hanging around in parks with youth gangs. The year I turned sixteen was also the year that I got my first conviction and taste of jail.

The trouble started when I was visiting some old friends at Wasaga Beach. We drove from there to Collingwood, about six miles away. When we got there, we went into a restaurant and got into a fight with three other guys. Two of my friends took off and left me on my own. But I was a tough kid by then, and I beat the hell out of them. As soon as I walked out of the restaurant, I was arrested.

Later that week I appeared in court with the three stiffs I'd beaten up. They got fifty-dollar fines each for causing a disturbance and fighting. But the judge had other plans for me. He didn't fine me. After giving me hell for being a troublemaker and a street tough, he told me I'd learn more if I spent some time behind bars. I got ten days in jail, even though it was my first time in court. It don't pay to win a fight sometimes.

Those ten days were no picnic. The judge sent me to the Barrie County Jail, fifty miles north of Toronto. On the second day there some guard handed me a rag to wash the floors with. I refused and wound up doing the next nine days in solitary confinement.

In the long run, spending nine days in the hole was probably better than spending them with the others in the jail, who were hard-core criminals. At least it was quiet, and I didn't have to fight my way out of some lousy creep's attempt at a jailhouse rape. They gave me a bible to read, and I fooled them — I read the whole thing. Those nine days in 1966 prepared me for what I had to face later.

The next time I was in jail I was seventeen, and it didn't have any impact on me at all. That time I went to Toronto's Don Jail for a weekend until I could raise bail. A year later, after I was convicted of a minor assault, the judge sentenced me to thirty days in the same jail.

When I got out of jail, I was still fighting and changing jobs. Then in late 1968 I started working for a concrete company on Wilson Avenue. It was there that I met Jimmy "Gee," who was a member of the Toronto chapter of Satan's Choice Motorcycle Club. At the time I owned a Triumph motorcycle, and I had a real love of cycling. But you don't do much cycling alone — not if you want to avoid trouble. You have to belong to a club of some kind, or an association. Other than the hell raisers I sometimes hung out with, I had no one to ride with. So after almost a year of associating with Jimmy and his friends, I asked him if he would help me become a member of Satan's Choice.

In August 1969, with Jimmy's sponsorship, I started "Striking." Striking is a probationary period that bikers go through before they are accepted into the club. For Satan's Choice the Striking period lasts eight weeks, and during that time I had to do whatever I was told to do, from cleaning the bikes of other members to proving that I could handle myself in fights, from going to the store for hamburgers for the whole club to stealing motorcycles.

As a Striker, you are at the lowest level of the club hierarchy. It's like being a plebe at West Point. All the upperclassmen can give him orders. It's that way with a Striker. All the club members can give you orders. It's a chance for them to see if you have what it takes to be a member, or if you're just an idiot who wants to get in on the pack's action.

Sometimes it takes a lot of guts to finish the Striking period, to pass all the tests the members want. I remember one Striker who was told to hold up pop bottles in his hands while members shot at them with a .22-calibre rifle. He survived with a few cuts and some bleeding, but he could have refused. If he had, he would probably not have made the club.

You are told when you start Striking that you do not have to break the law if someone asks you to. But you have to be nuts if you think you are going to join a motorcycle club like Satan's Choice and not break the law.

Striking was something like being initiated into the Mafia. Your sponsor had to be a member, he had to be willing to be responsible for you, and you had to go through a probationary period before you were accepted. If you cheated a member, violated his rights, or became an informer, you could be voted out by the membership, or you could be—and very often members were—killed. And outlaw bikers like myself had codes of silence that we had to live by. Those that didn't could get beaten to a bloody pulp or even killed.

There were a couple of big differences between joining Satan's Choice and joining the Mafia, of course. You didn't have to be Italian or from one ethnic group to be a member, although blacks were usually banned, and instead of a blood rite on initiation, Strikers sometimes had to actually eat shit while swearing loyalty to the club. There was one biker who loved to make new recruits squirm by dumping buckets of pig shit and urine over their heads and not letting them clean themselves off all day or night.

There is an image in the public's mind of the biker as a hairy ape, with long, smelly hair, wearing a World War II helmet, iron cross, full beard and mustache, dirty pants and boots, with a total disregard for people, their feelings, and property, and with no sense of morality. All of this is true, and then some. When I joined Satan's Choice in 1969, I joined a gang that conformed very much to that public image. The violence, the smells, the dirty clothes — all these were part of Satan's Choice. We were intimidating, and the public feared us. Fear was, and is, our principal weapon. It's the bikers' badge of honour, our way of intimidating the common folk and the businessman and making it pay off.

I knew from the beginning that trouble and violence were part of life in Satan's Choice. I knew that I could be present when someone got shot; I knew that I might be in the same room or the same house when someone raped some broad, and we'd all be charged with it; I knew there would be other crimes that I'd probably participate in. I didn't care. It wasn't that I joined the gang to do something like that. It was just that I wanted the excitement.

Satan's Choice was by then Canada's largest and strongest motorcycle gang. It had fifteen chapters in places like Montreal, Ottawa, Kingston, Toronto, Richmond Hill, Peterborough, Hamilton, Kitchener, St. Catharines, and Windsor. Each chapter had a membership of from ten to fifteen members, but a lot of people in the community thought a chapter had as many as three or four hundred because they were so loud and violent and because the members of other chapters would often join one chapter on a run on a town. But the most that were in Satan's Choice while I was in was about 220 active, full-time members.

Today all that's changed. Now there are only a few chapters left, because the club split up in 1977 and half the members went over to the Outlaws or Hell's Angels. There are maybe fifty or sixty Satan's Choice members now in Toronto, Kitchener, and Peterborough. The rest belong to the Stateside Outlaws and Hell's Angels gangs, which set up chapters in Canada and are now fighting and killing each other, mostly in Quebec.

The image of the hairy, smelly, scraggly bunch of bikers who went around grabbing and raping girls has also changed, because some bikers have gotten smarter and richer. A lot of bikers wear neat three-piece suits, they invest in business and real estate, they run narcotics rings, they appear at public hearings and testify, and they often present an acceptable public appearance. But they are still just as violent as they ever were. They have no intention of blending into the mainstream of society. They are outrageous outcasts, and they love it.

Jimmy "Gee" told me when I joined Satan's Choice that I would find I would always have very close and reliable friends in the chapter. Members helped each other out when they had trouble, and they always stuck together wherever they were, whether in Canada, the States, or anywhere else in the world. That was true, but only up to a point, as I was to discover.

The Toronto chapter had among its members a diversified group. Jimmy was a labourer. I was a truck driver. We had a plumber, a stock market office executive, an electrician, three narcotics dealers, an insulation installer, a couple of professional motorcycle thieves, some safecrackers, and an explosives expert. It was within this group that I got my baptism of fire and learned my skills as a bike thief, a burglar, and an enforcer. And it was here that I saw my first murder.

3

IN MEMORY OF JOHN FOOTE

There is a patch that some members of Satan's Choice wear on the backs of their jackets. It says, "In Memory of John Foote." I never wore that patch, but it was John Foote and maybe two or three other members of Satan's Choice who trained me in the fine art of crime.

Before he became a member of Satan's Choice, Foote was what they call a "Rounder." Moreover, he was one of the toughest of the Rounders. Foote was a vicious street fighter when challenged —homicidal, in fact. He'd killed more than one man in his travels. He was also a brutal enforcer for those who paid him enough. For years Foote had worked for a well-known Toronto bail bondsman when bondsmen were still used in the Canadian court system. Because of that association, he got to know a lot of the criminals in Toronto, including outlaw bikers, and he often dealt with them when they were setting up safecracking jobs, when they wanted to use explosives to scare the hell out of some businessman who wasn't paying tribute to Satan's Choice club members, or when they were doing break and entries of businesses and homes. He also collected loan-shark debts from street hoods and businessmen who sought out an ex-bondsman for loans. Those who were delinquent in payments frequently got visits from Foote, and he could get very violent about poor excuses for not paying—and all excuses were poor excuses.

When I first met Foote, he wasn't a member of Satan's Choice, but he was often at the clubhouse, and he frequently turned up at field day events when biker clubs and bikers showed off their skills by competing against each other. It was just before one of these events, a field day in the summer of 1973 at a popular resort known as Rice Lake, that Foote introduced me to the first murder victim I'd ever seen. The victim was a Satan's Choice biker whose body was hidden beneath a blanket in the trunk of Foote's car.

I'd arrived at the clubhouse early one morning to get ready to leave for the field event when Foote arrived and confessed to bike member Larry MacIlroy and me that he had the body of a Choice club member in the trunk of his car. The victim was a popular biker named James Lyons.

"We were doing this B and E at a farmhouse in Pickering," he said, "when Jim opened the door to the house and was shot in the shoulder by this farmer. I was hiding in the brush when I saw the farmer walk over to where Jim had staggered and fallen, and I saw him shoot him in the head. When the farmer went back to the house, I ran over, picked Jim up, and carried his body to the car. When I left, I could hear sirens in the distance," he added.

At first we didn't believe him, but then we went to his house in Scarborough. He took us to the rear of the driveway where his car was parked. Also present were three other Choice members. Foote opened the trunk, lifted up a blanket, and I saw Lyons lying crumpled in the trunk with a bad wound to his shoulder and his head distorted and bloodied from what looked like a shotgun blast. Then Foote and one of the Choice members, a burly, bearded character also named Jim, took Lyons's body and buried it on a farm in Brighton. The body has never been found, and in fact, Lyons's murder has never been reported as a murder. None of us believed Foote's tale about the farmer shooting Lyons. We all thought he'd killed Lyons himself. Foote had a terrible temper, and he was homicidal when he was riled. Lyons cheated Foote on a drug deal, so Foote blew him away, blew away half his head with a shotgun at close range.

Foote himself is dead now. But before he died, he taught me much of what I needed to know about handling explosives and using them to crack safes, extort contractors, and blow up buildings. He used to keep large quantities of explosives in a warehouse he had in Scarborough. If they'd all gone off at one time, he'd probably have blown half the town up with the warehouse. He didn't keep just dynamite there. He had C-4 plastic explosives and all kinds of timing devices. It was impressive. Most of it was stolen.

By the time I met Foote, I knew something about explosives, but not a hellava lot. I'd learned a little from a gang member we called Rupert, who showed me how to handle dynamite and put blasting caps in with fuses. The fuses I'd used with Rupert were crude fuses made with gunpowder. I learned to figure, by the length of the fuse, how long it would take for the spark to reach the percussion blasting cap to explode the dynamite. The trouble was, some fuses burned faster than others, and that could be a real hazard.

My first experience with an explosive as a bombing device involved the 12th Division of the Metropolitan Toronto Police. I was with a biker called Joey, who had a reputation for killing people and dumping them in unmarked graves. He hated a captain at the 12th Division because the cops under him were always hassling Joey. He wanted to throw a bomb in the captain's office.

"I'm gonna blow that bastard sky high," he said.

"Whaddaya, nuts, Joey?" I asked. "You do that, and they'll be on us forever. You give me that bomb — I'll blow up his goddamned car. He'll get the message."

Joey agreed, but for the moment I had visions of a bunch of coppers being blown up and our becoming the object of a continent-wide manhunt. I took the bomb from him, put it in a bag, and lit my cigar. Then I walked toward the police station, lighting the fuse as I got near it. The fuse was shorter than it should have been. Just as I got near the captain's car, another police car drove up. I heaved the bomb like a bag of garbage. It never made the car, dropping about five feet short. I walked, then ran, across the park. It went off, shaking the whole neighbourhood. It was the first bomb I ever lit. At the time I remember thinking, "Nothing to it — just light the fuse and throw it." The whole incident was hushed up by the cops, who never reported it to the newspapers. No one was busted or hurt, but a hole in the ground served as a reminder to cops and bikers alike that Satan's Choice had tried to blow up Metro's 12th Division.

Foote taught me a lot about different timing devices at his warehouse. There I learned how to hook explosives to alarm clocks, how to use pressure switches to set off bombs, and how to set mercury switches. He constantly reminded me, "In this business, Cec, your first mistake is always your last mistake. You never get a second chance." I found that wasn't always true. I made a number of mistakes in rigging bombs and survived, but I admit I was damned lucky.

Without Foote's instructions — and he spent three years on and off teaching me the ropes with various devices at the warehouse, in isolated areas outside of Toronto, and while doing safe-cracking jobs — I would never have been equipped to do the kind of extortion bombings that the Calabrian Mafia wanted me to do later on. A lot of the techniques he taught me, a lot of the devices he showed me how to use, I used later when Cosimo Commisso and his Calabrian buddies hired me to intimidate rivals and contractors who stood in their way.

Foote was finally killed in 1975 by a close friend of his and mine, biker John Harvey. Harvey has a long record of convictions for obstructing justice, theft, assault, possession of stolen property, and manslaughter. The manslaughter conviction came in April 1977 and was the result of the shooting of Foote.

Both Harvey and Foote were dealing speed (methamphetamines) that had been manufactured in one of the club's secret drug laboratories. The speed, sometimes called "Canadian Blue," was popular with bikers and other street people both in Canada and the States. For a long while the Choice labs were among the chief drug suppliers for the Stateside Outlaws until they teamed up with the Choice and took members from more than half a dozen Choice clubs into their gang.

It was an argument over a split on the take in one of their drug deals that led to the shooting death of Foote. Harvey told me that they were in an apartment that Satan's Choice was leasing. Foote suddenly went wild as they argued, shouting, "I'm gonna kill you just like I killed Lyons."

Harvey walked up to his apartment in the same building and got his gun, a .38-calibre revolver that I'd sold him about a year before. He then walked back downstairs. Foote was still there. Harvey shot him once in the chest, but that didn't stop Foote. He just kept coming at Harvey. He had to shoot him two more times before he stopped him and killed him.

There were three other members of Satan's Choice in the room at the time who saw the shooting. Harvey then ran back upstairs and dropped the gun in a hole in the wall near the stairs. The cops investigated the shooting, and three weeks later Harvey was charged with the murder of Foote. He got two consecutive two-year jail terms for manslaughter instead of a life murder rap because he had a smart lawyer to defend him.

Murder was almost a way of life for members of motorcycle gangs. The same summer that I saw Lyons's body in the trunk of Foote's car, I saw two members of Satan's Choice stuff the body of a young white male into the trunk of a car at the Choice clubhouse in Toronto. The kid (he was in his early twenties) was a victim of club discipline — a discipline that warns that if you testify about club members being involved in crimes, expect to get killed. In the world of bikers, whether they are Outlaws in Florida, Hell's Angels in New York or California, or Pagans in Philadelphia or Long Island, people who want to testify against outlaw bikers can expect to be the targets of intimidation, beatings, and even murder.

Intimidation of witnesses is a technique that outlaw bikers have used for a long time in Canada and the States to beat charges against them. Most of the bikers I knew, whether they were in Toronto or Fort Lauderdale, had long arrest records, but very few convictions. The reason was simple. We all used threats and bribery and beatings to make witnesses disappear. Sometimes witnesses ended up at the bottom of a lake, but more often than not it was the fear of what we might do that made witnesses lose their memories or take long vacations out of town.

I remember back in 1974 I stabbed a guy during a fight in a west end bar. I had been in there drinking with a girl when about ten Indians started mouthing off. They were high on firewater. A couple of them shouted something at the girl, so I calmly got up, walked over to them, and motioned to them saying, "You — outside. Not just one of you — all of you fuckin' assholes. All of you outside!"

The first guy I said something to followed me and walked outside with me. As I got outside the door, I wheeled and stabbed him twice, right in the gut the first time and in the chest the second time. He stood there, dumbfounded for a minute, then he stumbled back and fell into the arms of some of his buddies, who by then had all started to come storming out the door to take me on. I started fighting like a wild man.

I had my van in the parking lot and a baseball bat inside. I made a dash for the van, got the bat out, and began dealing with it. Two other guys who were in the tavern came out to help me fight the mob — three of us against ten.

I remember one of the Indians shouted, "Oh, you think you're tough with a bat, eh?"

I said, "Yeah, I'm tough — you take the bat," and I gave it to him. I beat the hell out of him without the bat, and within two minutes I had the bat back and was working some of the others over. And the guy I'd stabbed — he'd returned to fight some more.

Two weeks later the cops charged me with assault and wounding. They had four witnesses against me. One of the Indians' girlfriends had gotten the licence plate number of my van before I took off after the fight ended. It took a little doing, but I found out where the witnesses lived and paid them a visit. I gave them $200. "Look," I said, "here's two hundred dollars. Take a vacation around court time." So the guy I stabbed, his girlfriend, and the rest of his family took off just before I had to appear in court.

When I did appear to face the charges, the cop that had filed the complaint took the stand and testified that the witnesses had disappeared. Explained the Crown prosecutor to the judge, "Your Honour, we're going to have to drop the charges. We can't find the witnesses to subpoena them." Then he added, looking over at me, "And I don't think I will ever find them." He made it sound as if I'd killed them and dumped them somewhere. He thought his remark would make me look bad, but in fact, the opposite occurred. The judge dismissed the charges because there was no evidence, and by intimating that I'd killed the witnesses, the prosecutor added to the mystique of fear that bikers had among the general public. After hearing or reading that, what member of the public in his right mind would testify against Cecil Kirby, outlaw biker — or any outlaw biker?

CHAPTER

4

CLUBHOUSE
OF CRIME

One of the earliest criminal ventures I got into after I joined
Satan's Choice was safecracking. I learned the business after
I transferred from the Toronto chapter to the Richmond Hill
chapter, where I met two brothers, Duke and Chuck Bernard.
Both had done a lot of time in jail, and both were safecrackers,
but the real expert was Chuck, who had spent half his life in jails
in Dorchester, New Brunswick, and Kingston, Ontario.

I didn't know the first thing about cracking a safe when I met
them, but it wasn't long before I realized that not only were they
experts, but they also had someone who was tipping them off on
the places to hit. Sometimes it was an employee of a company
who wanted to make a quick buck. Sometimes it was a girlfriend
who worked in the place or knew someone who worked there.
Sometimes it was a delivery man or a salesman who told them
what to look for or that the company kept more cash than usual
in the safe on certain nights or on weekends. Whatever information they could get they gathered and used to their advantage,
and I learned that technique, as well as others, from them. I also
learned that safecracking isn't the safest criminal activity to get
involved in.

My first job with the Bernards was a bearing company in
Malton, Ontario. We cased the place for a couple of days before

we did the job. By "casing the place," I mean we'd find a way to gain access to a place either by applying for work, by posing as delivery men or salesmen, or by shopping in the area. The idea was to see where the safe was located and what type it was and to check out the burglar alarm systems. We'd also carefully check to find out if there were guards or dogs and when they might be around. If a place looked too well protected, we'd pass.

The bearing company wasn't, and we got $1,500. On that job I was "keeping six." Keeping six is a safecracker's code name for the person who is assigned to watch at a window for cops or to check out and deactivate any alarm system that might screw up the job. While one man is keeping six, two others are either "peeling" or blowing the safe.

In the more than a dozen jobs I went on with them, we almost always went through the roof to bypass the alarm system and get to the safe. To cut through the roof, we'd use a fireman's axe and a railway bar. Most roofs were made of sheet metal and were easy to cut open. The exceptions were wooden roofs, which took a lot longer to break through.

Once inside, we already knew the whereabouts of any alarms because we had cased the place in advance. We'd either deactivate or bypass the alarm, then we'd lift the safe over on its front and cut the back open with an axe. That's called "peeling" the safe. The safes that we picked to work on were generally made of the same material — sheet metal on the outside, three inches of asbestos rock with wire mesh after that, and then one more sheet of metal and you're inside. At least most of the time. A notable exception was a safe we hit at a supermarket named Food City in the town of Oakville.

When we cased the Food City job, we noticed that there was a wire going into the safe, but we figured it was just a door wire. Although I didn't have the Bernards' experience, I had a funny feeling about the wire. As one of the brothers started working around the safe, cutting the wood away around it, I told him not to hit the safe.

"Let's use a torch this time," I said. "Let's cut it open with a torch. Don't hit the safe — I got a feeling there might be a sensor inside there, or a bugged line."

They didn't listen. They hit the safe, and suddenly all hell broke loose. Alarms went off at the safe. We grabbed our equipment and ran like hell out the fire door. More alarms went off. There were alarms going off everywhere. We ran to the backyard behind the store, jumped into our car, and saw the cops coming. There was no way we could outrun them on the road, so we pulled the car into a nearby driveway and lay down in the seats while the cops came from every direction, passing us on the way to the store. Then while the cops searched the area around the store, we drove off quietly, unseen and empty-handed, but at least we weren't heading for the jail house.

Weather very often played an important role in planning a job. We did most of our jobs in bad weather, when it was raining or when there was a snowstorm. We hit restaurants, supermarkets, catering establishments, and bakeries, and in the dozen jobs we did, we got maybe a total of $32,000. It wasn't a very profitable way to make a living, but it gave us pocket money. With all the new technology and alarm systems today, safecracking is the crime of a dying breed of criminals. It just isn't worth taking the risks for the kind of money involved.

The job I remember most was the Community Credit Union in Collingwood, a job we did in September 1971. I remember it for two reasons: it was the first safe job that I was convicted of being involved in, and Collingwood was a town where I left a lasting impression as a biker on the community.

The reason I got convicted was that I was recognized by someone who saw me at the rear of the credit union, four hours before we broke into it, just before I cut the Bell Telephone wires going into the place. I had cased the place pretty well. I'd walked into the credit union and, using a phony name, asked a bank employee about opening an account. He took me to the safe to show me how secure my money would be. It was a Dominion safe, about five feet high and four feet long. There were obviously no alarm wires going to it, but there was a silent alarm system for tellers to alert police to a holdup. Later in the day, as I said, I went around back and cut the telephone wires going into the place. My mistake and that of my partners was not noticing whether there was anyone in the area when I went to the rear of the building.

After I cut the wires, the Bernard brothers and I sat in a grocery store parking lot and watched to see if the police would come. Nothing happened, so we figured it was safe to go do it. We went back that night and broke in through a basement window that was hidden in the rear of the building. Then we went back upstairs. There were no wires on the window then, but you can bet there are now — it's really bugged today to prevent theft. Anyhow, we rolled the safe over into the corner and peeled it apart with fire axes and a big crowbar. It was just like opening a can with a big can opener.

We were expecting to find a lot more money than we did. We opened all the cash boxes, and all that was inside was $5,000. There was another lower part to the safe where I was sure there was a lot more money, but we'd already been in the place fifteen minutes, and we couldn't spend more time breaking that lower drawer open, so we left it.

A few days after we broke into the credit union, I was arrested by the police. They had a witness who had remembered seeing me in the back where the wires were cut and had reported it to police. My lawyer told me that it was a tough case to beat and that I'd be better off pleading guilty.

"The most you'll get is six months," he said. He was right. I had been charged with breaking and entering and theft, but he cut a deal, and I pleaded guilty to willful damage of a public improvement — cutting the telephone wires. I got a year's probation. I had to do six months in Guelph Reformatory anyhow for a break and entry of a motorcycle shop.

The copper who had charged me with the credit union job was furious when he heard the judge sentenced me to probation.

"You get the hell out of this town, Kirby!" he shouted. "And don't you ever fuckin' come back! I'm sick of you and all your biker cronies."

He had good reason to be sick of me. A year before I was sentenced, I'd partied with some Satan's Choice gang members and gotten a little high. I told them I was going to make Collingwood remember the Choice. So I got a bucket of special paint, went to the town's tallest water tower, climbed to the top, and, while standing on the railing, painted the name "Satan's Choice" all over the tower. Next to it I added the phrase, "Fuck the World." It stayed up there for years. I don't know why they didn't remove it, but it took about three years before they painted it over. For all those years, every daylight hour, the police chief of that town and the people who lived and worked there had to look at "Satan's Choice—Fuck the World." It drove him crazy. He knew I'd done it, but he couldn't prove it. He couldn't even remove it. All he could do was look at it and fume and listen to the protests of angry residents.

Between safecracking and other crimes, I was moving up in the organizational structure of the Satan's Choice, first at the Toronto chapter and then at the Richmond Hill branch.

In my first year as a gang member, I was made road captain, a very important post in any outlaw biker gang. It's the road captain who, with the chapter president and other officers, is responsible for mapping out the route that the chapter members are to follow when they ride to a function. But mapping out the route is only part of the job. You have to ride up and down the line of bikes to keep them in formation, divert traffic, and stop it at intersections if necessary. The road captain always rides up front at the left side of the chapter president. To do all that, you've really got to know how to handle a bike, and you have to move at speeds of up to eighty and ninety miles per hour to check out intersections and keep everyone in line. Later on I also acted as sergeant at arms — a sort of enforcer who walks around with a baseball bat or some other instrument to whack guys in the head when they get out of order at club meetings. And I was vice-president of the Richmond Hill chapter. But it was as road captain that I got my spurs in field events.

Field events are competitions where outlaw biker club members who aren't warring get together in Canada and the States or in Australia and Europe to test their skills as cyclists. It's also a place where bikers have a hellava party. They get drunk or stoned on drugs, they play cards and gamble, and sometimes they tear up the nearest town if they're not properly welcomed. For the most part, though, it's a time and place to test your skills as a biker and have a good time.

On the day of the competition we'd have ten or twelve events, and winners would get trophies for first and second places. The events were in two classes, an A class for Harley-Davidson motorcycles with 1200-cc engines and a B class for the smaller bikes, 500 to 750 ccs. There were competitions for individuals and for teams.

There were drag races for a quarter mile or less. Then there was the Body Pickup Race, where we had to race to one end of the field, pick up a passenger, and race to the other end, with the first one crossing the finish line being the winner. And of course, there were the power turn races, where you lean your bike over and go around in circles, tearing up the ground with your wheel in high-speed power turns. I won a couple of those.

One of the most popular events was a competition called the Balloon Race, where the biker's passenger tied a balloon around his neck or his back. Each of the competing bikers' passengers had a paper baseball bat, and the biker would ride around in circles while his passenger tried to destroy the balloons of others with the bat. The last biker and passenger with a balloon was the winner. Very often people got hurt in these events, because you'd have twenty, thirty, or more bikes whirling around in a cloud of dust, breaking balloons and running into each other.

The most controversial race of all was the Chicken Race. That was a race that got the Humane Society all over us—they stopped the race for a while when they found out what we were doing. The event called for having a live chicken or turkey staked out at one end of the field and the bikers at the other. Everyone would race up, and the passenger on each bike would jump off and try to grab the chicken or turkey. Whoever came back with the biggest piece of the chicken or the whole chicken was declared the winner. Very few chickens or turkeys survived. They were usually torn apart by the bikers' passengers, who'd return to the finish line covered with blood.

Then for laughs there was a Shit Race. We'd put a golf ball in a bag of manure, usually pig or cow shit. Bikers were to race into the field, and the first one to find the ball and come back with it was the winner. I remember seeing one guy come back with the ball in his mouth. There were some real weirdos in these competitions.

The best cyclist I ever saw at any of these field competitions was Larry MacIntyre. While he was a member of the Choice, he made cycles do tricks for him that no one else could ever do. He had two bikes so he could compete in both classes, and he'd clean up. I can't ever remember him going home with fewer than ten or twelve trophies.

As good as he was, Larry used to watch in awe when my father rode a motorcycle in front of the members at the club. Dad didn't like the outlaw club, and he didn't like my being a member, but he accepted the fact that I was a member and that I loved motorcycle riding. He was the one who first gave me my love of biking. When I started riding a bike full-time, Dad would ride next to me, teaching me the finer points of riding. The last time I remember seeing him ride before I became a witness was when he was riding one of my bikes at the Richmond Hill clubhouse, where he'd come to see me. While all the club members watched in absolute awe, he rode down the street first with no hands, then standing on the seat. Dad's in his seventies now, but he can still tear down the street with the best of them on a bike. When I was competing in field events, many of the trophies I won, I won because the tricks and techniques he taught me made me a skilled and daring rider.

Another top competitor was Bob Gray of the Paradise Riders. He was my chief competition in drag races with Harley-Davidsons. He was also the best motorcycle thief I've ever known.

It doesn't matter whether you live in Canada or the United States — motorcycle theft is a major problem for insurance companies and law enforcement agencies. Almost every biker I knew from Toronto to Fort Lauderdale had a stolen Harley-Davidson or was using parts from a stolen Harley to keep his bike running. Bike theft is also big business for outlaw bikers, who sell the parts from stolen bikes through motorcycle shops they own either openly or secretly in nearly every town on both sides of the border where bikers operate. The theft of motorcycles got so bad in Manitoba that insurance plans there no longer include coverage for bike theft.

The best of the outlaw biker thieves was Gray, who was about six feet four, 250 pounds, very muscular, and extremely strong. He was also a man with a very loud mouth. Whenever he was at a party, he was always the centre of attention. As loud as he was, he had the stealth of a fox approaching a henhouse when he was stealing motorcycles. I don't think there was anyone in North America who had successfully heisted as many bikes as Gray had. For a time I helped him, but I was a piker next to him. In my time as a biker, I stole maybe thirty or forty motorcycles. That might be a month's work for him when he was moving around. But as good as he was as a thief, if you were his partner in a deal, you had to watch him. Greed would go to his head. He'd take the gold out of your tooth if you kept your mouth open too long. I learned to keep my eye on him in any deal after he slid one by me at a pop festival in 1971.

The festival was being held at Rock Hill, and by the time I got there, Gray had already stolen one bike. That was no small trick when you consider that the festival was guarded by police, who covered every entrance and exit to watch for trouble. It seemed like there were hundreds of coppers from the Ontario Provincial Police there that day.

When I saw Gray, he was looking for a way to get the bike off the festival grounds without having the coppers inspect it and discover it was stolen. He said he wasn't the only one who'd stolen a bike, that a biker called Al from Satan's Choice had also taken one.

"Look, Bob," I said, "wait here awhile while I think of a way to get you and the bike outta here."

"Okay," he said, "you figure a way, and we split what I get."

So I checked out the festival grounds and found a barn that was near the entrance. When no one was looking, I set the barn on fire and returned to where Gray was. By that time flames were roaring up into the sky, and smoke was curling overhead. People were yelling and screaming, while the coppers and firemen raced to the barn to put the fire out.

I hopped on my bike and shouted to Gray, "Bob, you follow me with that bike, right now!"

He was laughing like hell. "Cec, you're a pisser!" he shouted, started the bike, and roared off behind me.

When we got to the gate, the coppers were just waving everybody through because of the fire. Right behind us was the Choice biker, Al, with his stolen bike, but he decided not to follow us. "I'll take it out later," he said. The next morning he tried to get the bike out, but he was stopped by the coppers and charged with theft.

Now when Gray and I got out, we couldn't get far because there wasn't enough gas in the stolen cycle, so Gray had to abandon it at a park on Airport Road that night.

"I'll go back and get it later," he said, hopping on the back of my bike.

It was two or three days later before I saw him again and asked him about the bike. He said he'd gone back and found the bike gone. I shrugged and didn't think much of it until another Paradise Rider stopped to talk to me about some bikes he'd stolen.

"You know, I went with Bob Gray out to this park on Airport Road one day, and damned if he didn't come up with a Harley he'd hidden in the bush there that he said he'd stolen at the festival."

So Gray had ripped me off. He'd gotten the bike, sold it, and kept everything for himself. Like I said, you had to keep your eyes on Gray all the time.

I remember one day we were in a suburb of Toronto when he saw a Harley sitting in a guy's driveway. The poor guy was cleaning the bike. Gray went over, watched the guy working on the bike for a minute, and then began talking to him. The bike owner was eating an ice cream cone and then suddenly turned to get something from his house. As soon as he walked through the door, Gray was on his bike and gone like the wind.

Gray had other techniques too. He used to read the newspapers like a hawk to see what bikes were on sale. When he found one that interested him, he'd visit the seller and convince him that he should take it for a test drive. That would be the last that seller ever saw of the bike.

Gray would even steal stolen bikes from the guys who sold him bike parts that he'd stolen in the first place — guys like Charles (Chuck) Yanover, who was for a while an enforcer for Toronto Mafia boss Paul Volpe and who later plotted the assassination of certain international leaders and the takeover of a couple of countries.

In 1970 Yanover was just a small-time hood like the rest of us. He owned the City Custom Cycle Co. on St. Clair Avenue in Toronto, and from there he sold stolen bike parts that bikers brought to him. Gray was selling him hot bikes, I was, dozens of guys were. One day I stole a brand new Triumph with only ten miles on it. I took it apart and sold the damned engine to him for only forty dollars. He was making a fortune on the deals, and bikers were getting ripped off when they sold to him.

One day Gray decided to go after Yanover's personal bike and steal it. Yanover went bonkers. He ran screaming to the police to complain. They laughed so hard they cried when they took his theft report. I ended up with the bike. A member of the Richmond Hill Satan's Choice sold it to me. Then Gray came to me and said he could make even more money and get back at Yanover for chiselling us on other bike deals. Together we stripped the bike down and sold the parts, piece by piece, back to Yanover. We sold him back all but the front end of his bike. When we were through, Gray told him he'd been buying back pieces of his own bike. Yanover didn't say a word. His face went red as a beet, but he didn't say a word. About five years later I showed him a bike I was riding and pointed to the front end. "There's your front end, Chuck," I said with a chuckle. He didn't think it was funny, but he didn't say anything; he just walked away.

Stealing motorcycles was one of the easiest rackets around. It was also very profitable. On the average, we'd get $800 to $1,000 a bike if we didn't have to take it apart. If we stripped it and sold it for parts, we'd get more than double — $2,000 to $3,000, depending on who we were dealing with. At that time Harleys were selling at from $6,000 to $7,000 apiece new.

To steal a bike, the most important thing to do was case the area—map out the easiest and safest routes of escape, check out neighbourhoods to prevent being spotted, and watch the bike owner to see how careless he was. A lot of bikes were spotted through newspaper classifieds, at motorcycle shops, or in neighbourhoods where bikers hung out. Once we spotted a bike, we'd case the area for a couple of days and then drive up in our van. We had a big set of bold cutters in the van that could cut any chain or lock. We'd break the lock, usually at night, wheel the bike down the street quietly, and put it in the waiting van.

Sometimes there were close calls, like one I had in Richmond Hill. The owner of the bike I'd selected to steal came home earlier than expected, and I got jammed between his car and the bike. I slid underneath his car to hide from sight. When he walked by, I could have put my hand out and grabbed his foot — that's how close he was to me. He went into the house, and within seconds I was out from under that car, on his bike, starting it, and taking off before he knew what happened.

When we stripped a bike, we'd usually sell the parts to other outlaw club members. Fenders, gas tanks, windshields — there was always someone in the biker gangs who needed parts for their bikes, and we could get those parts faster than any motorcycle shop could, even those that had the franchises for the Harley-Davidsons and Triumphs. But I preferred selling bikes as is, without stripping them. It was a pain in the ass to strip a Harley. It could take eight hours, and my back would be killing me afterwards. A lot of the time was taken up pounding the identification numbers away with a ballpin hammer or drilling the numbers out, placing an aluminum weld over the hole, and restamping the casing with new numbers.

When we did a strip job—and most biker clubs wherever they are do this — we took the bikes right down to their nuts and bolts. We'd drill the numbers out of the transmission casings, out of the frame, and sometimes out of the engine casings. But most of the time we'd throw away the engine casing because it was too difficult to get the numbers off. When it was too much trouble to drill the numbers off the engine or transmission, we'd take it to a lake or a construction site and dump it. Any one we kept we'd weld over the top where the numbers were, grind down, and leave like that. Then we'd sell it to someone who was interested in making a customized bike, someone who was willing to put the motor over the frame numbers. He'd know he was getting a hot product but didn't ask questions—just paid the price. Or we'd restamp the engine casing, which was made of aluminum, and repaint it.

There were times when we suspected the stolen bike hadn't been reported, so we'd send someone down to the local police station and ask them to check the numbers of the bike on their hot list to see if it was stolen before we bought it. If it wasn't on their hot list, we'd get a document from the police to show that the numbers had been checked for theft and therefore the bike couldn't be a stolen one.

There were also insurance scams that outlaw bikers used to screw the insurance companies. One member of a club would report a bike stolen, while another would cannibalize it, rebuild it, and sell it as a home-built bike. They'd get the $8,000 from the insurance claim plus the selling price of the home-built, maybe $4,000 to $5,000. Some of the Harleys were valued at as much as $12,000, and the insurance companies paid out. I made thousands that way. I also landed in Guelph Reformatory in 1972 with some other bikers because we had stolen motorcycles from a cycle shop.

Guelph Reformatory is a medium-security prison located about sixty miles west of Toronto. It's not the worst prison in the Canadian prison system, and it's not the best. The food is terrible, and they make you work hard on the bush gang. The bush gang, I guess, is a bastardized version of the southern American prison chain gangs, only without the chains. It gets the name *bush* from the fact that heavily guarded prisoners work in cedar bush and forests in parks owned by the Ontario provincial government, cutting down the cedar trees. Some parts are sectioned off into fence-post-sized pieces, which are sent back to the reformatory and stripped by other prisoners. Other parts of the trees are stripped, finished, formed, and made into picnic tables, which are sent to Ontario parks for use by the public.

When I started on the bush gang, I wasn't the strongest guy around, but working with axes and saws and lifting the trees started to build me up. It also gave me some incentive to work out with weights with another Satan's Choice member, John Murdoch. When I started, I couldn't press much more than 120 pounds. By the time I left Guelph less than a year later, I was pressing nearly 330 pounds, and I was as strong as an ox. I was also ready, through associations I made at the prison with other outlaw biker members, to graduate to the higher and more violent levels of crime.

CHAPTER
5

GIRLS FOR SALE

Girls are as much a part of outlaw biker life as drugs and violence, and they are probably our weakest link. They often carry our guns, hide our drugs, front for our businesses, gather information for us about cops and other bikers or places we want to rob, and act as our couriers in drug deals and other crimes. That gives them access to a lot of information and evidence that could put members of biker clubs in jail. So cops do their damnedest to get them to become informers. In fact, bikers often kill some of the women to protect themselves, because they think they've become informers or might become informers.

That's one of the reasons a lot of girls, some of them from Canada, have disappeared or been tortured and murdered in Florida by members of the Outlaws. The cops would find them in pieces, or crucified, or they'd just never find anything because the bodies were dumped in the Everglades, where the swamps and animals and alligators finished off the remains.

Girls disappeared for other reasons too. Sometimes they had to work as prostitutes and dancers in topless bars too long, and they became too old and used physically at sixteen and seventeen and eighteen. Others tried to run away from the club members who owned them. Some cheated on the money they were supposed to turn over, and some just weren't making enough money. So they'd get wasted. The bikers didn't want them running to cops and talking about what had happened to them. That could mean long stretches in jail.

A copper I know once said to me that there was no way of knowing how many had disappeared from Canada into white slavery or had been killed. "It's like trying to document missing children," he said. "They're just swallowed up in the traffic, and there's no one around to trace them." He was right. Bikers from the Canadian clubs were selling girls across the border for from $500 to $2,000 apiece. A biker just had to make the right arrangements in the States, deliver the girl to the border, and other gang members from the Outlaws or Satan's Escorts or some other gang would take over. Some of the girls were as ugly as sin or so spaced out they never knew where they were, but they still brought bucks to the bikers, who made them work for still more bucks. "If they got four limbs and a hole, they're worth money," a biker friend of mine once said.

The Outlaws gang is one of the two biggest cycle gangs in the United States, and now they're very big in Canada. In the seventies they were our allies, and they would come to Canada to buy drugs from the members of Satan's Choice who had drug labs that were turning out big amounts of speed (methamphetamines) and "Canadian Blue." But drugs weren't the only thing they bought from us. They bought and sold weapons, they bought and sold counterfeit money, and they bought some of our women. Sometimes the women were given to them to hustle in their body rub shops and topless bars in Florida and Chicago.

The public thinks we get most of our broads through fear or rape or kidnapping. That's what the media likes to play up—the gang bangs in a clubhouse of some young chick or the kidnapping of some girl who ends up held captive and raped by all the gang members. Well, there is some of that, but for the most part bikers don't need to grab women off the street and rape them—the women flock to them like bees to honey. That's the truth. For some reason, girls fall all over bikers, no matter how scroungy they look or how bad they smell. Biker women are worse than rock star groupies. Most of them come asking for sex and companionship and wanting to be someone's "old lady." They have no families, or they're on drugs and they need money. So what happens to them happens to them. Most people don't care. Their families don't even care enough to tell the cops they're missing.

In 1970, and even today, a lot of bikers hung around Yorkville, with all its hippie hangouts. The girls hanging around the clubs always needed money to buy dope. So a lot of the bikers, myself included, would show these girls where to go to peddle their bodies for a price.

We'd send them to special hotels and bars on Front Street and Charles Street where there were a lot of men looking for action. We told them that they had to give us a percentage of what they made to guarantee protection from pimps hassling them. Some guys took 50 per cent; some guys took it all and gave the girls drugs to keep them working. When the girls weren't making enough money for them, or when they said something like they wanted to go on a trip with their biker-pimp-boyfriend, they'd be taken to the border and sold to an Outlaw or some other biker gang member. The Outlaws and Satan's Escorts Stateside chapters ended up with a lot of hookers from Canada that way. Once the girls were sold, it was unlikely that they'd ever be seen in Canada again. The Outlaws or other gangs would use them for a while and either sell them again to someone else or kill them because they'd seen or heard too much.

The Satan's Escorts gang members would come to Canada to socialize a lot with members of Satan's Choice. Some of the Choice would set them up with girls to take back to the States with them. They'd just deal them to the Escorts as a favour or sell them for as little as $100 or $200. Some of the broads were sold a bill of goods — promises of a vacation, a trip to sunny Florida, a good time. "Work for them [the Escorts]," our people would say, "and come back in six months if you want." They were conned. I never saw one of them come back, and dozens of them left.

It worked in reverse too. There were times when the Escorts and Outlaws sent American girls to Canada to work for us. A lot of them also disappeared.

I wasn't any better than the rest of the bikers who had their own stables of girls working for them. The only difference was that I didn't sell any of the girls who worked for me, and I only took 20 per cent from them, but I was doing pretty much the same thing as everyone else. I had four girls working for me at one time whom I protected in those days, but I only did it for six months.

In good weeks the girls were pulling down from $200 to $500 a day each, and I was collecting from $200 to $800 a day. That wasn't every day in the week, maybe three or four, but it was a nice income — with some fringe benefits, like making love to them. That was sometimes a problem because they were all jealous of each other. I was making it with all of them — sure I was. I'd be a fool if I didn't. I'm human, and I don't need to rape some broad to get what I want. But they were a pain in the ass with their jealousy, and after a few months I got tired of it and just had one working for me. The others took off.

I didn't go after them, chase them down, beat the hell out of them, and make them go back to work for me like most of the bikers would have. What was the sense? If they don't want to work for you, they don't want to work for you, and they weren't really working for me. I was their insurance policy, not their pimp. I got a percentage of all their tricks, and in return I gave them the protection they needed. If anybody tried to beat them up or rip them off, they'd reach out for me, and I'd catch up with the guy and beat the hell out of him.

Most of the girls I had, I'd met in Toronto's downtown area — in Yorkville and around some nightclubs. I remember one of them was a really gorgeous blond called Cindy. She was about twenty-three. She wasn't a hippy, just a good-looking woman who wanted to hustle her ass for a buck. I met her in Cedar Beach, where she was working in the hotel. Cindy was drinking at this bar when I picked her up. We started talking, and before long she told me she wanted to leave waitressing and get back into being a hooker. I told her I knew some good spots she could work, spots some of my other ladies worked.

Cindy went right to work. I'd drive her downtown and drop her off at the places where she'd pick up the johns and work them. She only had trouble once. One of her johns beat her up. She called me, and I found out who he was. I called him at his home. His wife was there and answered the phone.

"I got some business with your husband," I said. "Lemme talk to him."

She didn't argue or give any excuse that he wasn't there, just called him to the phone. When he got on the phone, I said, "Friend, you got a choice. I can talk to you, or I can talk to your wife about the girl you went out with last night." He didn't answer. So I continued talking. "I'm her boyfriend. You can come out and talk to me privately, or I can come to your house and talk — and your wife can hear it all. Either way."

"No, no, no!" he said excitedly. "I'll come."

"Okay," I answered. "Meet me at the North Hill parking lot and bring some money. Come alone if you're smart."

He hung up, got in his car, and met me where I'd told him I'd be. I got into his car, grabbed him by the collar, and put a gun to the side of his head.

"You beat my girl up when you got through," I said, "and you didn't even pay her, louse. Give me the two hundred bucks."

He was shaking as he handed me the money. Right then I punched him hard in the jaw. You could hear it crack as I broke it. I left him lying there, got in my car, and drove away. I never heard a word from him again, and neither did Cindy. I gave her all but fifty bucks.

The hippies-turned-hooker were always high and always having problems with some john or pimp who wanted to muscle them. I'd have to come in at all hours of the day and night to settle the problem. All the bikers did. Back in the late sixties there were a number of bikers who would pick up one or two girls who were hanging around Yorkville, take them back to the clubhouse nearby, put some clothes on them, and then send them back out on the street. When they came back, the biker would take some of the money, give them some dope, and send them back on the street again. It was real easy.

While they were working the streets, these girls would sometimes find themselves in trouble with some professional pimps, mostly black, who'd try to take them over by beating them up and hassling them. We didn't have that kind of trouble too often with the professional pimps. They knew the girls were biker broads, protected by the bikers, and they would stay away. They didn't want the trouble, but occasionally there was an exception, like in 1971 when some members of Satan's Choice beat the hell out of a whole bunch of them at a black club.

The pimps had roughed up one of the old ladies of a Choice member, something that is even more serious than going after the prostitutes we were protecting. Old ladies are the girlfriends of bikers who sometimes work the streets for them and are trusted to do a lot of other things you'd never think of letting some whore do. Old ladies are also a lot better looking than the average hooker. About fifty of us went to this black club to teach those bastards a lesson. A lot of them wound up in the hospital. We didn't have any trouble with the black pimps after that—or any other pimps, for that matter.

Some of the bikers weren't satisfied with shaking down the hippies and regular prostitutes for their street money and getting free lays. They had a thing about taking women off the street or grabbing them in the clubhouse and raping them, getting clubhouse gang bangs going. I knew one biker like that. We called him Nutty. If he found a broad alone in the clubhouse, he'd rape her—you could count on it. Almost 99 per cent of the rapes that took place in the clubhouse in Richmond Hill were by him.

When we were hanging around Yorkville and the women were all doped up on the street, some gang members would grab them, drag them back to the clubhouse, and start screwing them. Before long everybody in the clubhouse was joining in. There were others that got jumped that way, usually broads who hung around with club members and fouled up. Their boyfriends would then tell the club members they were fair game, and they'd get raped. Very few of them who were raped ever went to the cops.

One of these women was attacked by two brothers and a biker they called Larry. They had gone to an apartment on Keele Street in Toronto. The brothers said that some girls had told them to stop by and see them.

So we stopped, and one of the brothers went into the bedroom with one of these girls and came out about a half hour later. We left without anyone saying a word. Two days later I was driving around, and I got stopped by the police for indecent assault. I said, "Hey, what the hell is this all about?" The cops asked me if I had been with Larry and these two brothers when they assaulted a woman in a Keele Street apartment. I didn't know what the hell they were talking about, but I found out. The brother who had come out of the apartment like nothing had happened didn't tell any of us he'd raped the woman. We were kept in jail for two weeks without bail. When we went back to court, the case had been withdrawn. I don't know who did it, but somebody had gotten to her—threatened her life, I guess—and she withdrew the charges.

The sale of women and drugs between the Outlaws of the United States and Canada's Satan's Choice really heated up in the seventies when we began associating closely with the Outlaws. When I first met and visited with a lot of the top Outlaw members in Florida back in 1974 and 1975, they weren't as big as they are today, but they were every bit as tough.

I went to Florida one time to meet some of the Outlaws with "Mother," then the national president of Satan's Choice. Mother's real name was Garnet McKuen, and he was about thirty years old. He was from St. Catharines and had a record of six convictions on charges including an assault on a cop and being caught with narcotics. He had to appear in court in Fort Lauderdale on a charge of possessing a handgun. With us was Drago Salajko of the Choice's Kitchener chapter. Once we arrived in Miami, we were treated like royalty by the president of the Outlaws, Big Jim Nolan. He and a guy named Pete of the Outlaws' Hollywood, Florida, chapter picked us up in a specially equipped van and drove us to Nolan's house in Hollywood.

Big Jim's house was small, nothing impressive, but it was like a fortress. It was a two-bedroom bungalow that was very efficiently protected by the latest in alarm systems. Big Jim also had two huge Great Danes who would chew you into pieces as soon as look at you unless you were friends with Big Jim. He always had a handgun in the living room, and there were two or more high-powered rifles in other rooms of the house. Two girls were living there with him, one who worked in a body rub place and was his special girlfriend, the other a broad who just worked and hustled for him but lived at the house. It seemed to me at the time that almost every broad associated with the Outlaws worked in body rub parlours or topless joints, screwing anyone and everyone willing to pay the price. All the money they made went back to Outlaw members like Big Jim, who provided them with places to live, clothes, food, booze, and whatever drugs they wanted, within reason.

The Outlaws were making a fortune off women. They had the body rub parlours and topless bars from Orlando to Fort Lauderdale, in Chicago, and all across the country, and they had an endless supply of women who danced and worked as prostitutes. Those broads, hundreds of them, were bringing in as much as $2,000 to $3,000 a week each.

Big Jim was an impressive man with an impressive reputation. Only a few months before I met him in Florida, he had been accused of ordering the execution of three Hell's Angels enforcers. He'd had them shotgunned to death in April 1974. Their bodies were found in Fort Lauderdale, face down at the water's edge, with their hands tied behind their backs and cement blocks tied to their feet.

There were stories that Big Jim had personally skinned other Hell's Angels alive at other executions. He certainly was big enough and tough enough to do a job like that if he wanted to. He stood about six foot eight in his stocking feet and weighed about 250 pounds. Whether his reputation was true or not — and he wasn't convicted on these stories — I found him to be a nice guy. It was obvious he had lots of money, profits from the hustle of his broads and from the sale of drugs by the club. On every finger of his two hands he wore rings of all shapes and sizes — all gold and all with diamonds, some big, some medium, but all expensive as hell. Mother, Drago, and I stayed at his place for two days before moving on to other places, but whatever we wanted we got, whether it was booze, women, or drugs.

After a few days we went to Key West with some of the Outlaws, one of whom was from Detroit. While we were there, we stopped at a house that was owned by their national president, a guy they called "Surfer," whom I had met once before at a field day in Kitchener. While we fished in Key West, Surfer told me he had a job teaching school there. He said he had lots of money. He was forty and he'd retired, but he entertained any of the Outlaws and their friends when they came through. I suspected the retirement was only partial. I figured they were moving things like guns and drugs through his area, but I didn't know for sure, and I had to take him at his word when he said he was retired. They had plenty of bucks, those Outlaws. Some of them had to be millionaires with the kind of places they lived in and the businesses they owned.

Just before I left Forida, I had a talk with Big Jim about bringing some girls from Canada down with me the next time I travelled south.

"Can you get them jobs in your body rub shops?" I asked.

He burst out laughing. "You mean the massage parlours?" he answered. "Sure. You're welcome to come back anytime with any of your girls. I'll get them jobs, and you'll make plenty of money."

I tried to get a couple of the girls across the border later in my van with one of my bikes, but I was turned back at the border by immigration officials. I should have worked something out with one of Big Jim's people, but I wasn't trying to sell these girls. I just wanted them to work for me in Florida while I took it easy. It wasn't worth it to keep trying. I didn't want to get busted on some Stateside white slavery rap.

Mother went back to Florida a few times. He also had a few broads that he'd shipped there from Canada to work in the joints the Outlaws controlled and ran. One of them died in a fire in a body rub place down there. When Mother came back, he was a little shook up over it, but he never explained what had happened. We all figured she'd probably seen something she wasn't supposed to see.

The last thing I heard about Big Jim was that he had come to Canada to be hidden by members of the Satan's Choice while he ducked a warrant in the States. He was eventually caught and returned to the States for trial, where he was convicted and sentenced to a double life jail term. Some of the evidence and testimony that helped send Big Jim to jail came from a Canadian member of the Outlaws, a kid named Willy Edson, who had been one of Big Jim's enforcers.

Before Edson became a protected federal witness in the States, he was supposed to have been one of the Outlaws who had worked out a deal to supply the Chicago Mafia with women for its topless joints and body rub parlours. He and some other Outlaw bikers met with some Chicago hoods and worked out a deal. When the law came after Edson, he was hidden by a number of Outlaw chapters in the States. Then they smuggled him across the border and hid him in Canada at Satan's Choice chapters in Windsor, Kitchener, and Montreal. Choice members gave him phony new identification, weapons, and a radio to monitor police calls, but he got caught by the cops going to a liquor store in Kitchener and was deported.

In November 1982 there was a trial of some Outlaws and their business associates in Chicago. Five were convicted, including a Canadian biker and drug supplier for the Chicago Outlaws named Robert Burroughs. I remember that Burroughs worked for the president of the Outlaws' Chicago chapter, Thomas Stimac, who was also jailed in the case. Stimac, who was a friend of Big Jim's and knew a lot of Satan's Choice bikers, was identified at the trial as one of those who met with members of the Chicago mobs way back in 1977 and worked out a deal whereby the Outlaws would supply women to work as prostitutes in mob nightclubs and bars.

One of the women they supplied was a girl named Betty Darlene Callahan. She'd been kidnapped in North Carolina when her boyfriend didn't come up with the money he owed them for drugs. They raped her and forced her to become a prostitute for them in Chicago. Her story was like that of a lot of girls who were grabbed in Canada and sent to the States, some to Florida, others to Chicago or Buffalo. The big difference was, the Callahan woman became a protected federal witness like Edson and testified against them. She was able to testify about the Outlaws handling millions of dollars in cocaine, marijuana, and "Canadian Blue" because she was around long enough to see a lot, and she remembered. When she got her chance to make a break and talk to the feds, she did. It saved her life. If Stimac or the others had had even a hint of what she was going to do, they'd have killed her, made her disappear. Like I said before, women are the weak link of bikers.

CHAPTER
6

NOTHING IS SECRET

If the police want to know what outlaw biker gangs are doing or which biker is dealing dope, stolen goods, or women, they usually turn to their special biker squads for information. The biker squads have informers on the street and in biker gangs who supply them with information. The biker squad cops talk to street people — pimps, prostitutes, burglars, bartenders, gamblers, and nightclub owners — who see and deal with bikers regularly. They also talk to a lot of the bikers themselves.

The information they gather from these people can't usually be used in a court of law. It's not evidence. It's what they call "raw intelligence." That's hearsay stuff that can provide valuable leads to dope pushers, bookie joints, holdups, burglary rings, and extortions. It can even prevent murders, stop gang fights that can lead to killings, and help cops find guys who are hiding out. Intelligence is what makes biker squads and other special police units tick. Without it, police wouldn't know a damned thing about bikers or any other crime group, for that matter. It's their eyes and ears on crime.

While cops use intelligence to catch crooks, bikers have their own intelligence system to help them survive on the street. Moreover, the system they have is probably better than the one the cops have, because they can get information illegally about what the cops and their other enemies are up to.

We need intelligence to keep tabs on each other as well as on the cops. The truth is that there is very little trust among outlaw biker gangs and even among bikers in the same clubhouse. Allegiances are always changing. Fifteen years ago Satan's Choice was Canada's most powerful and toughest motorcycle club. Five years later it was an ally of the Outlaws Motorcycle Club in the States. Today some of its members are old-time Satan's Choice, some have become Hell's Angels, and others have become Outlaws. So yesterday's friend may be tomorrow's enemy, and it's best you have a record on him. The way we do that is through intelligence. When you know more about your enemy than he does about you, you win battles, and you win wars between gangs. While the cops are using us, we're using the cops to get information and eliminate our enemies either through firefights or the cops themselves. All biker gangs do the same thing. The Choice, the Outlaws, and the Hell's Angels were the best at the intelligence game in Canada and the States.

One of the best intelligence sources Satan's Choice had was a woman who had access to the combined Canadian police computer. Gary Cuomo of the Choice had acquired this source and dealt her number out to other members to help them in emergencies. Club members carried her number around in their wallets. If a member was worried about the cops, all he had to do was call her number, and she'd access the police computer to see if there were any warrants on him. When we spotted a rival gang member, we'd also use her to see if there were outstanding fugitive warrants on him. If there were, we'd have someone in the club call the cops and tip them off to where that rival was and who was with him. It was a good way of avoiding trouble and getting rid of rival gang members. We could also check out anyone's criminal record through that computer. This helped us spot people trying to infiltrate us from rival gangs or from the cops.

A lot of biker clubs use their sergeant at arms to rap with cops and pump them for information. Sometimes we used club members whom cops had hassled a lot. The cops figured they had them hooked, that they would be afraid of going to jail. Club officers would tell them to cozy up to cops to get information, even if it meant giving up some themselves. So while the cops were pushing those bikers for information, the bikers would be using them to find out who they were looking for, what bikers were in trouble, where the cops were concentrating their power

— all kinds of tidbits that would help us avoid arrests or other trouble with the cops.

For quite a while Satan's Choice had a gal working in the police dispatch office of the Ontario Provincial Police. She tipped us off for years about the movements of OPP vehicles, especially when they were going to raid a biker clubhouse or biker homes. A lot of guys were able to skip out before raids, and large amounts of guns and drugs were moved and hidden before raids because of tips we got from her.

There are many other ways we gather intelligence. One of the most important is through pictures. Bikers are forever taking pictures of each other — screwing broads at parties, high on drugs, at field events, and at funerals. Pictures, pictures, pictures — biker pictures fill album after album; they fill desk drawers and closets in clubhouses. Cops grab them on raids, and more pictures are taken. Why? Pictures are a record of what a guy looks like. Descriptions are never adequate; they can't fill the bill like a picture can. If the day comes that you decide you want to have a guy hit and you need an outsider to get next to him, what's better — a description or a picture?

In 1979 two members of the Rebels Motorcycle Club and myself went to burn down the Last Chance clubhouse. The Rebels were fighting with the Last Chance, and they'd asked me to help them because there was bad blood between me and members of the Last Chance. We never did burn down the clubhouse because the Rebel gang members changed their minds. But the bad blood remained.

At the time I was looking for a former member of the Toronto Outlaws because I wanted to beat him up. I found out that the Last Chance club members were hiding him, but they wouldn't turn him over, and I couldn't break into their clubhouse because they had it so well secured against break-ins. So I did the next best thing. I took a bat, smashed in the windows of four of their cars, and bent a few fenders as well. The Last Chance bikers never forgot. They had pictures of me that they'd taken at a field event or some other affair. They had one picture enlarged, and I'm told it now hangs in their clubhouse with large block letters underneath saying, "WANTED, DEAD OR ALIVE — REWARD $200,000."

There are a lot of outlaw bikers in North America who have

pictures of me in their clubhouse or in their wallets. Then if they spot me, they will recognize me and inform club members so a death squad can come after me and kill me. There are a lot of pictures of every biker in every club floating around. Someday they may be used the way the Last Chance bikers and other clubs are using my pictures — as a way of hunting me down.

Every biker club has its friends, its associates, and its hangers-on, people the cops like to call our "support group." The cops say that for every biker, there are ten support group members. They're probably right, although I think they are low on the estimate. It's a lot more than ten. When I was a biker, part of that support group were the citizens who got us inside information from the government. Some were employees of the government in key jobs with access to special and sensitive information. For example, for years I have had a source in the driver suspensions section of the Ontario Ministry of Transportation who would go to the department's computer and check out auto licence plates for me. On more than one occasion I have had information checked out for bikers and for Cosimo Commisso after I began working for him. We were able to identify unmarked Royal Canadian Mounted Police cars that way and spot other people who were doing surveillances on us.

I never overused that source, and it never cost me that much. Cops like to think that big bribes are paid to sources like that, but it's just not so. I used to have plate numbers checked out maybe twice a month, and all it cost me was a bottle of good booze. My source was just a good friend. You don't really have to pay off good friends, and that source still checks out information for me when I need it.

My government source has really been valuable, a lifesaver, especially today. If I didn't have that source, I'd be in a lot of trouble, particularly if there was someone tailing me or watching my house to set me up for a hit. I could call cops I know who are supposed to be available to help me in an emergency, but by the time I got to them, if I could find them, and had them check out a licence number, I could be dead. It takes them a hellava lot longer to do a licence check than it takes me.

I wasn't the only biker with a source in the Ministry of Transportation. There were bikers from the Vagabonds, Satan's Choice, the Paradise Riders, and other gangs who had girlfriends or associates who either worked in the department or had contacts there to check out plate numbers whenever they wanted to. The wife of a Choice biker was working in a government office like that. The cops found out about it and had her fired. But she was just one of the wives of Choice members working in that office, so the cops didn't stop the flow of information.

What information we couldn't get from corrupt government employees we sometimes got from people we dealt with in banks and at Bell Canada. My banking source, for example, could check the records of any bank to give me information on how much some guy or gal had in their accounts. Information like that was very useful when I wanted to set up an extortion or put pressure on someone to take on a "new partner." It also gave me a way of finding out if a guy was really what he said he was in business. It stopped a lot of ringers from trying to slip through the cracks.

The tipster I had in Bell Canada was equally important. Within two hours of receiving my request, she could provide me with any unlisted telephone number in Canada. She could get me the numbers and addresses of people I wanted to check out, and she often did. That made her very valuable, particularly when I wanted to harass or threaten someone in an extortion, or when I wanted to bomb a location and needed to be sure that I had the right address. I know of a number of bikers who had sources in Bell Canada. Some sources provided the information because they liked the biker, others because they were paid, and still others because they were afraid the biker would hurt them or their families.

Very often bikers need new identification, like driver's licences and credit cards, to change their identities and hide from the cops, or to run up tabs of thousands of dollars using somebody else's credit. While I was a biker, one of my best sources was a Canadian postal worker. He could come up with Ontario driver's licences and major credit cards — American Express, Visa, and Mastercard — whenever I needed them. He'd snatch them from the mails for me, and all he wanted for his troubles was a bottle of whisky. At one time I had five different driver's licences and a whole slew of credit cards I got from him and used to buy thousands of dollars' worth of goods. There were scores of other bikers who had similar sources to get them the documents they needed for identity changes.

We even supplied other bikers, including a lot from the States, with driver's licences and credit cards and other identity documents they needed to hide from the cops. Sometimes documents like that would cost us a bottle of liquor or tickets to a sporting event or a couple of twenty-dollar bills. That's all it ever cost me. There were other biker sources who gave information for drugs, like cocaine or speed or qualudes. Still others wanted to be entertained by women, and that's something all biker clubs had plenty of — women who did what they were told. Whatever the price, bikers in every club had networks that provided documents and information to keep them aware of what the cops were doing, who they were looking for, and what rival biker gangs were up to.

To hide from cops or rival gang members, you needed more than new identities. Just as important were "safehouses," places to hide. Every gang in Canada and the United States has safehouses — safe harbours or cool-off areas that wanted members of gangs can hide out in. Because of our relationship with the Outlaws in the States, members of the Satan's Choice had places they could hide in North Carolina, Florida, Indiana and Illinois, and the southwest. The Outlaws in turn could smuggle their "hot" gang members into Canada to hide in our safehouses in Richmond Hill, Concord, or up in the remote areas of northern Ontario, where we owned farmhouses and other places under the names of people who fronted for us.

We had one Choice member from the St. Catharines chapter who was easily identifiable because of his tattoos. We called him "Charlie Brown" after the Peanuts cartoon character, but that wasn't his real name. We had to hide him and provide new identification for him. So Mother, who was a tattoo expert, redid all his tattoos. The club even got him a job for a transfer company in St. Catharines and told him to keep a low profile and stay away from the clubhouse.

Charlie Brown did what he was told, and for a long time he was able to stay hidden. It was as though he had disappeared from the face of the earth. Charlie finally broke the rules, went out when he shouldn't have, and was eventually caught and sent back to the States, where he was wanted for a number of crimes. If he had paid attention to the rules, the cops would still be looking for him. We knew every move the cops made to try to find him through sources who kept tabs on car dispatches, fugitive warrants, and police computer information. Charlie Brown could have been safe for years, but he didn't follow the rules, and he was caught.

Then there was the case of Howard Berry of the Choice's Peterborough chapter. Berry was wanted in Ontario for shooting a guy in Peterborough at point-blank range with a .303-calibre rifle, so he took off. He was smuggled across the border down to Georgia and a safehouse run by the Outlaws. I heard later that the Georgia Outlaws tested Berry to see how tough he was. They beat him up once, but not before he'd beaten the hell out of some of them. They accepted him after that.

Berry had always been tough, one of the toughest of the Choice. But in Georgia he went bananas. He got involved in some homicides with the Outlaws, and he was charged by the cops with stealing automatic weapons and a tank from an army base. When they grabbed him, they found he was wanted in Canada, so he was deported. He got eight years for attempted murder and assault. Like Charlie Brown, he didn't stay cool, so the cops caught him. I guess nobody can stay cooped up in safehouses for long. Bikers have to be out doing things, usually bad, and that leads to their downfall.

The network of information that the biker gangs had helped Satan's Choice survive a couple of outlaw biker wars.

One of the most violent started in Quebec back in the midsixties between the Montreal chapter of Satan's Choice and the Popeyes Motorcycle Club. The fighting was over drugs and territories. The Montreal Choice members had a big speed lab, and they controlled the supply and distribution of speed for years without letting the Popeyes in on any of the action. The war ended for a while in 1969, when a member of the Popeye gang was found hanged in a graveyard.

But that war is continuing today — only the club names are different. Most of the Montreal Choice members became members of the Outlaws Motorcycle Club, and the Popeyes joined up with the Hell's Angels. The result is that the war between the Outlaws and the Angels heated up old hates between what was the Popeyes and the Choice. Bodies started dropping in a fight for control of the territory the Outlaws held in Montreal. At least twelve Angels have been executed in the war, and some Outlaws have been killed too.

There have been wars going on like that in Quebec for as long as I can remember. They've got a lot of biker gangs there, all fighting for a piece of the pie. In 1979 one gang called the Flambeurs took over the town of Mont-Joli and made drivers and tourists coming in and out of the town pay a toll. They partied in the streets, shook down businesses, and chased and raped women, but nothing happened for a long time. The local cops couldn't handle them, so they had to bring in some high-powered Quebec Provincial Police to get things under control. It was gangs like that and the killings that caused the formation of a Quebec commission that held hearings on the biker gangs and put a lot of heat on them.

In the late sixties, when the Montreal Choice and the Popeyes cooled their war, another biker war began between Satan's Choice and a bunch of smaller biker gangs that included the Vagabonds, the Wild Ones from Hamilton, the Cross Breeds from Niagara Falls, and the Henchmen from Kitchener.

It all started at the Cross Breeds' clubhouse in Niagara Falls. Some Choice members were thrown out of the clubhouse along with a member of the Paradise Riders. Members of the Choice came back later and blew up part of the house. There were some members of the Wild Ones and the Vagabonds in the house when it was bombed. That set the war going. In the months that followed, Satan's Choice bombed other clubhouses and shot a Wild One in front of his clubhouse in Hamilton. The coppers arrested a member of the St. Catharines chapter of Satan's Choice, but he was acquitted in a trial. The guy that really handled the shooting was a member of the Richmond Hill chapter of the Choice.

The war ended about two years later without anybody being killed. Some bikers were shot, including one member of the Choice, and a number of biker gang clubhouses were blown up, so the cops really put the heat on. Members of all the gangs were getting busted for possession of dynamite, for bombings — for all kinds of charges. Things mellowed out and cooled down because of the heat from the cops, and the fighting ended. But no one trusted anyone after that.

Although the war ended, people still held grudges, and a few years later members of the Henchmen who had been involved in the war were dealt with by Choice members who didn't forget. Members of the Choice grabbed two Henchmen and held them hostage. To get their buddies back in one piece, the Henchmen had to deliver their colours to the Choice. The two Henchmen were released after that, but not before one guy got his legs broken. He was put against a wall, and a member of the Choice ran a car into him. After that the Henchmen pretty much folded as a biker gang. The Choice drove them out.

The Choice always had the upper hand in Toronto because we had the best intelligence network around. We were able to move on the other gangs faster than they could move on us because we had such good sources and good information on the habits of the other gangs. A lot of that changed when the Choice split up. The sources of information that were pooled among Choice members dried up because Choice members joined different gangs. When they left, they took their information sources with them. The network was never the same after that; it never recovered, and the cops started getting the upper hand.

Before 1977 Satan's Choice was the best organized, biggest, and toughest motorcycle gang in Canada. Our primary base was Ontario, but we also had chapters in Quebec. We had over two hundred members then, and every chapter had a president, a vice-president, a secretary-treasurer, a sergeant at arms, and a road captain. These were the officers with the power, who kept club members in line. But it was the chapter members who voted them into office every year, so they had to have earned the respect of the membership to get where they were. At various points in my membership in the Choice I held the posts of road captain, sergeant at arms, and vice-president of the Richmond Hill chapter. No one handed the jobs to me. I earned them, and I was proud of it then.

At the national level we had "Mother" — Garnet McKuen — who was the national president, and we had Bernie Guindon, who was the national chairman. It was McKuen who brought the Outlaws to Canada and developed the close relationship between the Outlaws and Satan's Choice. There was no other motorcycle gang in the States that we had an alliance with. Once we started associating with the Outlaws, that was it.

Bernie, however, wasn't in favour of the association with the Outlaws. He partied with Big Jim Nolan and other Outlaws in Florida and dealt drugs with them, but he didn't like them. Before he got a seventeen-year sentence for selling narcotics in 1976, he was the kind of guy who travelled a lot in the biker world and was trusted by the leaders. Before Bernie went to jail, the associations with the Outlaws were just that — associations, nothing more. We dealt drugs together, traded and sold women and weapons, competed in field events, and sometimes did crimes together on either side of the border. But once he was behind bars, the associations with the Outlaws by different chapters of the Choice changed.

It started with the members of the Windsor chapter. They wanted to join up with the Outlaws. They went to St. Catharines, then to Ottawa and Montreal, until finally the Choice was split and a vote was taken. These four chapters decided to join the Outlaws.

The members of these chapters were, as far as I'm concerned, the real nuts of Satan's Choice. If there was going to be a shooting, these were the guys who would do it. They were the guys who killed and enjoyed it. They wanted to be Outlaws because the Outlaws had a big membership, lots of money, and widespread contacts for the sale of the drugs that the Choice members were manufacturing in their labs. And a lot of them hated the Hell's Angels and wanted to fight them with the Outlaws. The rest of us saw no point in getting into a war between gangs like that. We'd just come through some biker wars without too much damage, so why get into new battles now? It didn't make sense.

There was a vote throughout the entire membership of Satan's Choice. The chapters in Hamilton, Toronto, Richmond Hill, and Peterborough voted to stay as Choice. Two members of the Toronto chapter and one from Richmond Hill joined the Outlaws. The vote was fair, but there were hard feelings. Suddenly there were disputes and fights among former Choice members in Ottawa and those in Toronto over drug deals. One guy from Toronto owed gang members in Ottawa over $10,000 for drugs and refused to pay. Others were beaten because they double-dealed on agreements that had worked smoothly before.

Before Satan's Choice split up, three motorcycle gangs—Satan's Choice, the Vagabonds, and the Paradise Riders — had pretty much carved up Toronto when it came to the narcotics traffic in speed, "Canadian Blue," and cocaine. Heroin was pretty much a Mafia trade, and bikers only rarely got into it. There were times when small biker gangs sprouted up and tried to move in on selling dope. They'd quickly get a visit from members of the Choice. We'd go down to their club and tell them to get outta the business. To make sure they got the message, we'd usually strip their colours right off their backs and beat the hell out of them. We weren't going to have any small clubs giving us competition in the dope trade or any other business. The Choice and the other gangs wanted complete control of the city. So when our spies, our intelligence system, told us there were newcomers competing in the dope trade, or extortion, or some other business that was ours, we moved in.

There were no killings that I know of because of this policy, but there were some bad beatings. I remember getting one guy at a motorcycle shop near Weston Road in Toronto. This biker was from the suburbs, and he was trying to operate in our territory.

"You're in Toronto, mister, not home," I said. "You can't wear your colours here."

The biker was big and muscular, and he had a long beard, patches that had the one-percenter emblem, the swastika that a lot of bikers wore, and an emblem that identified the club as the Coffin Wheelers from Sudbury.

"Look, wise guy," I said, "you were told before that you're not supposed to start a club here — you were told that a long time ago. Now you got a choice. You can take your colours off and hand them to me, or I'm gonna beat your face in and take them off."

"Go to hell, Curly," he said. "I'm stayin' put."

"Step outside," I said. "I don't want to ruin this shop."

Now my hand had been broken in another fight a short time before I met this guy. So when he stepped out the door, I had a big wrench from my tool box located right where I could reach it as I stepped outside. He saw me with the wrench, and he started to take off his colours. Then he stopped. That's when I let him have it with the wrench. I took off his colours and left him lying in the street.

The cops were at the motorcycle shop a good part of the time. They saw the fight, but they didn't do anything. They just walked into the shop and waited until it was all over. They watched as the biker got up off the street, staggered to his car, and drove off with blood streaming down his face. His club became associated with the Hell's Angels later on, but they never came back to set up a club in Toronto.

There were some members of the Coffin Wheelers who joined the Windsor chapter of Satan's Choice. They were a tough bunch, mostly shooters. When they got together as a chapter in Sudbury back in 1972, they grabbed some people one day in a fight over a drug deal and tortured them — beat the hell out of them and burned them with a cigarette lighter all over their bodies. The bikers who did the burning, ten of them, got twelve years in jail. It just wiped out the whole chapter in Sudbury. When they got out of the pen, they all went down to Windsor.

While the bikers from Sudbury took stiff raps, and they should have, there is a biker gang that seems to walk around with a horseshoe up their ass whenever they get caught doing something. That gang is the Vagabonds, Toronto's second biggest biker gang.

In all the years I was a biker gang member, it seemed to me that the Vagabonds got off with light raps when they were arrested by the cops. They had a hellava good lawyer, but it was more than that that kept them doing light time on big raps. There was one Vagabond who robbed a mail truck looking for dope. He got caught in the act and was charged with armed robbery. All he got was two years. There were two other Vagabonds who worked for Super Disposal Services Ltd., a garbage company. Their job was to beat up people and burn some houses in Hamilton. But they had a fight with someone in the company and wound up being convicted of extorting the owners. All they got was probation. There were lots of Vagabond cases like that — contract killers who got light sentences in murder cases that wound up as manslaughter charges, extortions, drug dealing. I always wondered whether they were fingering other biker gangs for the coppers and getting deals for themselves.

CHAPTER
7

WORLD OF THE ROUNDERS

B etween the tight-knit organizations of outlaw biker gangs
and the secrecy and tradition of the Calabrian Mafia is a
strange, independent criminal world the public knows little or
nothing about — the world of the Rounders. It's a world I grew
close to early in my life as a biker and later as an enforcer and hit
man for the Calabrians. Rounders in Canada are somewhat like
the crime associates of Cosa Nostra or the Mafia in the States.
They both operate independently in gambling and loan-sharking,
they set up dope deals and hijackings, and they sell their services
to organized groups like the Mafia. But they are different in two
ways: Canadian Rounders, unlike the Stateside crime associates,
don't owe their allegiance to anybody but themselves, and they
deal with all types of organized groups, whether it's Chinese tongs
and triads, outlaw bikers, or Calabrian and Sicilian Mafia crime
families.

The term "Rounder" is one that has been used in Canada for the
last twenty years or more. A Rounder is a street person who
knows hundreds of other people who operate around bars and
clubs, sell dope, gamble, and deal back and forth in stolen or
hijacked goods. Rounders almost always dress well. No matter
where you go — whether to a high-class or average hotel, whether
you bar-hop, or whether you go to the best clubs — you'll find a

Rounder or maybe several Rounders, and you'll usually find them in classy, expensive clothes.

They are the people with connections. They're rough, they're tough, and they know where to get the things you need and want. There's Joe the Rounder over on Yonge Street sitting at one of the better bars. He can get you a pound of grass at a moment's notice if you've got the money and if someone's vouched for you. And there's Ken the Rounder at one of the class hotel discos. If you come up with the right word and enough money, he can hustle up an ounce or more of coke faster than you can reach for your wallet.

Rounders are all independents. They answer to no one — not to the Commisso brothers, not to Paul Volpe when he was alive, not to Vincent Cotroni before he died, not to Danny Mo of Toronto's Kung Lok triad before he went to jail for robbery, not to members of Satan's Choice or Hell's Angels or any other gang. They answer to themselves. They're on the street to make money and to survive. They deal with other street people, but it's the connections they have — for guns, drugs, women, gambling, and stolen goods — that make them important to Canada's criminal world.

Go to a racetrack where everybody seems to know each other, and you'll see little cliques there, groups of ten guys or less hanging around, working out deals. These are the people that the Italian mobs would come to see and talk to if they wanted to find out something. They are the people to whom those of us in the cycle gangs would go to learn about jobs or places to deal speed or people to unload guns and counterfeit currency with. The Rounders are not particularly keen about being around bikers. They'd rather stay away from them, but they can't, because a lot of Rounders you see operating in Toronto or Hamilton or other cities were bikers before they became Rounders.

One of the toughest Rounders I ever knew was a guy named Tough Andy. He and two of his fellow Rounders, a guy they called Bobby and a black man named Billy, were tough enough to take on eight of the toughest members of the Toronto chapter of Satan's Choice in a Yonge Street bar called the Trick. The Choice bikers beat the shit out of them — dragged them into the parking lot and beat them in a car and then ran over one or two of them. Andy kept on fighting, even though he was outnumbered four or five to one. He really mauled one of the bikers — broke his jaw with just one punch. This was Mike Evert, a Choice biker with a long record for assault and trafficking in drugs. When he got through wrecking Evert, Andy went after the biker who had tried to run him down. The biker finally escaped, but not before Andy smashed his car windows and windshield with his fists.

Andy was about five feet nine inches tall, 170 pounds, with curly blond hair. Sometimes he wore a beard, and sometimes he was clean shaven, but he was always neatly dressed in a suit or slacks with a sharp shirt. I personally found out how tough he was at a hotel up at Wasaga Beach. I was at the hotel with another Rounder who was a sort of friend and business associate when I heard some loud yelling and screaming in a hotel across the street. I went over to see what was going on and found a member of the Toronto Choice screaming all kinds of curse words at Andy.

Right then and there I should have turned around, walked back to the hotel, and minded my own business. I didn't. Suddenly the Choice biker jumped Andy and knocked him down and began pounding his head on the floor. My Rounder friend decided to jump in to help Andy. The next thing I knew, I was in the middle. A friend of Andy's decided I was the enemy and took a swing at me. I belted him and knocked him out. Then Andy turned on me and came after me. He said something I didn't like, and I hit him as hard as I could and knocked him down. He got right up, and I knocked him down again. This time I kicked him in the head to keep him down. It was like kicking a block of wood.

Whew!! What a guy! No matter how many times I knocked him down, he got up. Now we were in the street, cars were roaring by, and we were still swinging. I grabbed him and tried to push his head into the wheel of a car that was going by. It didn't work. By then the cops were at the scene, and Andy was now fighting them.

I saw no point in hanging around. I took off down the street to get away from the cops. But I learned that day that Andy was one tough man with a violent, violent temper. What set him off that night? He just didn't like bikers, and he was in the hotel drinking when some members of the Toronto Choice came in. He decided he was going to fight them. Funny thing. About a year after that brawl, Andy started hanging around with some members of the Choice whom I knew, and they began bringing him to the clubhouse, where he started to make some friends. By then he had calmed down and was busy making dope deals with the bikers.

During the late seventies Tough Andy and a lot of the more important Rounders hung out at one of the more popular bars at the Hyatt Regency Hotel. The Hyatt bar was popular with the Rounders because one of them, a guy I'll call Roger, had two waitresses at the bar working for him. The job of the waitresses was to spot trouble, usually in the form of cops trying to slip in undercover. When they spotted the cops or some other people who might be there to cause trouble, they were to tip Roger off. He in turn would tip us off and the Rounders he dealt with, so we could cool any deals we had working before the coppers got on to us. Only Roger knew who the waitresses were, and he never identified them to any of the Rounders. Roger controlled the distribution of cocaine to Rounders at that bar. It wasn't unusual to see a dozen or more Rounders meet with Roger and make multi-ounce buys from him. Sometimes they'd buy more.

Now none of these Rounders were controlled. They all did their own thing, worked independently of each other and of the gangs that operated in the city. They would move around and sell to whomever was buying in the city. They'd sell multiple pounds of speed, which they bought from one particular biker who ran a big speed lab for the Satan's Choice. Sometimes Roger the Rounder was a buyer instead of a seller, particularly when it came to speed. He could handle two, three, or more pounds at a time. The trouble was, he wanted pure speed, not speed that had been stepped on or cut.

Roger's demand for pure speed and the willingness of Satan's Choice to supply it to him was what eventually brought the heat down on everyone, costing a lot of people some really big money. Roger caught the attention of some crooked narcotics investigators, who began following him around. They eventually caught him with a big load of the pure speed, but instead of busting him, they took his supply as a patch and said goodbye. A "patch" was the term the Rounders and others on the street used to mean a payoff. It was the beginning of a lot of patches for dope dealers after that. Roger kept his mouth shut and took the loss as part of the cost of business. Later on he went to jail on another big speed bust. Other dealers, most of them Rounders, had the same business expense, because these narcs started hustling everyone.

Giving up patches to some of the narcs who were working the

city went on for years in the seventies. The favoured technique was to hit a gambler or drug dealer with a minor charge that could land the Rounder six months or more in jail. If he gave them the patch without any trouble, they would either drop the charge in court or make sure the Rounder got probation or a fine with no jail sentence. That way they covered their ass on the bust, and no one was the wiser that they were taking patches. A patch meant they took your proceeds from crime — drugs, illegal guns, or gambling money — and kept it; you said nothing about what they did if you wanted to stay out of jail. It wasn't only the narcs who were pulling that scam. There were other coppers involved too, and none of them ever got caught to my knowledge.

The charges that the crooked cops filed to get their patches weren't usually felonies or indictable charges, just minor summary charges. I recall one time when I was charged with a break and entry on a house on Woodbine Avenue. The house I broke into was the wrong one to hit. The guy I had with me had picked the wrong place, the home of a cop's sister. Someone spotted us leaving the house and got the licence plate number of the car we were driving. Two weeks later I was arrested and charged with break and entry.

The day I was arrested was the day I found out that the house I'd hit was that of the arresting cop's sister. Now this cop was no graft taker. He wasn't looking for a patch, but he played the same kind of game that some of the patch takers did.

"You know the house you broke into was my sister's," the cop said.

"No, I didn't know — honest," I replied, and I didn't.

"No, eh?" he grunted. "Well, listen to me, Cec. You just make sure that everything you took gets back. If you do, I'll see to it the charges get dropped."

I got the message loud and clear. As soon as I got out of the courthouse, I went and gathered all the stuff that we'd taken and put it in a plastic bag. Then I placed it on the side of the road in front of an old Satan's Choice clubhouse on Yonge Street and called the detective involved. He picked it up. A few days later I appeared in court in Richmond Hill, and the charges were dropped. The detective stood up and told the judge that the police had no way of identifying me with the case and that, as a result, they wanted to withdraw the charge. And that's what the judge did.

There were a lot of rules that we played by with the cops that were unusual. There were times, for example, when we — bikers, Rounders, or Mafia hoods — got caught cold turkey on a crime by the cops. We'd try to cut a deal with them through our attorneys before the preliminary hearing. We might want to plead guilty and take a six-month jail sentence rather than go to trial and face a long jail term or an extended trial that would cost a lot of money and take us out of circulation for a long time.

I remember one time when six members of Satan's Choice and myself were charged with break and entry and the theft of motorcycles and other stolen property, including a handgun. I wasn't there when the cops raided the Choice garage and found the stolen motorcycle parts, but I got charged with a couple of deals, and they said they'd found my handgun. To make sure they'd nail me, the cops took the handgun they'd found in the raid and wrote my name on the back of the holster so they would be certain I would be convicted. Our attorney came to all of us after the preliminary hearing and told us we were cooked, that we'd better make a deal before the case went to a higher court for trial. If we fought it, he said, we'd get a minimum two years in the pen. If we didn't fight it, we'd get between four and six months each. It was clear to all of us that we couldn't beat the charges. What evidence the cops didn't get, they'd rigged. So we made the deal, and I got six months.

One of the areas where Rounders are most active is Toronto's airport strip, an area that's filled with bars and motels and hotels. There were several popular hangouts there in the early seventies — Attilla's Cave at the Hilton Hotel and the Skyline Hotel on Dixon Road, where most of the gambler Rounders used to hang their hats. One of the most active was Walter (Wally) Chomski, a professional gambler and loan shark who worked with a Greek gambler who always made sure Wally won in the high-stakes card games at the Skyline. Chomski and the gambler Rounders worked a strictly nighttime operation, ending their games at five or six in the morning after $50,000 or more had changed hands during the night.

For a long time Chomski was close to John (Johnny Pops) Papalia, one of Ontario's most important crime bosses. While he was operating around the Skyline and other Rounder hangouts, Chomski got in some heavy trouble with Johnny Pops. The word among the Rounders was that he owed Johnny Pops a lot of money. Then in December 1974 Chomski had his right leg torn off when a bomb exploded in his Lincoln Continental. The cops said the force of the explosion tore the transmission loose and sent it up through the car, tearing off Chomski's leg. The cops never solved the bombing. There were too many suspects, they said, and no one was talking, least of all Chomski. He survived, and I heard he took care of his problem, whatever it was. He must have. He was allowed to keep operating, and he had no more trouble with the mob.

There were a number of gambler Rounder operations going every night. Chomski and his partner might work the Skyline on a given night, and while they worked there, other groups of two to four Rounders would be working games at the Cambridge Hotel across the street.

There were other groups working games at banquet halls like the Casa Commisso, where a relative of the Commissos controlled the action. The relative knew all the card sharks; sometimes he'd let them in, and sometimes he wouldn't. When he did, he'd tell them that they had to pay a kickback on all their winnings to the Commissos. Then he'd let the suckers sit down and get taken — all but his close friends and relatives.

The gambler Rounders had games all over town — at the Royal York, the Cara Inn, the Holiday Inn, the Bristol Place Hotel, and the Constellation. Their general routine was to hang out in the hotel bars or the coffee shops to make their connections. They weren't big drinkers — they had to keep their minds on business. They didn't cut deals with the hotel employees or management because they didn't want to share their money with anyone. They trusted no one. I've seen them search each other after playing cards to see if they were cheating each other. It was crazy.

To set up their games, they'd get rooms to play in, sometimes through hotel security people, whom they paid off to make sure they wouldn't be raided or ripped off. They would target particular hotels when they knew there were to be big banquets or conventions or stag dinners. Some of the Rounders were members of Kiwanis, the Lions Club, and the Rotary Club, and through those memberships they would get lists of upcoming stag events and banquets to hit. They would know a week or two ahead of time where to go for the action, whether it was Ottawa, Montreal, St. Catharines, Niagara Falls, St. Thomas, or London.

No matter where the gambler Rounders played, they rigged the games, "set the gaff." They always had a gaff for something. Maybe they used crooked dice that were mercury-loaded and bounced to the numbers they wanted because they squeezed them, using the heat from their hands to make the mercury set on the numbers they wanted to turn up. Or sometimes they switched the dice in and out of the game. They did it so fast, no one spotted what they were doing.

I remember one Rounder playing a high-stakes dice game at the Beverly Hills Hotel in Toronto. He was throwing the dice out, and everyone was losing. It was about 2 A.M. when he rolled the dice out again, and this time three of the suckers came clicking out. His hands moved like greased lightning. He grabbed the fuckin' things so fast no one noticed it, but I saw it, and I thought to myself, "Oh shit, nobody saw it because they were too busy drinking." He was palming two dice as he threw the dice out to make the number he wanted, and that time one of those palmed dice slipped.

Then there was a game where they spun a top. The way the Rounder spun it, he always won. The sucker always spun it the wrong way and lost. The cards were rarely marked — they didn't have to be. They had Rounders dealing who could make any card they wanted come up, and I defy anyone to spot what they were doing.

There is one event that stands out in my memory above all others. It happened on the Mariposa Belle, a charter boat owned by Don Pressey, one of Cosimo Commisso's associates. The event was a stag party held for a Rounder named George. George was one of several guys who had robbed a bank in Winchester, getting more than a million bucks in cash, money that was for the payroll of the Windsor racetrack. After George and his friends had tied up all the bank employees to take the payroll, they were caught. So he went to jail. When he was paroled, he was broke, so the Rounders of Toronto decided to hold a stag for him and raise money to give him a new start.

At the time I was working for the Commissos, and they knew I was going to work with the Rounders to help raise money for

George. At the party were a lot of outlaw bikers from Toronto and Kitchener. Among other things, most bikers are degenerate gamblers. They piss their money away in games, and half the time they know those games are rigged. In this case they didn't believe the games were rigged because I was playing in them and I wasn't known to be a gambler — in fact, I had never played poker before.

I sat down at a table with one of the Rounders I knew who had given me some general instructions on how to play. A number of bikers were playing, among them the president of the Toronto chapter of Satan's Choice. He was blowing $500 every hand. So were some others in the game. I just sat there drinking, almost drunk, as the Rounders dealt me winner after winner. Flushes, full houses, three aces, straights — you name it, I got it. Finally Ernie, the Toronto chapter president, stood up and started to leave, but before he did he looked me up and down and shook his head.

"Kirby," he said, "I never seen you play before, but I gotta tell you — you are the luckiest mother I ever saw pick up a card." Then he turned around without another word and left the club. He had dropped more than $4,000 in the game.

That night I won over $10,000. I was sitting in the game for a Rounder who couldn't make the party. The other Rounders in the game dealt me hands that couldn't lose. They knew no one would suspect it was a crooked game with me as the big winner, but it wasn't because I knew anything about the game. Several times they deliberately tried to deal me some losers so it wouldn't look too bad. I almost screwed up their strategy by drawing cards when I wasn't supposed to. A couple of times one of the Rounders had to kick me under the table, hard, to make me play the way they wanted me to. They had to kick me real hard to make me stop playing bad hands that didn't have a prayer of winning and that I was supposed to fold with or only lose a small amount on.

When the game was all over, I met the Rounders and gave them all but $100 of the money I'd won.

"Look," I told them, "just give me a hundred bucks, and you keep the rest for George."

They all laughed, shook my hand, and bought me a few drinks. I was supposed to have kept half, but I'd had a hellava lot of fun doing what I'd done, and they'd really done all the work. It was worth it for me to see some of those bikers get ripped off, especially Ernie. He'd figured he was gonna clean me out in that game. It was worth it to see the expression on his face when he left with his pockets empty.

Ernie should have known better in the first place. When you start gambling with the Rounder card sharks, you'd better check your belt to see if you've still got your pants when you get up from a game. They can't play without cheating. It's in their blood. They've just gotta have that extra edge — they gotta get something for nothing.

Ron the Rounder was like that. He was one of the best Italian Rounders in the business, and he was an expert gambler. I met him while I was a biker, and we quickly became friends. He had style, Ron did. He did everything with flair. He made and lost literally millions of dollars in card games he played in from Buffalo and Niagara Falls to Toronto and Montreal. He survived because he was close to the Italian mob — Cosa Nostra in Buffalo and the Calabrians in Niagara Falls. He played high-stakes card games with them, but unlike his operations in games at banquets and clubs and stag parties, Ron never cheated while playing his mob friends. That's when he lost big sometimes — playing with them. They hustled him, but he didn't hustle them. It wasn't healthy.

Because of his close association with the different Italian mob groups, Ron had a lot of action steered his way, suckers the Italian mob dealt with and used but told him it was okay to work over and take. Of course, they expected and got a piece of his action.

Sometimes Ron worked the suckers with the best gambler in all of Toronto, Eddie Neuff. I could introduce you to a dozen gambler Rounders, and they'd all tell you the same thing: before he was killed, Eddie Neuff was *the best*. He was an independent, a Rounder, but he lacked the protection some of the Rounders had who worked with different mobs like Ron did. Eddie was well known in the States, where he'd been barred from a number of casinos in Las Vegas and Atlantic City because he was too quick. He was a professional counter who could tell you how many aces or how many fives or whatever numbered card had been dealt by a casino dealer and would use that ability to his advantage to make big bets on hands when the percentages favoured him.

One of the suckers Ron and Neuff really worked over was the

owner of a prominent Italian Toronto food company. The food dealer — I'll call him Giuseppe — was the kind of guy who'd bet when the next raindrop would fall. He wouldn't listen to anyone — not his brother, not his family, not his friends — he just had to play in the high-stakes card games that Ron and Neuff were operating in a room at the Seaway Hotel. Ron told me later that he had never played with a sucker for punishment like Giuseppe. Night after night he would show up and play, and each night Ron and Neuff would take him off for $20,000, $50,000, $80,000 at a time. It was a dream come true for them.

Then one night Ronnie told me that Giuseppe had paid off in tens and twenties the night before at the hotel game. "He had a bag full of cash," he said, "and when he left he was still carrying a lot with him, maybe twenty thousand or more."

"Does he keep all that money at home?" I asked.

Ronnie looked up at the ceiling like he saw a pot of gold on top of the rainbow instead of at the end. He reached into his pocket, took out Giuseppe's address, and handed it to me.

"Why don't you break into his house some night," he said. "There's a hellava lot of money in there. This guy always pays in cash, and he comes to the games straight from his home." He paused for a minute, letting what he said sink in. "You get into his place and sack it, and whatever you get, just give me half. The rest is yours."

I knew I couldn't handle it alone, so I called a biker friend of mine to help me, and we headed for Giuseppe's home off Bayview Avenue in Toronto. No one was there, and we broke in. We couldn't have been inside ten minutes when Giuseppe pulled in his driveway. We both ran out the back door, and as we ran my friend shouted, "Cec, I got some money out of a fuckin' bag—I don't know how much. There was a lot more, but I didn't have time to grab it, goddamnit."

We got back to the car we'd parked near a school and started counting the money. There was over $8,000 in fifty- and one-hundred-dollar bills. The night before he'd paid Ronnie off in tens and twenties, and he'd still left with a bag full. We'd missed the big bundle, the big stash, because we hadn't cased the place the way we should have. We should have made sure he was gonna be gone for a lot longer before we broke in. I gave Ronnie $4,000, and my partner and I split the rest.

Ronnie laughed when I told him what happened, but not so

hard that he didn't take his cut. Later he told me that every gambler Rounder in town tried to get in on the action, get a piece of this food dealer. Ronnie and Eddie had milked him for hundreds of thousands, but like all good things it came to an end. Giuseppe's family found out he was squandering the family profits at the card tables, and they forced him to stop. Not long after that Giuseppe died.

Ronnie was so good at card cheating that he started to run his own school for card cheats, particularly for some of his Italian mob friends. He got a lot of people hot at him for doing that. It was really stupid. He was teaching newcomers a technique that's supposed to be kept inside the gambler Rounders' organization. The reason they wanted to keep it tight was because there were maybe thirty professional card cheats in the city who worked the big card games. For a lousy $100 a lesson, Ron was giving away the road map to a gold mine.

Neuff, on the other hand, wasn't so lucky. He became the target of a gunslinger friend of mine named Billy the Rounder, who was also a member of Satan's Choice for a while, and his sidekick, Al.

The last Neuff was seen alive was in a Toronto restaurant on December 12, 1978. He was supposed to be married three days later to his girlfriend. His frozen body was found on January 5, 1979, stuffed in the trunk of a car at Toronto International Airport. He'd been shot repeatedly. It took four days to thaw out his body at the Metro morgue and figure out how he'd been killed, but they never figured out who killed him.

Now for years the coppers thought that Neuff had crossed some Mafia bigwig or some other big organized-crime guy and been knocked off. Then five years later, on November 14, 1983, they found the body of Toronto Mafia boss Paul Volpe shot and stuffed in the trunk of his parked car at the same airport. For a while some cops speculated that Volpe may have been killed by the same assassin.

Well, Al told me before he was killed himself that Billy the Rounder did Neuff, and although I wasn't there to witness it, I know he was telling the truth.

It seems Al and Billy the Rounder had a guy in New York who was giving them some terrific tips on football games, on what teams were going to win and by how many points. This guy from New York was right about 90 per cent of the time, according to

Al. He and Billy were paying this tipster in New York for his information. His payoff was a kickback on the money they won by taking off all the bookies in Canada with their bets.

For weeks they were having a field day busting out a lot of bookies. One of those they busted took off before paying off thousands of dollars, and Billy and Al went looking for him. They searched for him at his home, at his clothing store, at all his regular haunts, but he was nowhere to be found.

Billy the Rounder was furious. "I'm gonna get that bastard, Cec!" he shouted one night. "So help me, I'm gonna get that little fuck and bury him." I don't know if he did, but he also made one other promise that night. "The next fuckin' bookie that rips me off, I'm gonna fuckin' do him," he said.

Al told me that that next guy who screwed them was Neuff, a professional gambler who was taking their bets. They started betting heavily with him and winning, but he smelled a rat and on the last bet wouldn't pay off. So they grabbed Neuff, shot him, took him out to the airport, and dumped him to make an example of him. The message that they were delivering was, "This is what happens to bookies who don't pay off." It was a message that bookies throughout Canada understood.

Like a lot of outlaw bikers, Rounders are also boosters, store thieves who either act like shoplifters or do the smash-and-grab bit at jewellery stores — they smash the front window, grab what they can, and are far from the scene in less than three minutes. Ron the Rounder was a great booster of Royal Doulton china and figurines, and he was good at it. He drove the Skyline Hotel crazy with his boosting. But one of the best smash-and-grab thieves around was a Satan's Choice biker by the name of Armand Sanguigni.

Armand was Italian. He'd grown up in Toronto's Little Italy, around St. Clair Avenue. When he wasn't racing around on his bike with members of the Choice, or peddling dope, or hustling counterfeit bills, he was busy on the street boosting from jewellery stores. He was really good at it. It was a sideline that made him $3,000 to $4,000 a month. Armand wasn't a particularly good fighter, but he sure as hell was no coward. He was only five feet seven in his stocking feet, and I can't remember him ever weighing over 145 pounds, even when he wore a heavy black beard, mustache, and long hair.

Armand was a fast talker, and his main topic was sports or gambling. He was always at the track when it was open, gabbing with friends and Rounders and betting his shirt. One day in 1978 he and a friend of his, a Rounder-turned-biker-turned-Rounder named Kenneth Goobie, went to the house of a friend of the Commissos to pick up some funny money. I was at the house when they made the pickup — $300,000 in counterfeit American currency. A day later they had sold it all off, peddled it all over Toronto after paying the Commissos fifteen cents on the dollar. It couldn't have been two days later when there was a story in the paper about the town being flooded with the counterfeit. It became so hot nobody wanted to touch it.

The funny thing was that the counterfeit money had been hot for a number of years. The Commissos and the Calabrian Mafia had peddled the stuff around New York, particularly in Long Island and Brooklyn. And they pushed it in Connecticut through pizza parlours the Calabrian Mafia controlled or could influence. They moved hundreds of thousands of dollars of the funny money in the States, and they moved a lot of it in Vancouver with the help of the Vancouver mob and an Italian friend of theirs named Carmelo Gallo. In 1976 the roof caved in on that operation because they sold the funny money to an undercover agent. They were all convicted.

For a while things cooled down over the money that Goobie and Sanguigni had flooded the market with. But a lot of people, bikers and Rounders, had to sit with thousands of dollars' worth of the phony bills. Tough Andy got stuck with a big bundle, and Goobie even got burned. He gave $20,000 in bills to a biker they called Jerry, who was a member of the Last Chance Motorcycle Club. Jerry was supposed to sell it, but he ended up losing it. Rather than face Goobie, he took off. Goobie tried to hunt him down. I even went with Goobie one night to try and find him. No luck. So Goobie did the next best thing. About a year later he took Jerry's bike and sold it. I got about $200 out of the deal.

But that didn't end the tale of the counterfeit twenties. About a year later, in 1979, I did a favour for Cosimo Commisso, and he told me he had some counterfeit money I could have if I wanted it. I thought, "What the hell, it's cool now. Maybe I can move it and make a quick buck." So I said sure.

"You know, Cec," he said, "that money's been nothing but a

pain in the ass. I got pinched with it. Remo, he got pinched with it. Everybody that's touched that fuckin stuff has been caught."

Cosimo let it sink in. He was letting me know I could land in trouble if I handled the money he was offering me.

"When we first got this stuff," he said, "we had a whole room just piled high with the money. We had about twenty million bucks."

Cosimo didn't say where they had kept the money, but he said he had a guy who was still holding $20,000. "You get in your van," he said, "and drive down to this place on Bloor Street. Park your van in the parking lot, leave your doors unlocked, and take a walk for about an hour. When you come back, the money, she'll be waiting for you. But you be careful. It's jinxed money."

I did what he told me, and when I came back to the van, the money was there waiting. It was the same kind of funny money that Goobie had gotten. I took it north to a cottage I had and buried it in a container. About a year later I came back to move it. When I dug it up, I found it was soaked, even though I'd wrapped it carefully and put it in the container. I didn't let a little water discourage me. I took the money back to the city, dried it out, and then examined it to see if it could be used. The bills must have been cut by a butcher. Some were short, some were long — it was terrible. I stacked and wrapped it and took it to Ron the Rounder, who gave me $300 for the whole load. The last time I saw that funny money was in November 1980, when biker Gary Barnes came out of prison. He stopped by my house to say hello and pulled out a roll of the bills.

"For chrissake, Gary," I shouted, "where the hell did you get that shit? Get that crap outta my house! I'm tired of seeing it. It's the same stuff we had years ago."

Gary had gotten the money from Goobie and Sanguigni, who were supposed to be his friends. The trouble was, they didn't tell him how hot the money was. It couldn't have been a week later when Barnes started passing the money. Somebody took the licence plate number off the car he was using, and the cops traced it back to him and busted him. I felt bad about that when I heard it. I liked Gary. He was a pretty easy-going guy, but not the world's smartest.

CHAPTER

8

CALL THEM TREACHEROUS

B urglary, safecracking, counterfeiting, murder, arson, extortion, prostitution, motorcycle theft, insurance fraud, gang warfare — all that and more was part of my everyday life as an outlaw biker. You either live with it, become part of the action, or you don't survive. You become an outcast, and sooner or later you become very dead.

At least some of these activities provided a source of income to the biker. But for the biker who was ambitious and wanted to make a bigger buck, moving narcotics was where the real action and the big money were. It was also where the violence could always be found, where gang wars started, and where killings were part of the territory.

I first got directly involved in the narcotics business through Ken Goobie. I knew a lot of bikers who dealt in narcotics, but until I hooked up with Goobie, I'd pretty much steered clear of it except for smoking a reefer now and then. I never thought much of dope dealers. I still don't. They can't be trusted, and Goobie was no exception, although it took me a little longer than usual to realize it.

I first met Goobie in 1970. He was only twenty-two then, but he was big and tough, with a quick and violent temper that had already cost him more than a year in jail for assault. We took an

71

almost immediate liking to each other, I think because he was such a good fighter and backed off from no man. He was six feet, 170 pounds, a little bald on top, with long hair down the sides and a mustache—he was never without that mustache. He had done some amateur boxing, winning two or three matches while fighting at the Lansdowne Boxing Club. And although he was relatively young, he had already earned a reputation as a tough Rounder in the downtown area of Toronto, where he battled in bars, dabbled in selling small quantities of dope, ran around with lots of women, and burglarized homes whenever he was broke. He was forever joking around and shadowboxing with everybody in the bars and restaurants that he frequented.

But behind that fun-loving exterior was a cool, calculating character with a brain that was always clicking over, figuring out ways to make money. Burglaries, coin thefts, hustling bike parts, gambling — if there was a way to make a quick buck, Goobie found it.

In 1972, after I'd introduced him to a number of Choice members, Goobie decided he wanted to join Satan's Choice. He did his Striking period, and within a year he'd stepped up the ladder to become one of the biggest outlaw biker dealers in narcotics. One of his sources of supply were my friends Harry the Hat and Patsy Perry, two gambler Rounders who had connections for large quantities of speed from biker methamphetamine labs on both sides of the border. Harry the Hat and Perry could come up with five to ten pounds of speed a week for Goobie. He was paying them $4,500 a pound and selling it to bikers and Rounders, to pimps and prostitutes, in the hotels and bars around Toronto's west end for more than $8,000 a pound after he'd stepped on it (diluted it) once or twice.

In the early stages of his operation, Armand Sanguigni was Goobie's number-one guy, his trusted courier and distributor. I became his banker and sometime courier. Many times I would have to take the money that Goobie and Sanguigni were pulling in to a restaurant, where I would meet Harry the Hat and pay him for dope that had been sold, thereby ensuring future deliveries.

It was an operation with high profits and equally high risks. Typical of these risks was a period when there was a lot of American money coming in to pay for drug buys. Goobie told me that he and Armand were selling quantities of speed to a Rounder and safecracker known as Irish Danny. Danny had some kid working for him named Larry, who was caught by the Horsemen (RCMP). The Horsemen turned this kid into an informer, and before long they were buying the narcotics from Goobie and others using American money. Eventually Harry the Hat, Perry, and Goobie were all busted for trafficking in speed, but Goobie beat the rap. They never got to me, although I was the one with the American money, and I was the one using about ten different banks to convert it to Canadian currency. The Horsemen never knew, or never had enough evidence to prove, that I was involved, and they never charged me with anything.

Before too long the Horsemen also got Armand. The day he got nailed, he'd been at my apartment on Jane Street. I watched him as he crossed the street from my apartment to his car. As he walked, he threw a gym bag he was carrying up in the air like a basketball — higher and higher — playing catch with himself. The bag was filled with better than two pounds of speed.

As I watched him, I remember thinking to myself, "What a dummy! He's walking across that goddamned parking lot without a care in the world, throwing $13,000 up in the air like it's nothing." He got into his car and made it almost to Yonge Street, in the heart of Toronto, before the Horsemen stopped him, smashed into him and drove him off the road. That ended his effectiveness as a courier for a while. He got two years in jail.

With Sanguigni in jail, I had to do a lot of the courier work for Goobie, and he had to watch over the money. By 1976 he had developed another major source of supply and was selling big amounts to the Peterborough Satan's Choice, to the Kitchener Choice, and to some of the more trusted Rounders, including one I called Roger the Dodger. I made most of the big deliveries to Roger the Dodger. I was storing the stuff in a gym that I had access to, which I later bought and turned into a health club. I used to stash the speed in the boiler room on top of the vents, usually ten pounds or more at a time.

Goobie would make the connection with the buyers and come to the gym to tell me where to meet them, and that was it. I'd take out the amounts he had sold and deliver them to a drop-off location. For every pound I transported I got a lousy hundred bucks. I was being hustled by Goobie and I knew it, but I wanted the money and I liked the excitement, so I did it even though I knew I was taking high risks for what amounted to pennies.

Goobie had an almost foolproof system. With one exception, he never touched the dope he was selling. As his courier, I never met the guy who was delivering the loads. That was my insurance policy. Goobie would send me to a place like a particular garbage can at York University, where a bag containing ten or fifteen pounds of the stuff had been dropped. If the cops showed up, all they would see was another bum, rifling through a bloody garbage can looking for some chicken parts or something.

Of course, I took precautions to make sure I wasn't being followed. Sometimes I'd use different cars for pickups, other times a van. When I made deliveries, I made them to people whom Goobie or I knew. We never made deliveries to strangers. I had to be confident enough to meet with a buyer. I'd have to have known him for at least two or three years. When you sell to people you know, it's less likely you're going to get caught. The best system in the world is to sell to those you've known a long time. If you're stupid enough to sell to strangers, you might as well go into the cop shop and give yourself up.

The speed we were getting was like a rock. It was being brought from a biker lab to drop-off points, and Goobie would be notified where it was stashed. Usually that was in a locker at Oakdale or at the Hillcrest Mall in Richmond Hill, or I'd find it underneath the rear of a trailer in a private parking lot late at night or inside a garbage container at York University. It was never the same location, always someplace new, and each load would be ten to fifteen pounds, about the size of a briefcase. The most I picked up in one day was fifteen pounds in a suitcase left at the Hillcrest Mall. It was four inches thick and twenty inches long, and it was so hard, I had to use a hammer to break it up for distribution.

I would put it in a special briefcase, take it back home or some other place, and chop it up into five- and ten-pound pieces. Then I'd hide it at the gym or in a tool shed at my dad's or high in the rafters of a garage we had down the street. When I'd get the call for a delivery, I'd drop it at prearranged locations that Goobie had set up with buyers we both knew. I'd make sure they picked it up, but I never took any of the money. Goobie saw to it that they paid him. Moving a fifteen-pound load meant $1,500 in my pocket on a pickup and a like amount when I delivered it to the locations that Goobie had set up. But while I was picking up three grand on pickups and delivery, he was pocketing ten times that amount for the same load.

Goobie never went near the dope himself except once that I can remember. He had decided to bypass me as a courier and save himself a couple of thousand dollars on one transaction. He sent the buyer to a trailer that was parked in a lot off Yonge Street, telling him the load was stashed under the trailer. When the buyer got there, he couldn't find it and came back to me and Goobie at the Beverly Hills Hotel, screaming, "The stash isn't there, you bastard!"

"It's gotta be there!" Goobie shouted back. "I'll get the shit myself."

Goobie calmed him down and took off for the parking lot on Yonge Street with me. When we got there, Goobie got out of the car and spent nearly an hour crawling around under trailers and cars until he finally found it. What had happened was that the guy who owned the trailer had moved it and parked another car in the spot where the load had been stashed. Goobie found it underneath the car. It was the only time I saw Goobie handle a load of narcotics himself. He always had someone else do the dirty work. Why should he do it? He was running the operation.

By 1977 I was pissed off about getting only $100 a pound, and I told Goobie how I felt.

"Look, Kenny," I said, "I want at least two hundred dollars a pound to handle this stuff. I'm doing a lot of work here, taking a lot of risks. I want a raise to two hundred."

He agreed to up the ante to $150, and I accepted it. It wasn't long after that, maybe a few weeks, that I was stopped by the cops as I was driving a black van I owned. In the van was better than two pounds. The cops searched and searched and searched, but they didn't find a thing. I drove away without being charged with anything. The load was stashed behind the panel of a back door.

It wasn't the first or the last time I had a close call. There was a time on Jane Street. I was following Sanguigni's car with my van when suddenly he speeded up and got about ten cars ahead of me. As I tried to keep sight of him, he went through an intersection. I had to stop for the light. Seconds later two Mountie cars went barrelling through the red light after him. About an hour later I phoned him and asked him what had happened.

"Whaddya mean, what happened?" he asked. "Nothing. What shoulda happened?"

"Didn't you see the Mounties chasing you?" I asked.

"Hell, no, there were no Mounties chasing me," he said.

"Armand, you're an asshole," I said angrily. I was transporting more than three pounds of speed in the van on a delivery. If the Mounties had stopped me after missing him, I'd have been cold meat. I was lucky that time.

Later on Goobie and a guy from the Vagabonds motorcycle gang developed a way to package speed that made it easy to slip it by the Mounties and other narcotics agents. What they did was develop a process to shape the speed into a pie plate shape; they called it "pie plate speed." It came in different sizes and weights, but the shape was the same, and for a long time the narcotics agents didn't realize that the "pies" that bikers were delivering and receiving were actually quantities of speed.

Goobie was making millions. I know because I was his banker for a long, long time. Every week I'd take $20,000 to $30,000 or more and move it through the banks, changing the money from Canadian to American. I can't remember ever being questioned by anyone at any of the banks. I'd usually change about $2,000 at each bank, never more than that, so they wouldn't ask questions. Once the money was changed, I'd arrange to wire it to relatives of Goobie's in the States, particularly in California. I was just one of his couriers, and I handled over three hundred pounds of speed in a two-year period. That alone represented more than $2.4 million in sales, and Armand must have handled double that or more for Goobie before he was jailed.

What Goobie and Armand didn't send across the border, they gambled away, especially Armand. They were being taken like any sucker at a black crap table in the Yorkville area. Those blacks just loved Goobie and Armand. Goobie dropped an average of $2,000 a night, sometimes more, for months. They were ripping him off and loving it, and he wasn't smart enough to figure it out. He had the fever, and they kept his temperature high. Armand was just as bad. He was blowing thousands a week on bookies and the tables. It was god-awful to see.

You would have thought that making money like that would

have satisfied Goobie. After all, he had the Satan's Choice colours, and that meant he was protected. It meant he wouldn't get ripped off. If an outsider tried, the gang would go after him. That protection was implicit while you were a member of the Choice. It was like an insurance policy for the narcotics business. Of course, there were exceptions. You could become the target of members of another motorcycle gang, who would rip off your stash, or worse — kill you doing it.

Dope rip-offs became a way of life in the narcotics trade, and outlaw bikers very often used techniques that they saw police use in busting dope rings. At Satan's Choice we had a number of techniques, but the most popular and successful one was to use a girl or someone known on the street to buy dope from the dealers we wanted to set up. That's the way the cops did it. They'd have an informer or undercover agent make a buy, and when they got the signal that the buy had been made and the dealer was carrying dope, they'd bust in to make the arrest.

Well, we did a variation on that technique. Our "agent" would be sent in to make a buy from the dealer, usually an ounce of speed or cocaine, and leave, making an arrangement to buy a couple of ounces on the next visit. The "agent" would reappear in a day or two to make the two-ounce buy. By then the dealer would have confidence in our agent and be ready to be set up. The agent would then make arrangements to buy a pound or more on a special date and at a prearranged place. Once he or she went in to make the buy, we would come charging in behind, our guns drawn, shouting, "This is the police!" as we flashed phony identification. The dealers would freeze without a fight. Convinced we were the cops, they would surrender their guns and say nothing as we confiscated their narcotics and weapons. It was only when we tied them up and left that they'd realize they'd been had.

Before we hit an operation, we would all know who the dope dealers were and what quantities they handled. We'd know if they had two or three pounds of hash or marijuana or speed or cocaine in their place. When I went on a job, I always made sure we had it thoroughly cased. Because of that, we never had a problem on a dope rip-off. Others who handled rip-offs weren't always that careful.

There were always reports of shootings and beatings, like in the Rice Lake case. That one started off as a drug rip-off. Two of the Choice bikers ended up shooting a guy called Randy, who they believed was a dealer. He was hit in the spine and ended up becoming a cripple. There were four witnesses in the case, and one of them just happened to turn up at a motorcycle shop that was used by a lot of the bikers. One of them was Armand Sanguigni, and he and another biker recognized the witness. They grabbed him, kidnapped him, and took him to the Satan's Choice clubhouse at 7 Woodbine Avenue.

When I drove up, they had just put him in the trunk of a car. I looked in the trunk, and he was gagged and tied up, but I couldn't be sure if he was alive or dead at that time. Armand told me the guy was a witness against William (Bill) Dollack and Bob Cousins, who'd been charged in the rip-off shooting. Armand said they'd beaten the witness up and hit him with battery acid. They were going to take him to Peterborough so the guys at the Peterborough chapter could dispose of him. About a week later I read in the paper that they'd found the guy in Rice Lake. The cops came and searched the clubhouse for the rope they used and other things, but nobody was ever charged with anything.

To me it didn't make sense to get rid of just one witness, but Sanguigni and the others thought it would scare off the other witnesses in the case. It didn't. They testified, and Dollack received seven years and Cousins six years for the shooting. The cops never did solve the murder of the witness they found in Rice Lake.

Goobie's biggest rip-off was one that involved a lucky circumstance and a phony story. The guy he took was our supplier and the chemist who manufactured the stuff for biker gangs, including the Vagabonds, at a hidden lab up near Sault Sainte Marie. In 1977 Goobie spotted an article in a newspaper that identified one of his biggest buyers, an associate of the Vagabonds, as having been arrested at the Detroit airport with "a large quantity" of speed. What the article didn't say was that the quantity was only two pounds. Now Goobie had just gotten fifteen pounds from our supplier, and he told him that the buyer he'd sold the fifteen-pound load to had been busted and the entire load seized. He showed him the article, and the supplier bought the story.

What really happened was that Goobie had sold off the fifteen pounds, including the two pounds to his Detroit biker buyer, collected the money, and lost it all at the gaming tables — more than $100,000. He lost so much at the black crap tables and with the bookies, in fact, that he fell behind in the mortgage payments on one of his houses. The next thing I knew, the house burned down, and Goobie collected on the insurance. Funny thing about that fire. The only things that didn't burn to a cinder were about ten or twelve of his photo albums.

About a year later the source Goobie had been using offered me the same deal he'd given Goobie when he'd supplied him. He'd provide me with the speed in whatever quantities I wanted, and when I'd sold it off, I'd pay him. He wanted the same $4,500 a pound he was getting from Goobie wholesale. I turned the deal down. The risks were too great, and after three years with Goobie and his crew, I knew you couldn't trust anyone you were dealing with. You never knew if you were dealing with cops or not or whether you were going to be set up for a rip-off. It wasn't worth it to me.

Until that happened, Goobie, Sanguigni, Mike Evert, and myself were a tight little clique in Satan's Choice. If one of us got into trouble, the rest would be there to help him. We were very close. If one of us got involved in a fight, everyone jumped in to help, even when the odds were heavily against us. Sometimes we got into trouble helping a friend. Like Gary Barnes.

When Barnes got out of prison, as I said before, he started passing some counterfeit money that he'd gotten from Goobie and Armand. He stayed with me for a short time, and he borrowed my .22-calibre pistol with a silencer. For some reason he went to Peterborough and got himself into trouble shooting up a tent full of people. He didn't hit anybody, but he was jailed for parole violation and then charged with possession of a weapon dangerous to public peace.

I went up to Gary's place the day after he'd shot up the tent to get the silencer, and that's when I found out he'd used my .22. I talked to Goobie, Mike, and Armand about what had happened and about the witnesses that were stacked up against Barnes. We decided to see if we could help him by seeing some of the people he was charged with shooting at and trying to persuade them not to testify in court. When we went to visit one of them, we ran into trouble we hadn't expected. We hadn't threatened him yet — we were just trying to talk to him through a partially opened door. But I could see through a crack in the door that he had a friend with a gun trained on us.

"Look," I tried to reason with him, "tell your friend we just came here to talk. We don't want trouble, we just want to talk."

The guy wasn't listening. His friend kept the rifle in his hands pointed at my belly. Then he started yelling and shouting at the four of us. I knew that if we stayed around, it could only end up in a shootout, so I told the guy we were going to leave and that we wanted no problems with him. Two months later we were charged with attempted obstruction of justice and attempted murder. We were all acquitted in a trial before a jury.

Under ordinary circumstances we might have pleaded to a lesser charge, but a source I had knew a cop in Metro Toronto Police who was involved in the investigation. The cop had talked to some people about the case before we were arrested and said we were going to be charged with a crime. He didn't say exactly what the crime was. After we were bailed out, the cop also predicted that we'd beat the case if we fought it, that there wasn't much evidence against us. My source heard about it and told us that all we had to do was get a good lawyer and fight the case. It was another instance of our sources being better than the cops, good enough to help us beat charges that might have cost us a jail term.

There were a lot of drug-smuggling operations going on in the late seventies between motorcycle gangs in Canada and the United States. One of the more profitable ones that I knew of was a hashish-smuggling business that operated from Jamaica via New York to Toronto. It was run by members of the Last Chance Motorcycle Club and the Toronto Outlaws, who later became the Rebels Motorcycle Club. At that time cocaine wasn't as big as it is now, and bikers zeroed in on things like grass, hash, and speed.

The bikers were moving large quantities of hashish and hash oil from Jamaica using their girlfriends as "mules." Three of the bikers, including a former president of the Toronto Outlaws, had each invested $10,000 in this smuggling business. They'd send one of their girlfriends to Jamaica, where she'd pick up the load, strap the stuff to her legs, fly to New York, and change flights for Toronto.

On one of the trips they sent three girls down at once after giving them $15,000 each to pay for the loads. The girls left

Jamaica without any problem, but en route to the States they started partying, and a sharp stewardess noticed that one of the girls had something taped to her legs.

With the help of the pilot, the stewardess tipped off customs before the plane landed in New York, and the customs agents pulled the girls off the plane, had them searched, and confiscated the hashish loads. The bikers who had the big investment wanted to have the girls killed because they'd been so stupid, but they didn't. Two of the girls got tried in the States and got three years. The third was never extradited or tried, but the bikers lost one hellava profitable smuggling business. In 1979 hash oil was selling for $500 an ounce in Canada. The bikers were buying the stuff for $500 a pound in Jamaica, and on each trip they were moving twenty pounds — loads worth $160,000. That was a hellava return on a $30,000 to $45,000 investment in those days. Now it's peanuts.

A couple of years before I got out of the narcotics business with Goobie, I gave up my membership in Satan's Choice. At the heart of the problem was dope.

It all happened in March 1976. At the time I was vice-president of the Richmond Hill chapter of Satan's Choice. The Choice was involved in several insurance frauds that involved the phony theft of motorcycles. What we would do was get some guy to register motorcycles in his name. He'd then report them stolen, and the insurance company would send him a cheque to cover the loss. Those motorcycles that we were collecting on were bringing in insurance claims of $7,000 or more each.

One of the front men we were using was a young guy who was rooming with a black kid. I'd had some trouble with both of them, and in front of the white guy I'd been a little nasty to his black roommate. I'd chewed out this white guy for being late on some payoffs to us. He noticed, I guess, that I didn't take to blacks, and he decided to use it.

A week or more after I'd had problems with this kid, my wife started getting threatening letters and phone calls. The letters were written in such a way as to make us think that a black had written them. I went wild. No black was going to threaten my wife or me. So I went to this black's house, but before I left, I tucked a gun in my belt and went to the Choice clubhouse to get some backup. There was just one guy there, Billy the Bum.

"I'm going down to face this nigger," I said to Billy, "and I wouldn't mind having you back me up in case something happens. All you gotta do is sit out in the car and keep an eye open in case some other people show up."

This bearded giant of courage looked up sort of lazily from where he was sitting and said, "Gee, Cec, I can't leave yet. I just ordered a pizza."

That blew my mind. I had helped this guy out of a few jams and never hesitated. I was steaming. It was a club rule that you always helped a fellow biker when he was facing trouble; you stood with him and fought with him. I'd always lived by that rule.

"You son of a bitch!" I shouted. "You just stay where you are and eat your fuckin' pizza. I'll do what I gotta do without you."

So I went to King Street alone that night to this black kid's boarding house. He'd moved to a different room away from his former white roommate after they'd had a fight. I went there and talked to him calmly, all the time fingering my gun in case I ran into trouble. First I pulled out the letters my wife had received and showed them to him. He looked them over and shook his head vigorously.

"I didn't write no letters to your wife," he said nervously. "I got no reason to."

"Maybe you did, and maybe you didn't," I said. "You willing to give me a sample of your signature and handwriting and come to the clubhouse later? I'll make sure your ex-roommate is there and make him sign a piece of paper. I think maybe he might have written them and tried to get you in trouble for it."

"Sure," he said. "I got nothin' to hide."

We set a time to meet, and as I left I was greeted by six big buck blacks standing out on the street in front of the boarding house waiting for me. Each of them had a gun. If anything had happened to the kid, they were going to gun me down. They let me pass without any trouble.

The next night the black kid and his ex-roommate showed up at the clubhouse. The roommate's girlfriend waited for him in a car outside. I shoved a piece of paper in front of the white kid and made him sign it. He was shaking like a leaf, but he signed his name. It was a match to the handwriting in the letters.

I grabbed a .410 shotgun, pulled the hammer back, and pointed it right in his face. As I did that, he pissed all over himself.

"You're the bastard who's been writing letters to my wife — not this kid," I said, pointing to the black. "I should blow your fuckin' brains out right here. Now there's the door. You better get outta here while you're still alive. If I ever see you in the west end again, I'll put you in the hospital for a year."

The kid ran out of the clubhouse, wet pants and all, straight to the car with his girlfriend and drove off like his life depended on it.

I met the next night with the chapter president, a guy we called Monk.

"Here's my colours," I said, throwing them on a chair in front of him.

"What's the matter, Cec?" he asked.

I pointed to Billy. "One, you see this guy here?" I said. He nodded. "I was in trouble, and I asked him to help. I'd helped the bastard before when he was in tight spots. He was a fuckin' coward. All he said was he was gonna eat some pizza. He's not a man. I won't be associated with someone like that." I paused a minute, letting what I said sink in. "You want me to stay?" I asked.

"Hell, yes, we want you to stay," Monk answered. "We don't want to lose you as a member."

"Well then, throw the bastard out," I said.

Monk took a vote of the chapter's membership, but there wasn't a high enough percentage of the members — you need 90 per cent — to vote him out. Seventy-five per cent wanted him out, but that wasn't enough. He had some friends who depended on him to get them dope that he was buying from some dealers, including Goobie.

So I quit. I was the vice-president and the road captain of the chapter at the time, but I quit. I just walked out after the vote and threw my colours on the chair as I left. The irony was that a year later Billy the Bum quit anyhow.

It wasn't long after that that I teamed up with Cosimo Commisso and the Calabrian Mafia to begin a new and even more violent career in crime.

CHAPTER

9

THE ENFORCER

It was Ron the Rounder who paved the way for me to team up with the Commissos. It wasn't anything that was planned. It was just a question of timing and need. I was the right person to fill the need, and Ron was around to recommend me. It was as simple as that.

In the spring of 1976 Ron found out that I had left Satan's Choice. I hadn't seen him for a while, and at the time I was busy hustling a buck in a part-time job as the driver of a tractor-trailer for a construction company. He had been out of town working high-stakes card games for the Niagara Falls Italian mob when we bumped into each other at one of the Rounders' hangouts in Toronto's west end.

"Where have you been hiding, Cec?" he asked. "I've been looking all over town for you for some friends of mine."

"What friends are you talking about?" I asked.

"The Commissos," he answered. "They'd like to have you working for them."

Now I had heard about the Commisso brothers. Anyone who worked the streets as I had, had heard about them. They were the bosses of a rough-and-tumble outfit that was shaking down contractors and businessmen in a large segment of Toronto. The guy who was their "godfather," the head man of respect for the Calabrians, was an old-timer named Michele (Mike) Racco.

Racco ran a popular bakery shop at the corner of St. Clair and Nairn in Toronto. It was a particularly popular meeting place for a lot of the old members of the Calabrian Honoured Society or Calabrian Mafia. They went there to see Racco, who was sort of the Carlo Gambino of Toronto. Gambino played the role of "godfather" at a popular bakery and confectionery in New York's Little Italy. The old and even some of the young Italians would come from all over New York to get Don Carlo's blessing and help. Well, Michele Racco was like that in Toronto. Everyone, including the Commissos, who needed the help of a "godfather" in the Calabrian community would go to the bakery to see Don Michele.

The Commissos bossed their own family, but when push came to shove, they took their orders from Don Michele Racco. So did the bosses of two other Canadian Calabrian families. Before he died in 1980, Racco was the *Capo Crimini*, the "boss of bosses," for the Calabrian Mafia in Canada and the United States. There was no one higher than him among the Calabrians over here, not even the Calabrian Mafia bosses in Siderno, Italy.

Nobody in Satan's Choice had ever dealt with anyone like Racco or the Commissos because up to then they lived in a different world, and bikers weren't included in that world. Calabrians stuck with Calabrians and kept to their own traditions and secret society. There was a frame of mind among the mafiosi that bikers and the mob didn't mix, they didn't have anything in common.

With that in mind, I wondered out loud why the Commissos would want to hire an ex-biker — and an Irishman to boot. I certainly didn't fit their mould. I also wondered what had happened to the guy who was their former enforcer. Where had he gone? Had he been killed?

"Come on, Ron. What the hell would the Commissos want with me?" I asked. "I'm not Italian. And worse — I was a biker."

Ron shook his head. "Look, Cec," he explained, "they've heard a lot about you. I've been talking to them about you." He paused for a minute, looked around to see if anybody was listening to us, and then kept talking. "You've got a good reputation as a solid person, a solid Rounder. They want me to bring you to the Casa Commisso. If things work out, you could make a lot of money." He reminded me that for years members of the Niagara Falls Italian mob had worked with members of the St. Catharines Outlaws in drug deals and occasional beatings that had to be given to street people.

So I agreed to go with Ron to meet the Commissos the next day. I was a real fish out of water there; I was the only non-Italian in the damned place. But it didn't bother me. I'd expected it to be that way.

The three of us sat down at a table near the kitchen where Cosimo felt nobody could listen in, and Ron introduced me to Cosimo. Then he got up and walked over to join some other men so Cosimo and I could talk privately.

"How you like to work for me?" Cosimo asked.

"Depends on what you have in mind and how much it pays," I answered matter-of-factly.

A trace of a smile crossed his face before he answered. "Ronnie, he says you can be trusted. He says you're tough, you do good work. I give you some jobs . . . we see how good you are." He was giving me the once-over as he talked. I think he was wondering what had happened to the long hair, the stubbles of beard, and the dirty jeans and black leather jacket he expected a biker to be wearing. I had changed that look even before leaving the Choice. I'd shortened my hair. I'd shaved the beard. All I had was a mustache, and I was always cleaned and dressed up when I went out. So I suppose I was a surprise to him and to his brothers, Remo and Michele, who had by now joined us at the table.

"Fine, but what about the money?" I asked.

"You be paid well," he said. "We put you on the payroll when we see how you do the first job."

I suspected they would test me on a few minor jobs first before giving me any major assignments, if they ever did. Ron had told me I'd probably make about $500 a week to start but that the price would escalate if I did well for them. I had other concerns besides money. I wondered where I would stand if there was trouble with other mobs as well as with the cops.

"Look," I said, "before I jump into this, I'd like to know something for my own protection. Just who is running Toronto? The Raccos, you, Johnny Pops, Paul Volpe? I don't want to get done myself 'cause I don't know the players."

Cosimo looked around and motioned to his brothers, Remo and Michele. "We run this area," he said. "We run it all. We control Toronto."

He and his brothers weren't saying they shared things with anybody or that they answered to anybody. He was saying they were running things and that Toronto was *their* pie, not something they shared with someone else. They were saying that if I worked for them, I wouldn't have trouble with other mobs.

I was impressed, and I nodded in agreement with what he had to say. "Okay, that's fine," I said. "I just wanted to know what position I'm in. What if I get caught doing anything for you in the future?"

Cosimo looked at his brothers and, still smiling, answered, "We have the lawyer for you, and we pay all your expenses. We'll look after you."

With that we shook hands, and I gave them a number where they could reach me. "Just call," I said, "and I'll meet you someplace to talk about whatever job you want done."

Cosimo nodded. "We be in touch."

In early August 1976 I met with Cosimo and received my first assignment. He had a contractor who owed him money, and he wanted me to give him a message to pay or else. He gave me the contractor's name, the location of his office, and a description of what he looked like. His instructions were to just deliver a message, not to hurt anyone — yet.

So I located this guy's office, and I went up to see him. I just walked into his office, strode up to his desk, and laid it on the table to him. No open threat, just a subtle intimidation.

"I don't want to say this more than once, my friend," I said. "You owe a friend of mine a considerable amount of money. Now I suggest you pay him, because I don't want to have to come back." I looked at him real hard, the muscles in my jaw twitching as I stared at him. "I hope you're smart enough to understand."

The contractor understood, but as I left I decided to leave a reminder — just in case. I walked to his car and flattened all of its tires. Cosimo never said how much the contractor owed, but when I saw Cosimo a couple of days later, he was obviously pleased.

"You on the payroll, Cec," he said.

The next job was on a bookie. It was sort of a spur-of-the-moment thing in which they called on me to help out. I was in a poolhall one evening when Cosimo walked in and came over to see me.

"There's this fella over here," he said. "We want him to pay the money to us, but he needs persuasion." He pointed to a middle-aged bookie whom I'd seen operating at the poolhall quite often and who was pocketing better than $10,000 a week in profits without paying anyone for the privilege. "That's him," Cosimo said. "Persuade him."

So I walked over to the bookie and pressed him pretty hard. He was up against the wall, shaking like a leaf, as I whispered in his ear and jabbed him hard in his lower gut. He got the drift and that night started paying the Commissos a percentage of his daily take.

He wasn't the only one to get a message like that that night. The Commissos had me go with them to visit a boxing promoter they called Bernie who had been holding out on them, not paying them a percentage of the money he was taking in promoting fights and loan-sharking some of his own fighters. The Commissos laid it on Bernie pretty heavy. While I held his arms, the Commissos stuck guns in his face and cocked the hammers. Suddenly Bernie smelled like a miniature cesspool. He'd crapped all over himself in fright.

All of these assignments were tests. There were four in all before I got a major assignment, but not all went off without a hitch. The last of the tests, one that I got paid $500 for, was one that had a few twists and gave Cosimo a big laugh.

My job was to beat the hell out of a guy who lived in an apartment on The West Mall and who apparently owed them a bundle of money. Cosimo had given me the guy's address and phone number, and I called to see if he was in. I couldn't tell him who I was or why I wanted to see him, not if I wanted to get him out of his apartment, so I came up with a tale I thought would make him come down.

"This Mr. Smith?" I asked.

"Yeah, you got him," he said.

"Look, I'm sorry, Mr. Smith, but I just backed into your car down in the parking lot," I said. "You want to come down and look at the damage and figure out how much I owe you?"

"I'll be right down," he said anxiously.

I already knew where his car was parked because I'd cased his operation pretty well beforehand and staked out his parking area. When he arrived at the car, I was standing with my head bent over, looking down to hide my face. When he reached out to turn me around, I whipped around suddenly with a blackjack in my hand and clobbered him across the head, knocking him cold. Then I worked him over good. He spent a few days in the hospital. Several days later I went over to see the Commissos. Cosimo greeted me, laughing like hell as he handed me the $500.

"You no do the right guy," he said, still laughing.

"I don't get it," I said. "If I did the wrong guy, why are you so happy?"

"It's all right," he said. "You do his partner. This smart ass — he sent his partner to meet you. The partner that you do, he's gonna spend two months in the hospital. So the guy we wanted done, he's paid up. He doesn't wanna go to hospital the same way."

What apparently happened was that my target had gotten suspicious, knowing the Commissos were after him, and had sent his partner to double-check the car damage, believing nothing would happen to him. Now I'd had a description of the guy I was supposed to beat up, but it was dark and hard to see, and so the wrong guy got worked over. The blackjack I'd used on him was eight or nine inches long — flat, thick at the end, and made in Brazil — and it didn't leave a muscle that wasn't blackened, not to mention a few bones that were broken in the process. While the wrong guy was put in the hospital, the results were the same: the Commissos got their money. I was now ready, they were convinced, for bigger, tougher, and more violent assignments. I didn't know it at that moment, but I was about to become their new top enforcer.

People like me aren't concerned with history. We probably should be. If I had known as much about the Calabrians then as I do now, I would probably never have gotten involved with them, and I wouldn't be in the situation I'm in now.

When I agreed to work for the Commissos in 1976, all I knew about the Calabrians were some stories I'd read about the arrest of an Italian named Francesco Caccamo. Toronto police had raided his home back in 1972 and found some guns and explosives, but more important, they had also found some papers that were supposed to describe the initiation ritual that people had to go through before they could become members of the Calabrian Mafia — the Honoured Society.

Those documents, which came to be known as the Caccamo Papers, were the first real evidence that the public in Canada or anywhere in North America had of the existence of the Calabrian crime organization. Caccamo was no informer like Joe Valachi, but those papers were as important as anything Valachi had to say about Cosa Nostra in the United States. Valachi could describe how he was "made" into a member, a soldier of Cosa Nostra, when he testified before the American Senate in 1963. But he had no document that supported his testimony. Caccamo didn't say anything, but the documents the cops grabbed said it all — more than he could have said — and made it more believable. There it was in black and white — an initiation ceremony for becoming a member of the Calabrian Mafia.

It was in October 1976 that Cosimo called me to the Casa Commisso. It had been quite a while between jobs, and I figured they were still testing me. I was living a fairly straight life then, still driving the tractor-trailer; working for the Commissos was only a sideline. This job was a little heavier than those in the past had been.

The target Cosimo and Remo wanted me to do a number on was a salesman by the name of Antonio Burgas Pinheiro. He was in his late thirties and lived in Brampton with his wife and four kids. He worked for the Appia Beverage Company on Queen Street West in Toronto.

"We don't want this man hurt," Cosimo explained. "Just blow up his car or his pop truck. We take care of things from there." Remo just stood there, nodding in agreement, letting Cosimo do the talking. Cosimo always did most of the talking.

Now if I'd known something about the Calabrians' history in Toronto, I'd have understood better what was involved when Cosimo told me to go after Pinheiro and Appia Beverage. According to the police, Italian soft-drink companies had been at the centre of some serious extortions by the Calabrians from Siderno back in the late sixties and early seventies. In fact, the Appia plant was bombed in 1972, and two officials of Cynar Dry Company, an Italian soft-drink company that employed a relative of the Commissos, were murdered.

The first official killed was Salvatore Triumbari, president of Cynar, who was gunned down as he left his home in a Toronto suburb in January 1967. The next guy killed was Filippo Vendemini, who was from Calabria and had been involved in delivering illegal alcohol for some big Calabrian Mafia hoods like Paolo Violi from Montreal and Vincenzo Melia. Vendemini was shot three times in front of his shoe store at 1086 Bloor Street West. The reasons behind their murders were never made clear by police or anyone else. It was part of a Calabrian problem and a fight for control of the Italian soft-drink market by people like the Raccos and the Commissos.

I found it interesting that Violi had been picked up and questioned about Vendemini's murder. Just as interesting was the fact that somebody had spotted a car with a Montreal licence plate leaving the area at the time of the murder. Cosimo told me later that the cops traced the plate and the car to a place where the car owner was supposed to be staying. The car owner was there with Cosimo and Remo playing cards. The cops grabbed him but had to release him because there was nothing to prove that he had been driving the car. The Commissos weren't charged with anything either. Still, it was quite a coincidence that they were all together and that they all had connections to Vendemini and Cynar employees. This was part of the history I didn't know about when the Commissos called me in to bomb Pinheiro's vehicle.

On October 23 I drove out to Brampton, where Pinheiro lived. His truck wasn't there that night, but his car was in the driveway. So after parking my truck where no one would notice it, I went back to his car with two sticks of dynamite under my coat and a five-foot-long fuse. In a matter of minutes I placed the two sticks of dynamite between the frame and gas tank of his car, stretched out the fuse, lit it, and drove off in my truck. I was far enough away when the bomb went off that I didn't even hear it — but half of Brampton did. It exploded at 11 P.M. and caused more than $1,000 damage to Pinheiro's 1974 Chevrolet. Later that evening I called Pinheiro's home and threatened him. The cops taped the call but could never identify who made it. They stayed that night and watched him for a couple of weeks because he was so badly shaken by the bombing.

Pinheiro told them he didn't have any idea who was behind the bombing. Maybe he didn't, but his boss, Liberato Simone, told the press that the people behind the bombing were trying to drive him out of business. He never identified the Commissos or anyone else. His problem was that his soft-drink company was competing with the companies that the Commissos wanted to control the business.

The Commissos were more than happy with the way I operated now, and they were busy shaking down people all over the city, using stories of the bombings and beatings I had handled for them to intimidate others. Sometimes it worked, and sometimes people needed personal object lessons. One who needed an object lesson, according to the Commissos, was a drywall contractor who lived in an expensive neighbourhood in the Kingcross estates in King City, Ontario.

I got the call to meet Cosimo and Remo at the Casa Commisso. As usual, I parked my car in the parking lot of a nearby Kentucky Fried Chicken place and went in through the rear entrance of the banquet hall so I wouldn't be spotted in the event the cops were watching the Commissos. The guy they wanted shaken up was a contractor named Andy Pozzebon, who owned the Pozzebon Construction Company at 225 Wildcat Road, North York. They told me that Pozzebon owed a large amount for a plastering job to a friend of theirs.

"If you do a good job and he pays his bill," Cosimo said, "you gonna make ten thousand dollars."

I smiled at that figure and nodded. "Sounds good," I said, looking at Remo to see if he was in agreement. "Where is this place?"

Cosimo said he would go with me to show me where it was and what he wanted me to do. We drove both to Pozzebon's home at 12 Blueberry Lane and to the business, so I would have a good feel for the area. He told me he wanted me to put a stick of dynamite in Pozzebon's mailbox in front of his home and then call his office.

On November 11 that's exactly what I did. I placed the stick of dynamite in the mailbox and called Pozzebon's secretary at the plant. I told her my name was Thompson and that she should call her boss at home and tell him to look in his mailbox for a special message that I'd left in it. She called Pozzebon, and when he went to the mailbox, he found the stick of dynamite. He called the York Regional Police in to handle it. A couple of days later I called the Pozzebon Construction Company again and talked to the same secretary.

"Did Mr. Pozzebon receive my message?" I asked.

The woman was nervous, obviously upset, and she struggled to answer, stuttering a little. "Ye-e-s, he—he got your message," she said.

"Good," I said. "Now tell him he'd better pay his plastering bill, or next time I'll blow up his car."

She delivered the message all right, and Pozzebon must have paid the Commissos. They paid me $1,000 with the promise of more to come. I never got the other $9,000, but they were famous for that. They were forever chiselling on the amounts they promised to pay.

Extortion, bombings, beatings, threats — they were becoming routine. But soon the Commissos changed the routine. This time their game was murder.

CHAPTER

10

THE CONTRACT IS MURDER

The games of push and shove, of phony names and telephone threats, came to an end in early December 1976 at a meeting between Cosimo and me at the Casa Commisso.

"Cec, I want you to do a guy for me," Cosimo said. "It's worth ten thousand dollars."

I was still ticked off about the payoff I'd received the month before, and I let him know I was still unhappy.

"You mean ten thousand like in the ten thousand you were going to give me last month for Pozzebon?" I said. "Come on, Cosimo — no more bullshit."

"Cec, that was not my fault, not Remo's fault," Cosimo explained. "We didn't get everything we were supposed to get. When we get it, you get it — you have my word."

"Okay, okay, Cosimo," I said, shaking my head. "Who do you want done?"

"This fink, this Dennis Mason," he said. "He's a witness against a friend of mine. I want him shut up — permanently and fast."

Mason was a relatively young guy who worked in a Pizza Pizza location in a shopping plaza off the Don Mills Parkway. He was a witness against a Commisso associate who had been charged with possession of counterfeit money. It was the same counterfeit junk that had put so many of the Calabrians, their friends, and some bikers behind bars. The associate was an assistant manager of a hotel, and he owned a charter boat moored on the harbourfront. He was involved in a lot of deals with the Commissos, but in this one he was facing long jail time because of Mason's testimony. He had supposedly sold $2,000 worth of counterfeit to Mason.

Cosimo gave me Mason's address, and we drove first to his home and then to the pizza place. We split up, and I began the process of stalking this guy and planning his murder.

It was cold, it was miserable, and it snowed most of the next couple of weeks as I watched this kid and plotted how I was going to do him. I watched him drive home and drive to work. I followed his routine until I had it down pat. Most of the time he delivered pizzas to private homes, and the pizza delivery became the cornerstone of my murder plan. My initial plan was to gun him down from a wooded area across the street from a home where I planned to have him deliver a pizza. The location was perfect, and I could be hidden under the large branch of a big Christmas tree. Both the house and the tree were located a short distance from the Prince Hotel in Toronto.

It was snowing the night I called the pizza place from a phone near the hotel. I parked the van and sat underneath the Christmas tree, waiting for Mason to show. It was very dark, about midnight, and I was almost certain he would be the one to deliver the pizza because it was so late. I sat underneath the tree for thirty or forty minutes. After a while the pizza delivery vehicle showed up at the house.

A young guy stepped from the truck and rang the doorbell of the house. Just as he had delivered the pizza and turned back to the truck, I got ready to step from underneath the Christmas tree and blow him away. As I looked down my gunsight at the door, I could see it wasn't Mason — it was someone he'd sent to make the delivery for him.

I tried a couple of other ambushes, but they didn't work either. Finally I decided on a bomb. I was going to blow this kid to kingdom come the day after Christmas in the driveway of his mother's home.

The dynamite I was using had been given to me by Cosimo. I should have known better. I took the five sticks he'd given me, wired them to the dash of Mason's car, and rigged it so that when he turned the ignition key, they would go off and send him up in a cloud of smoke. The hookup was relatively simple. One wire went to the windshield wiper fuse under the dash, and the other wire was wound around a bolt connected to the master cylinder. The wiper fuse remains dead, inactive, until you turn that ignition switch. Once on, an electrical circuit is made, and BOOM! — off goes the bomb.

After wiring the car and making sure everything was set, I left for home. A day later the front page of a newspaper had a story about a guy who got minor injuries in a car bomb explosion.

Minor injuries! "Jesus Christ," I shouted, "how the hell can you get minor injuries with five sticks of dynamite!" This kid must have had a guardian angel sitting on his shoulder that day. All he got out of it were some minor cuts when one good stick of dynamite should have killed him. The five bad sticks that Cosimo gave me just gave him some cuts. And to add insult to injury, the kid I had been stalking and almost killed was the *wrong* Dennis Mason. Cosimo had given me not only bad dynamite but also bad information. He had taken me to the wrong address, shown me the wrong guy — he'd screwed up from start to finish. For all my troubles I got a lousy $2,000, not the $10,000 promised, but then I hadn't done Dennis Mason the witness. As for Cosimo's friend, he went to court two weeks later, and the real Mason showed up to testify. When the friend saw him, he pleaded guilty in a plea-bargaining deal and got seven months.

I didn't get another major murder contract until 1978, when the Commissos wanted a Montreal financier killed. But before that there was a homicide that I was responsible for. It happened on May 3, 1977, when I blew up the Wah Kew Chop Suey House at 111 Elizabeth Street in Toronto's Chinatown. The murder was accidental, but it was a murder nevertheless, and it could have been avoided if the Commissos had done their homework better before handing out the bombing contract.

The Commissos had taken a contract to blow up this place through members of the Kung Lok triad, the Chinese crime syndicate that controlled gambling, extortions, and drug peddling in Chinatown. The Kung Lok is kind of a Chinese Mafia, a secret society complete with bloody initiation rites and secret oaths that came to Canada from Hong Kong and, like the Calabrians, shakes down the people of its own community.

Restaurant owners, gambling dens, tailors — all kinds of small shops pay some sort of protection money to members of the Kung Lok. Those that don't get visits from their enforcers. The next thing you know, there are merchants and customers who've been beaten up and sometimes killed. That triad had Chinatown locked up tight. Even the old Chinese tongs who used to run Chinatown knuckled under to the Kung Lok and hired their enforcers for protection. All the Oriental gambling dens along Elizabeth and Dundas streets then were supposed to be protected by the Kung Lok.

One of the gamblers who wasn't paying for protection was a big shot at the Wah Kew Chop Suey House. This restaurant hot-shot had been using the place for some gambling, running phony dice games and Chinese games after hours without the Kung Lok's permission. In fact, he was cutting into the business receipts of one of the gambling dens they were providing protection for.

Because the Kung Lok was under pressure from Toronto's finest, the triad apparently decided to get somebody outside Chinatown to handle the job for them. Cosimo got the contract, and that's when he called me to the Casa Commisso in late April to tell me about the job.

"You gonna get paid fifteen thousand for this job," he said. "When you do the job, make sure there's nothin' left. Level it. Do it late, at six A.M. Nobody be there then." Remo stood there nodding. He was certain no one would be there when the bomb went off.

Famous last words!

I had to case the layout of the Wah Kew to find the best place to set the bomb. The next day I went there and gave them a takeout order. While they were busy cooking it up, I walked around, looking for rooms where I might set the charge. Finally I checked out the washroom, and I noticed there were some loose ceiling tiles. After jamming the door shut to be sure no one would surprise me, I stood on the toilet seat and pushed the ceiling tiles up. It was perfect. Plenty of space to put a bomb and timer where nobody would spot them. I also checked to see when the restaurant emptied out. By 3 A.M. it was closed, and everybody was gone.

The next order of business was to get the dynamite I needed and the blasting caps. I figured it would take about 100 sticks with a couple of blasting caps made up into two separate but identical bombs. Each bomb was to have fifty sticks of dynamite, a blasting cap, a standard twelve-volt flashlight battery, a small clock, and a positive and negative wire that ran from the blasting cap to the clock. I drove to Windsor and got the dynamite from the Satan's Choice chapter. They always had dynamite available because of extortions they handled and gang wars. It was usually stolen stuff, but it was dependable.

At about 7 P.M. on the night of May 2, I put on some glasses, changed my hairstyle, and went back to the restaurant carrying a gym bag and a briefcase with the two bombs. The reason for two bombs with two clocks was that if one bomb didn't work, the other would.

I ordered a couple of egg rolls and a coffee to take out and went back to the washroom with a doorstop in my pocket to jam the door shut while I worked. I stood on top of the toilet seat again, lifted up the ceiling tiles, and gently eased the bombs, one by one, into place. On each bomb I left a wire loose. I always left a wire loose — the final wire that made the connection for the bomb to go off. I kept it loose until the last minute, until I was sure everything was ready to go, just in case something screwed up. I was lucky I followed that procedure that night. If I hadn't, I probably wouldn't be around today.

One bomb had the connecting device taped on but not hooked up, and it was resting in place on a ceiling tile ledge that had a slight downward slant to it. I kept one hand on it. I had something in my pocket — I can't remember what the hell it was — that I took out with the other hand and dropped. I started to bend down to retrieve it and took my hand off the bomb for a split second. I looked and saw it falling as if in slow motion — falling, falling — and I said to myself, "Oh, my God." I heard it hit the floor. I blinked, involuntarily threw up my arms to protect myself — a foolish act in itself — and looked down at the floor. There was a momentary silence, but I could hear my heart pounding like a sledgehammer, and I thought to myself as I looked at the bomb, "Christ, I'm still here."

I was breathing again. When my hands stopped shaking, I wiped the sweat from my brow and my hands with a handkerchief. Then I gently lifted the bomb back up and put it back in place on the ceiling tiles. When everything was in place, I set the clocks to go off at about 6 A.M. and hooked up the final wires, letting the ceiling tiles carefully down. Then I left the Wah Kew, picking up my takeout order as I went.

I guess it was at about 2 A.M., four hours before the bombs were to go off, that I telephoned the restaurant just to be sure that nobody was there. The phone rang and rang, but there was no answer. If someone had answered, I would have told them, "Hey, get the hell outta there. There's a bomb about to go off!" But there was no answer, and as I hung up the phone I thought no more about it.

The bombs went off about half an hour early. Official reports said the explosion occurred at 5:33 A.M.. The bombs tore the hell out of the place. Working in the kitchen, which shared a wall with the washroom, was a cook, who was later identified as Chong Yim Quan. He was killed by the blast. Three other employees were injured. None of them was supposed to be there, according to the Commissos. They were wrong as usual. The employees had come to the restaurant in the early morning hours to begin preparing meals for the day's customers. I'll never know why any of them didn't answer that damned phone.

I heard about the homicide on the morning news, but I didn't see Cosimo and Remo until about a week after the bombing. We were in the Casa Commisso.

"Great information you and Remo gave me, Cosimo," I said. "I thought you said no one was gonna be in the restaurant."

"Ah, Cec, so what," Cosimo said nonchalantly. "It's no big deal. It was just a Chink."

That was typical of Cosimo and his brothers. They didn't give a damn who got killed or who got hurt as long as the contract was fulfilled and they got their money. They didn't care how many arms and legs were blown off a body or how badly someone was burned as long as it wasn't someone in their family.

I shrugged at his answer and figured I could be just as calculating as Cosimo and his brothers. "You got my money?" I asked.

He nodded and shoved an envelope across the table. "Here's your money," he said.

I opened the envelope and counted it out. There was $18,000 in cash. For the first time he'd paid me more than he'd promised. I didn't ask why. I knew. I pocketed the money and left without another word.

I never found out how much Cosimo and his brothers got for the job, but the restaurant damage was estimated at more than $168,000. He probably pocketed twice what he paid me. But then that's what crime bosses do. They take the lion's share. That's why they're bosses.

If the murder of the Chinese cook was accidental, there was nothing accidental about the Commissos' plot to murder Montreal millionaire stock promoter Irving Kott in April 1978. The planned murder of Kott was undoubtedly the most important hit assignment the Commissos had come up with.

For more than twenty years Kott had wheeled and dealed in the securities business in both the United States and Canada. In 1962 he'd been fined $10,000 by the Quebec Securities Commission for trading in stocks that were unregistered. Police thought at the time that he was being financed by Montreal Calabrian Mafia boss Vincent Cotroni. The Cotroni brothers, Vincent and Frank, were close to the Commissos.

In 1967 the Quebec Securities Commission ordered a halt to the sale of stock for a company known as Allegheny Mining and Exploration Co. because its owners were dealing with Kott, who was involved in stock deals that were under investigation in Florida, New York, Denver, Toronto, Vancouver, and Montreal. Then in 1973, while he was living in New York, Kott was sued in U.S. District Court by a British millionaire for more than $8 million. The millionaire, Ian Jones, claimed that Kott had defrauded him out of a multi-million-dollar calculator business.

A year later Kott and eight others were arrested for fraud in the sale of Somed Mines Ltd. stock to investors in Ontario, Quebec, and Europe. In 1975 Kott pleaded guilty to conspiracy in the case and paid a $500,000 fine, but not before he and eighteen others were charged in a $5.5-million swindle of Continental Financial Corp. of Montreal, an American-owned subsidiary of Industrial National Corp., the owner of the Industrial National Bank of Rhode Island. Throughout all this Kott was supposed to be operating with the blessing of the Cotronis.

The price to hit Kott, Cosimo said, was $25,000. He said he was acting as a broker in the deal for Kott's partner, who would benefit from Kott's death. I just never believed that was the real reason for the contract. I was convinced then, as I am now, that the Cotroni mob had given the Commissos the contract to kill

Kott because they believed Kott had swindled them in one of his stock operations.

Cosimo gave the Kott hit plot a personal touch.

"This is a very important job, Cec," he said. "I'm gonna meet you in Montreal, and I'm gonna show you where this guy works, where he lives—I'm gonna show you everything about this Kott." He paused for a moment and looked straight into my eyes. "I'm not gonna rush you," he continued. "You can kill this guy wherever you feel it's right. But we want him killed soon. Capice?"

I understood, and for $25,000 I'd put icing on the job if he wanted it. He was saying, "Don't rush, but hurry." It's not good when you have to hurry jobs like that.

Cosimo's plan was for me to fly to Montreal. He was going to drive. The following day we were to meet in front of the Bonaventure Hotel. We met as planned, and for the next day or so he drove me to every haunt of Kott's. He knew the guy inside out. We went to his home, which was in a Jewish neighbourhood, and to the small place not far from there where he had breakfast every morning.

While we were casing the house, Kott suddenly came out, climbed into his gleaming new 1978 Mercedes Benz, and drove right past us. Cosimo was furious.

"If I'd had a gun," he shouted, "I'da killed the no-good son of a bitch right then!"

That's when I realized there was something very personal in this contract. For Cosimo to say that he'd have handled the hit personally, on the spur of the moment, was extremely unusual. He wanted this done, and done right, to impress someone, not just to collect a fee from Kott's so-called partner.

After we finished casing Kott's business location, his home, and his hangouts, Cosimo gave me the address of a girlfriend of Kott's who was also his employee. "He stays at the girlfriend's sometimes," he said quietly. "Sometimes he stays the night, sometimes a coupla nights."

Then we split. I flew back to Toronto to construct the bomb I'd need and get a .22 silencer to go with a special .22 handgun I'd acquired for the hit. I also went to a Mercedes Benz dealership in Toronto to look over their cars—check them out to find the best place to put the bomb. Before I was ready to handle the job, I drove back and forth to Montreal a couple of times, staying at different places each time as I stalked Kott and his every move. I wanted this guy's moves down pat before I blew him away. All my expenses were paid. The Commissos had given me $1,000 for expenses.

The first time I tried to do him I took the .22, the silencer, and the dynamite with me, all ready to hook up to his car. I planned to either go through a side window of his house and hit him inside or wire his car to blow up when he started it in the morning. Just as I was going through the window, somebody walking his dog on the street spotted me, and I had to leave in a hurry. That caused a little unexpected heat, and I had to leave the area. Everyone thought it was a burglar. They didn't see the gun or the bag containing the dynamite. So I had to lie low for about two weeks. Then in late August I returned to Montreal. This time I planned to attach the bomb to Kott's car and rig it so it would explode when he turned on the ignition. Later I had to change that plan.

When I got to Montreal, I found out that Kott was in court. I drove to the courthouse, parked nearby, and walked around most of the afternoon trying to find his car in the parking lot. It might have been in the underground garage, but I wasn't about to look. There were too many cops in the area, so I walked on by, got to my car, and left.

I was concerned about being seen. I remember driving by a cop at one point. I had the dynamite and the gun in the car and stolen plates on it. It was early morning. As the cop went by, I was figuring, "I might have to shoot him if he stops me here." He kept on going, never looked at me, so I just took off out of the area.

Every time I went to Montreal to case Kott's movements, I stole a new set of plates off a Quebec car and put them on mine. I figured I'd have at least twelve to twenty-four hours before the theft was discovered and reported to the cops, then it would take them another couple of hours to alert their cars to the stolen plates. I needed that time to keep tabs on Kott's movements.

I took other precautions too. I had no photograph of Kott. I never carried photos of the targets I was after. I memorized the addresses and directions that Cosimo handed me on pieces of paper. And I kept unlisted phone numbers, ones I couldn't look up, inside my sock. Each day I changed the type of clothes I'd wear and my general appearance. Sometimes I'd comb my hair

down or wear a baseball cap or winter hat with a tassle. Sometimes I'd wear sunglasses or tinted eyeglasses and dark clothes.
Always it was different, and always I'd look for the quickest way
to exit an area before parking or walking around.

One day I sat outside Kott's office for six hours, waiting for
him to go to lunch. I didn't realize it, but he had a kitchen in his
office, and he rarely went out for lunch.

The next day I called his office to make sure he was there, then
I went to his place of business, the Highland Knitting Mills, and
spotted his car parked in an underground parking lot at 5425
rue Casgrain. I took the bomb from my car, set the wiring, and
returned to his parked Mercedes. There was a parking lot attendant maybe two hundred feet away from where I was working
underneath Kott's car. He never spotted me.

I placed the bomb — five sticks of 75 per cent nitroglycerin
taped together — on top of the exhaust pipe, almost exactly
beneath where he sat. I ran electrical wires back to a battery that
I hid behind one of the car wheels, on the inside below the axle. I
had put a pressure-sensitive ignition starter button on top of the
battery, and I placed it under his tire so that at the slightest move-
ment of the tire against the button, the bomb would go off. Once it
was in place, I slipped out quietly and drove back to Toronto.

I figured Kott would get into his car within a couple of hours,
and poof! — up he'd go. If he was sitting in his car on top of that
dynamite, his asshole would be on the third floor of the warehouse of his firm. Wrong.

Kott never used the Mercedes. Instead he climbed into his wife's
Jaguar and drove to the airport. While he was away, the parking
attendant was working in the parking lot, sweeping under the
cars, when he saw the button under the Mercedes. I still don't
understand how he saw it — it was very dark under there. I should
have put it on top of the tire, not under — it was my mistake. I
had hurried the job.

It was about 5:10 A.M. on August 28, nearly nine hours after I
had set the bomb in place. The attendant looked at the button,
pushed it, and ba-boom! — the bomb went off, sending him flying
halfway across the parking lot. Another person who was walking nearby at the time was knocked to the ground. The attendant lost part of his hearing in the explosion, but other than that
he wasn't badly hurt. Neither was the bystander. Kott's car was

demolished, and two other cars parked nearby were badly damaged.

I didn't know that Kott had escaped injury when I returned to Toronto and told Cosimo what I had done. He was pleased. Then he found out that Kott wasn't hurt.

I saw Cosimo about three weeks later. Surprisingly, he wasn't all that upset. I guess those who had ordered Kott hit weren't that upset either. Maybe the explosion had sent a message to Kott that he understood, and as a result he had taken care of his problems. Whatever happened, Cosimo handed me $3,000 more for my trouble. It wasn't the $25,000 I'd been promised, but then I hadn't nailed Kott either. I hadn't expected to get anything.

"Well, I guess Kott knows who's after him now," I said.

"Well," Cosimo said, "he knows who he owes money to, but there's others who are after him."

"You want me to go back and do the job right?" I asked.

"No. Never mind, Cec," he said. "Remo, he'll go there to kill him."

I know Remo never went to Montreal to kill Kott, and Kott is still alive. I never did figure out why Cosimo said that. Whatever the reason, I was $3,000 richer for botching a job.

CHAPTER
11

EVERYTHING HAS A PRICE

W hether it was concrete or cement, plumbing or plastering, electrical wiring or trucking — if it had anything to
do with the construction industry, the Commissos and their
Calabrian Mafia friends had a hand in it somewhere, and usually that hand was reaching in and taking.

Michele Racco and his family had a piece, Paul Volpe and his
people were in it, and so was the Luppino crime family of
Hamilton. The infiltration of the construction industry in the
early seventies by mobsters, some of them from the Mafia, some
of them associated with the Mafia, was so widespread that it
resulted in a Royal Commission investigation under Judge Harry
Waisberg. This Royal Commission held hearings for more than
a year on some of the bombings and shootings in the construction industry and documented them in 1974 in a 770-page report.

But neither the investigation nor the report produced public evidence of the Raccos' and Commissos' involvement in construction at that time. That was probably because the coppers knew
little about the Calabrian Mafia and even less about the Commissos. The Commissos were pretty young then and hadn't yet
reached the status of bosses of a crime family that could rattle
the cages of other mobs from Long Island to British Columbia.

When I started working for the Commissos in 1976, I learned

quickly that their big thing for making money was the construction industry. They probably made more from extortions in the construction industry than they did from trafficking in heroin — and it was a hellava lot safer.

They had a lot of ways to make money in construction. One of their most successful was taking over where the law failed for contractors who wanted to collect debts. The law was very slow to act. It could take years for a guy to collect through the courts. In fact, contractors could and did go broke trying to collect monies owing them by waiting for the law and civil suits to settle their claims. And even when the courts made awards favouring a contractor, he often found out that the guy he was suing had a dozen different corporations, and the corporation he'd been dealing with was legally bankrupt and had no money to pay him. The debtor had simply moved his money from one corporate account to another to get out of paying bills.

What this situation did was make room for guys like the Commissos to become "collection agencies" for contractors. The Commissos would collect money owed to a contractor and take a percentage of it. They didn't let legal technicalities or stalling tactics get in the way.

Take a major contractor — let's call him Builder X. To complete his project, he subcontracts electrical, plumbing, and plastering work to smaller, specialized contractors who are experts in those fields. Mr. X promises to pay these contractors $200,000 or $300,000 to complete their work. Now the electrical contractor finishes his job, goes to Mr. X, and says, "Pay me." Mr. X doesn't have the cash right then, so he says to the electrical contractor, "I'll have to pay you later."

The electrical contractor has employees to pay, supplies to pay for, bills to meet. He sues in court to recover his money. Maybe two or three years down the road he collects, maybe he doesn't. Meanwhile Mr. X has used the electrical contractor's $200,000, and similar amounts from the plumbing and plastering and cement contractors, to invest in some other project that makes him an even bigger profit on their money.

That was the system for a long time in the construction industry. It took the Commissos to find a way to make big money out of it. Now instead of going to court and waiting two or three or more years to collect, the electrical contractor or the plasterer goes to his friend down the street "who knows the Mafia . . .

who knows the Commissos." The Commissos then go to see Mr. X or send someone like me to hassle and threaten him. They collect, and they get a piece. The electrical contractor gets most of his money back. That's the way it's done here — through extortions.

By 1978 I was getting a number of contracts from the Commissos to squeeze contractors from whom they wanted to extort money, who they told me were not paying bills they owed to subcontractors. The first of these extortions involved a contractor named Ben Freedman.

Freedman was the main contractor on a construction project in Toronto. He had hired a couple of subcontractors to do some electrical work that cost more than $175,000, but when it came time to pay, Freedman suddenly came up with short arms and long pockets. There was no money, he told them; they could either wait or take him to court. The subcontractors, both of them Italian, turned to Remo and Cosimo for help. They wanted their money and they wanted it right away, and they didn't care what had to be done to get it for them. That's when Cosimo called me in.

We met at the Casa Commisso on February 13 and then drove to Freedman's home at 41 Shenstone Road in North York.

"Bomb his house," Cosimo said, "but don't hurt anyone. I just wanna shake this guy so he pays up what he owes."

The fee to do the job was $2,000. Originally Cosimo wanted me to put the bomb on the side door of the house, and I didn't see any problem until I got there that night. I was in a jogging suit, which I wore so that anyone who saw me would think I was just another one of those health nuts jogging up and down streets in the area. People don't take much notice of joggers, and the jogging suits I wore were usually black or dark blue, making it even harder for anyone to see enough to remember. I also wore running shoes and a cap over my head.

I had two sticks of dynamite with me and a five-foot-long fuse that I connected to a percussion cap hooked to the dynamite. When I got to Freedman's house, I spotted some kids' bicycles and a baby carriage around the front of the house. Because there were kids in the house, I decided against a bomb at the door. I didn't want some kid to get maimed or killed because they were playing at the wrong place at the wrong time. So instead of the house, I chose to bomb Freedman's car, which was parked in the driveway. I put the bomb between the wiper blades and the windshield, set the fuse, and jogged off. I was long gone when the bomb went off. The next day I read in the paper that the car had been totalled by the bomb but that no one had been injured.

A couple of days later Cosimo went to a public telephone booth on Davenport Road and called Freedman to explain why the car had been blown up.

"Be smart, Mr. Freedman," he said, carefully speaking the words so his Italian accent wouldn't be obvious. "Pay your bills. That way no one — no kids — get hurt."

Cosimo paid me the $2,000 he owed me and said I'd done a good job. But he didn't keep his word to me. He had told me that when I handled these extortions for him, I would get a percentage, as much as one-third of what was collected as a result of my intimidation of their victims. I never got anything beyond the $2,000. That was another pipe dream they fed me.

Once the Commissos had delivered for a subcontractor like they did in the Freedman case, they were in a position to muscle that subcontractor or make deals to collect for him on other projects where he was owed money. They became, in effect, his private collection agency and silent partner. That was the case with the electrical contractor who had collected from Freedman because of my bomb. There were other contractors who owed him money, big money, and the Commissos intended to cash in by collecting those debts.

The biggest of the targeted contractors was a pair of apartment building and condominium owners named Jerry and Roman Humeniuk. They were brothers and partners in a condominium complex called the Fairways at 1400 Dixie Road in Mississauga.

In March 1978 I got the first of several assignments from Cosimo and Remo to shake up the brothers and force them to pay the more than $196,000 they owed the same electrical contractor who'd been stung by Freedman. The contractor had done a lot of work at the Fairways and hadn't been paid for it.

Before taking on the job, I checked out the area to see what the best escape routes were and how many people were around at different times of the day and night. I finally settled on doing the job in the underground parking lot of the condo, where I figured it would be least likely to kill anyone.

I'd gotten two sticks of dynamite with a three-foot-long fuse from the Commissos, and I lit the fuse a few minutes before 9

P.M.. When the dynamite went off, it blew out the plate glass windows that separated the underground parking area from an underground lobby. Shortly afterward I telephoned some people who were living in the condominium complex, people whose names I'd gotten out of the telephone book.

They were pretty shaky when I started talking. "Look — you don't want to get hurt, right?" I asked.

A woman in the room was crying, and the man who was on the phone was asking, "Why us — why are you calling us? We haven't done anything."

"Just tell that landlord of yours to pay the money he owes to his contractor," I snarled. "He'll know who I'm talking about. Tell him to give up the money he owes, or I'm coming back to blow the fucking apartment house apart — and I'll blow up your fucking place with it."

The woman was hysterical now, screaming into the extension, "He isn't here! Please! Leave us alone!"

"Lady," I answered, "just give him the message." I hung up.

The Commissos gave me $2,000 for the job. Two months later they wanted me to go back. This time Cosimo wanted me to zero in on the home of Dr. Roman Humeniuk, at 313 Pinegrove Road in Oakville.

"This building owner," he said, "he's no paid up. We want you to go back again — blow up his car."

I drove by the place first to look around. There were kids in the yard and in neighbouring yards. I didn't think it would be safe. If I blew up his car, I might cause a fire, because the car was parked very close to Dr. Humeniuk's garage. The explosion of the car and the fire that was bound to result would spread to the house. I didn't want some kid trapped in that house by fire. So I figured out an alternative plan.

In the early morning of May 15 I threw one stick of dynamite on the lawn, and the explosion put a big hole in it. I almost screwed up with that one. I used a short fuse, about a foot long. That gives you about forty seconds after you light it to get the hell out of the area. I hit a red light just as the dynamite went off at about 12:15 A.M., and I could hear the explosion, feel the van rock a little, as I waited to get on the Queen Elizabeth Way. Humeniuk's house was just a short distance from the expressway exit.

Still nothing. The Commissos were mad as hell. Humeniuk

didn't pay, and the contractor was pressing them for results. So in July I went back to the condominium complex in Mississauga again, this time to the other side of the garage, where there were two concrete supporting pillars. I rigged a bomb with four sticks of dynamite, a six-foot-long fuse, and a blasting cap. When it went off at 12:05 A.M. on the morning of July 21, it shook the entire complex and sent debris flying more than sixty feet onto the golf course at the nearby Lakeview Golf Club. It was designed to cause more fear than damage, and that's exactly what it did.

I called the same tenants again and went through the same routine. The woman was almost a basket case by now. The idea was to get the people to tell the Humeniuks to pay what they owed, or they'd move out. When they move out, he loses money. Rather than lose money and have an empty condo, he pays what he owes.

I don't know if it worked. The Commissos claimed the Humeniuks never paid up, but they never called me back to squeeze him any more either. This made me believe that they'd accomplished what they wanted and that their contractor was a satisfied customer. I figured they were just trying to get out of paying me any part of the $196,000 that the Humeniuks owed the contractor. All I got for all my work was about $3,000. I'm positive the Commissos got ten times that for what I did.

It was apparent to me by the time I got the Humeniuks' extortion contract that the Commissos had a lot of construction industry subcontractors lined up, ready to pay them to do what the courts weren't doing. Even as I was handling the Humeniuk bombings, I got the nod to start extorting money from Montreal developer Max Zentner and his millionaire partner, John Ryan, the owner of the engineering firm of John J. Ryan and Associates of Bay Street, Toronto.

In May Cosimo told me to try to go after Ryan, who he said owed an electrical contractor "friend" of his more than $200,000 for work he'd done on a project. The contractor was supposed to be suing Ryan in court to recover the money owed him, but Ryan's lawyers were stalling.

Cosimo showed me Ryan's home on Bay Street South in Hamilton, his Cadillac, which was usually parked in the driveway, and his office at the Commerce Court in Toronto. He said Ryan also had a partner I should muscle, a developer named Zentner who lived in Montreal.

"Break his legs," Cosimo said of Ryan. "You break his legs and rough him up good."

So one morning I went to Ryan's home at about 5 A.M. and flattened the left rear tire of his car. I waited outside in my car, figuring I'd waylay him when he tried to change the tire. The trouble was, by 9 A.M. he still hadn't come out of his house. So I left. About five days later I returned to his mansion. I had changed my facial appearance with a mustache and a wig and glasses. I walked up to the front door and knocked. When he opened the door, I knocked him flat with a blackjack to his face.

I then travelled to Montreal. I telephoned Zentner and told him to get his partner, Ryan, to pay up, or he'd get the same treatment Ryan had just gotten. Nothing happened, but Cosimo gave me $1,000 in cash. The money was to cover my expenses.

About two weeks later I returned to Hamilton. It was about 1:30 A.M. when I got there with two sticks of dynamite and a five-foot-long fuse. I spotted a 1977 Firebird in the driveway, and I knew it belonged to Ryan's daughter. I put the bomb on top of one of the rear tires, set the fuse, and took off. I heard it go off just before I hit Main Street in Hamilton. It sounded like two trains colliding.

Later I saw a picture of the car in the Hamilton *Spectator*. The car was wrecked. Pieces of it were found two or three houses away, and the bedroom window of a neighbouring home was cracked, but no one was injured. The Ryans and their daughter were away, staying at some cottage near Parry Sound. Some witness said she'd seen a sports car leave the scene when the bomb went off. Hell, I was driving a sports car, but she couldn't have seen me. Like I said, I was crossing Main Street about a mile away when that bomb went off. Witnesses sometimes have vivid imaginations.

After the bomb went off, Cosimo wanted me to call Ryan and tell him that the next time a bomb went off, his son or his daughter would be in the car that was blown up. I tried getting Ryan, but his secretary never let me talk to him. I was never certain whether he'd paid the $200,000 to the contractor, but the Commissos never asked me to go back and shake him up. They just paid me the $2,000 they said they'd pay, and that was that.

That was one thing that drove me wild with the Commissos. They were full of promises of big money, but they rarely delivered. Sometimes I'd get so pissed off by their promises that I'd pull out of jobs I'd promised to do unless they paid me the money up front. Take the case of Alphonso Gallucci, the owner of Gallucci Construction in Toronto.

Gallucci owed a friend of the Commissos more than $54,000 from a project and had stalled paying it. Cosimo's face was flushed with anger when he told me what he wanted.

"You break this guy's arms and legs," he said angrily. "You break them slow, so he feels the pain longer."

"How much am I going to get for this?" I asked.

"We give you a percentage," Cosimo said.

"No good, Cosimo," I said. "I'm tired of promises. I want my fee up front. Like the Chinamen say, 'No tickee, no shirtee.' No money, no legs broken."

Finally, after a couple of months of haggling with Cosimo and Remo about up-front payment, I pulled out of the deal. I was tired of Cosimo's promises of big payoffs and only winding up with peanuts. I knew he'd collected a fortune in the shake-downs I was involved in, but I'd got nothing but the short change. So I walked away from the Gallucci contract, and as far as I know, he never got anyone else who was willing to do the job.

Shaking down contractors accounted for only a small part of the Commissos' take from the construction industry. They were also very active in bid rigging on municipal contracts like hydro-electric projects or buildings or highways that the government was putting up. When they wanted to rig bids, the Commissos would threaten the competition facing the contractors they were dealing with. Once their man got the bid, they became his partners, and their people — plasterers, electricians, plumbers, cement suppliers — would be used on the job. They'd inflate the cost of the job, pocket the profits, and run like thieves while the public or business paid the price.

There was a dam project in British Columbia that the Commissos wanted to control, and they wanted to use a friend of mine to do it. The friend was "Charlie Tuna." He was a member of the Rebels Motorcycle Club, and he used to hang around and work out at an athletic club that I owned and operated. He was also the son of the owner of one of Canada's largest construction companies. This company had apparently bid on the dam project, in competition with a company that Cosimo said he and "the family" were into. If they could rig the bid, it would mean big bucks for everyone. They wanted me to shake down Charlie Tuna, rough him up if need be, to put pressure on his old man.

"Look, Cosimo," I said, "I don't do friends. I'm not extorting him or his family."

"Cec, don't say no," he said. "Think about it."

"There's nothing to think about, Cosimo," I said. "I'm not shaking down Charlie or his family. That's it."

"Okay, okay, Cec," he said. "We gotta see if we can get through to this company some other way, work something out with them."

He smiled as he looked at me. "If they don't co-operate, I get my friends in the unions in British Columbia, and we close this company down with a strike. You'll see. They'll fall in line."

I don't know if they did fall in line or if the Commissos got a piece of the pie at the dam project, but there was no doubt in my mind about his influence with the unions, particularly the plasterers' union.

One day Cosimo gave me the address of the plasterers' union hall and told me to go there and sign up. "Once you sign up, you'll be a member," he said. "You get a check for five hundred dollars every week."

I said no to the offer. I knew that if I went to that union and signed up, sooner or later the guys in the union would know who I was working for and start talking. Then one night the guy who ran the union would come to me and say, "You're Cosimo's friend. I want you to burn this house or break this guy's head." It would have been stupid. I could have taken down an easy $500 a week, but why take the chance? It wasn't worth it.

The plasterers' union was only one of several that the Commissos had their hooks into, and just before I left them and began working as an informer, I heard them talk about forming some sort of protection union for the construction industry. Their plan was simple. They were going to use this union to shake down contractors who were being short-changed by companies they did work for. For a fee or a percentage of what was owed the contractor, they were going to send union goons to the company that owed the money. The company or contractor would either pay up or face beatings of the employees by union muscle, wild-cat strikes, and other forms of intimidation.

I never found out what union they took over to operate their protection racket from or whether they actually put the plan into operation. By that time I'd become a witness against them and others, and I was no longer able to get inside information.

While they were extorting contractors and using unions to muscle in on municipal contracts, the Commissos were also busy controlling the mobile lunch trucks that provided workers with sandwiches, coffee, pop, and other goodies at construction sites. It's a damned lucrative way to make a buck if you're sitting at a catering hall like the Casa Commisso, pressing all the buttons and hauling in the profits while everyone else does the work.

The mobile lunch truck business is so lucrative that the boss of the Joseph Bonanno family in New York, Philip (Rusty) Rastelli, got into it and wound up in jail after a federal jury in Brooklyn found him guilty of extortion. Rastelli was more than once a guest of mob members in Toronto and Montreal, where the Bonanno family had a lot of friends and connections for their narcotics business and for other rackets they were involved in here in Canada.

The Commisso version of Rastelli's mobile-lunch extortion racket was geared toward the construction sites themselves. The Commissos and the Raccos controlled most of the mobile catering trucks that operated in Toronto. When there was competition, they didn't usually blow up the competitor's trucks or threaten him. Instead they went after the construction site superintendent and squeezed him, made him keep the competition off the construction site.

Cosimo brought me in to help the owner of one of the mobile catering companies who was close to Michele Racco. He was having a problem with a construction site superintendent who wasn't letting his trucks on the site but was, instead, letting the trucks of a rival company service the workers.

"What my friend wants," Cosimo said, "you do for him. You get paid well."

There was something about this friend of Cosimo's and Michele Racco's that rubbed me wrong. I didn't trust him. He wanted me to rough up the site superintendent, break his legs if I had to, to make him open the site to his mobile lunch trucks. When I was through with that, he said, he wanted me to burn some trucks of another catering company in another part of the city. There was something about the way this guy talked, the way he put down his competitors and wanted to grind them under his heels, that made me uneasy. I figured he'd double-cross his mother, let alone me, so I refused to handle his work. Cosimo wasn't happy about it, but he didn't press me. He knew I'd made up my mind.

The lunch company caterer was greedy. He already had lunch trucks operating all over the city — at construction sites, industrial complexes, garages, you name it — and he wasn't afraid to handle hot goods to increase his profit margin. Sometime after I had turned down this assignment, Cosimo said this guy's lunch trucks would handle a $100,000 load of cigarettes stolen from the Imperial Tobacco Company that I was arranging to sell to Cosimo for some friends. The cigarettes were from a trailerload that Ken Goobie and Armand Sanguigni were trying to peddle for $40,000 through a middleman named Richard Corbett. Cosimo finally agreed to take the load for $30,000. With all those lunch trucks, he said, they could move a truckload of stolen cigarettes in a day, and no one would ever be the wiser, least of all the cops.

Funny thing about the hijacked-cigarette deal. At the last minute Cosimo had second thoughts about his mobile catering company friend. When he got the cigarettes, he arranged to sell them to another mobile lunch company owner, a rival. The guy promised Cosimo a bigger profit than the guy Cosimo had wanted me to work for. That was always Cosimo's downfall — his greed.

In the end the whole deal blew up in Cosimo's face. After paying about $12,000 of what he owed on the cigarettes, he lost everything when some of his Calabrian flunkies were spotted by a sharp-eyed citizen unloading 127 of the original 317 cases of cigarettes in a run-down garage in Toronto. The citizen called the police, and they seized the cigarettes and arrested four men, who later pleaded guilty to possessing stolen cigarettes. The Commissos had to provide lawyers and bail money and expenses for the four, including one who was deported. It was a fiasco for the Commissos, for Goobie and Sanguigni, for Corbett, and for me. I'd expected to make a good piece of change out of the deal, but all I got for my troubles was a headache and a lousy $100.

CHAPTER
12

HUSTLING A BUCK

W orking as an enforcer and hired assassin for the Commissos had some good paydays, but it wasn't exactly lining my pockets with enough gold to live on easy street. The money I received for blowing up the Chinese restaurant and for contractor extortions and the attempted murders of Mason and Kott went fast. Too fast. There was a new Chevrolet Corvette sports car, there were a lot of fast women, and worse, there were even more slow horses. I went to the track too often and bet more often than not on the wrong nag.

I recognized early in my relationship with the Commissos that I'd have to supplement my income with side deals of my own. For a while I continued acting as a courier in Goobie's narcotics operation, and I handled a number of drug rip-offs with some bikers that added thousands to the stash in my safety deposit box. I was averaging $75,000 to $80,000 a year, but it wasn't nearly enough. I had become a Rounder of sorts myself, and I was always looking for new ways to make money.

It was through a chance meeting with two international gambler friends, Bob and Roman, that opportunity came knocking. Roman was a good friend of Eddie Neuff, and he was pretty close to Ron the Rounder, who had introduced us. We'd all done some drug rip-offs together. On this particular night we were in a hotel in downtown Toronto tossing down a few when Roman asked me if I'd be interested in taking a trip to Bogota, Colombia.

Now Roman's objective was to locate a source for quantities

of cocaine, which he and Bob planned to smuggle into Canada. They had a front they were convinced could get them through customs with a couple of pounds of coke. They were leaving for Colombia to have some parts made for a plumbing operation they were running. Their plan was to have the parts produced on a massive scale and shipped to them with the coke hidden inside. It wasn't a foolproof plan, but as it turned out, it was a successful one.

I decided to go along for the hell of it. I'd just finished blowing up the Chinese restaurant, and I wanted some high living without worrying about coppers or the Commissos or anyone else looking over my shoulder. I wasn't the least bit interested in smuggling narcotics. I considered it too risky.

We spent about a week in Bogota, sightseeing and living it up. During this time the three of us met a high-ranking official of the Bogota Chamber of Commerce at a Colombian bank, where we were changing Canadian currency into pesos. One thing led to another, and before I knew it, the discussion went from pesos to plumbing supply parts, to cocaine, and finally to guns.

"Can any of you get guns?" he asked. "We need guns, all kinds of guns — rifles, machine guns, bazookas, ammunition . . ."

Roman and Bob were dumbfounded. They were trying to set up a supply source for a cocaine-smuggling operation, and here was this guy talking about reverse smuggling — moving guns from Canada to Colombia. They both shook their heads, figuring that their lack of contacts for weapons was going to cost them in their attempt to set up the drug-smuggling operation. At that point I surprised them with an unexpected offer of help.

"There's a guy I know," I said. "He's sort of a friend. His name is Chuck [Charles] Yanover." Roman's face brightened as I spoke, and the Colombian business official leaned close to listen to what I had to say.

Of course I knew Yanover, but we weren't close friends, just sometime business associates. Like a lot of members of Satan's Choice and other biker gangs, I had sold stolen motorcycle parts to Yanover for years. Then in 1971 Yanover was convicted of possessing seventy stolen motorcycles, bike parts, and a gun. He was sentenced to two years in jail.

I lost track of him, but while he was in prison, he apparently graduated to the big time. He got hooked up with Nathan (Nate)

Klegerman, a convicted diamond swindler and international con man who was Paul Volpe's right arm. The Royal Commission that investigated the construction industry in 1974 identified Yanover as part of the Volpe mob that was shaking down and bombing contractors. Two years later he was busted with Volpe, Klegerman, and three others for trying to smuggle $1.5 million in diamonds into Canada.

In spite of all that, Yanover still managed to get an arms dealer's licence. He used to brag about that to me whenever I saw him. He was the Ontario agent for Fabrique Nationale, a Belgian arms manufacturer. The joke was that as the agent for this supplier, he was helping arm the Ontario Provincial Police. He once told me he was negotiating a contract to sell the OPP a special rifle they were after, but I didn't know whether to believe him or figure it was just another one of his bullshit tales. Chuckie was always bragging, talking about million-dollar deals and international plots to take over countries.

To look at him, no one would expect that Yanover was an international mercenary. There's nothing swashbuckling about his looks. He stands about five feet nine inches tall and wears thick glasses that hide ferret-like eyes. He has receding brown hair with a bald spot at the top rear of his head. Thick, heavy lips and a long nose fill out a weasel-like face. Some say he has the looks of a caveman. I always said he looked like a weasel. From the tip of his balding head to his pudgy feet, there was nothing to remind you of a cold-blooded mercenary ready to kill whoever stood in his way of overthrowing governments. Yet that was exactly what Yanover was. And he had a lot of mercenary friends, gunmen for hire whom he'd met while peddling arms for the Belgians.

Yanover was full of schemes in those days. At the time he was living at King and Parliament streets, on the fifth floor of an apartment building owned by Volpe. We used to meet there occasionally, usually in the boiler room, when I wanted to buy some diamonds from him or some guns. It was at one of these meetings in the boiler room that Yanover offered me a murder contract.

"I got a couple of things for you to do if you want some work, Cec," Yanover said.

With Yanover you never knew what to expect, so I was cautious in expressing any real interest.

"Yeah? Well, what have you got in mind?" I asked.

"First of all," he said, "I can guarantee you a million bucks if you'll handle a contract to kill Fidel Castro."

I looked at Yanover as if he'd lost all his marbles. "Come on, Chuck, you're not serious," I said.

"I sure as hell am!" he snapped. "The only thing is, it's going to take a hellava good shot. You're going to have to take the shot at him from a quarter of a mile away. That's as close as you'll be able to get."

I started to chuckle, but I saw Yanover getting almost beet red with anger, so I coughed and frowned and speculated the job was a suicide mission.

"Chuck, be reasonable," I said. "I don't speak Spanish. I wouldn't last ten seconds after taking a shot at Castro. The people would tear me apart. Even for a million bucks I don't think I'd be interested. I don't have a secret desire to kill myself — not yet."

He never said much more about the plot, but I got the impression that the plan to hit Castro was something hatched up by some mob guys who wanted to get back into the casino business in Cuba. Castro had cost the Italian and Jewish mobs millions when he took over their casino hotels and threw them out of the country. Since that discussion the newspapers and American congressional committees have reported a number of plots to kill Castro, some sponsored by the Central Intelligence Agency, who wanted to use the mob, others planned by Stateside mobsters themselves, who had dreams of getting back their casinos.

When I turned Yanover down, he didn't bat an eye in switching to another contract hit.

"Okay, maybe I got something else for you," he said. "I got something personal you can handle. I'll give you ten thousand dollars, and all your expenses will be paid."

The target of his vendetta was some poor slob who was working a Caribbean cruise ship. The guy had made the mistake of taking off with a girlfriend of Yanover's. Chuck didn't like people chasing his women, even if he was chasing three or four at a time himself.

"You go down to Miami, and you get on this cruise ship," he said. "You grab him and just dump him off the boat and forget about it. You'll get ten grand and all expenses if you handle the job."

Later on he had a guy he wanted me to get rid of in Switzerland.

I don't remember his name, but he wanted this guy hit in the worst way. Friends of mine and the cops told me later that some guy who was a witness against Yanover was shot in Switzerland and nearly killed. I was never certain whether that was the same guy that Yanover had wanted me to hit.

About a month after I'd talked to Roman, Bob, and the official from the Bogota Chamber of Commerce, I arranged a meeting with Yanover at the Prince Hotel. Roman, Yanover, and I sat down. I was acting as the middleman, figuring I'd collect from both sides on the deal.

"I have this Colombian," Roman explained to Yanover. "He wants to buy automatic weapons, bazookas, tanks, and whatever else he can get his hands on, and he's willing to pay whatever it takes to get them."

Yanover sat there nodding, wiping the eyeglasses that he'd taken from his nose. "You just have him send the money up, and I ship them whatever they want. Planeloads of tanks, guns, munitions — you name it, I'll get it, and the prices will be right."

Both Roman and Yanover glided over the costs. Nobody got specific about the price of a tank or a machine gun or anything. They just talked in generalities.

"How are you going to get weapons like that to them in the quantities they want without attracting too much attention?" Roman asked.

"Look," answered Yanover with just a hint of anger to his voice. "I've handled shipments like this lots of times before. We just report the plane lost at sea after we deliver the weapons. Just go back to Bogota and have them draft some money to a bank here, and we'll start delivering them the guns and tanks they want."

But after all this, Roman backed off. He never went back, and he never saw Yanover again to my knowledge. As for Yanover, we kept on dealing together. From guns and cocaine to arson and other plots — one to overthrow a Caribbean island called Dominica and another to assassinate the president of South Korea. The government overthrow plots happened later, after I had become an informer and witness. But in the late seventies Yanover's biggest value was as a gun supplier.

Yanover had a ready supply of handguns and machine guns available on almost a moment's notice. He could get anything I wanted — grenades, machine guns, plastic explosives, antitank guns, even tanks themselves. His suppliers weren't just the Belgian arms manufacturer. He also had supply sources in New York and Chicago, sources he kept to himself and didn't talk about. I used to buy a lot of guns from him and sell them to bikers, to the Commissos, to Rounders I knew.

Cosimo Commisso was always in the market for guns. If he wasn't buying them from me, he was getting them from two Italian gunsmiths who had a shop in downtown Toronto. The gunshop owners themselves were in the market for special guns, even those that were hot. I recall selling one of the owners a collector's Winchester carbine. It was hot — stolen in a burglary — but they didn't care. They had a customer who wanted it, no questions asked. Cosimo sometimes bought hot guns from the younger gunshop owner. I remember one occasion when the owner promised Cosimo that within a couple of days he could have ten guns that were coming in from a source he had in the States.

Collectors' guns, any guns, were wanted by Rounders and bikers, who were always checking out gun collectors and gun stores that they could heist later. There were times it seemed to me that everyone in Toronto was in the market for a gun of some kind, and no one asked questions. If someone really wants a gun, he can always buy one on the street — whether it's in Toronto, Montreal, New York, or Miami. They are out there for people who know people, and it doesn't take too much to find and get to know the right people.

Between 1978 and 1980, when I was dealing heaviest in guns, I always had two or three guns of my own just sitting around for possible sales or possible jobs. Keeping them around like that sometimes got me in trouble. The worst incident came out of my giving a .32-calibre handgun to a Rounder friend of mine, James Munro, in May 1980.

Munro was short on money, and he was an old associate, so when he asked me for a gun and said he'd take care of me later, I didn't ask any questions about how he planned to use it. Munro was a hustler. I knew he handled burglaries and heists, but that was his business, not mine.

On May 14 Jimmy and his brother, Craig, tried robbing Bourbon Street, a Toronto nightclub. While they were holding up the place, a cop, Const. Michael Sweet, interrupted the robbery and was shot. That brought out an army of cops, and for a couple of hours Craig, who was older and crazier than Jimmy, held the cops at bay with the gun I'd given Jimmy. All that time Constable Sweet was bleeding; he bled to death from the wounds that Craig later admitted inflicting on him. Both Craig and Jimmy got life for murder. I wasn't charged in the case because the Munros didn't implicate me. When I became a witness and got immunity for past crimes, I admitted giving Jimmy Munro the gun just one day before the shootout. I didn't know, however, that they were going to rob the nightclub or shoot a cop. I felt bad about Sweet. He was a good cop with a wife and three kids. He was just in the wrong place at the wrong time.

Yanover hustled a lot of things besides guns. One of the items he could always sell cheap were diamonds, quality diamonds. I don't know exactly who supplied him, but I know he had developed some terrific sources for them through Klegerman and some of the Jewish diamond cutters in New York's diamond market. He also handled diamonds that bikers got for him from burglaries and robberies, bikers like Joe Veterre.

Veterre was an associate of the Vagabonds Motorcycle Club. He worked with another biker, a junkie, stealing and fronting diamonds. The two of them would break into houses and pull armed robberies and drug rip-offs. Veterre would sometimes unload his diamonds through Yanover, who had close ties to some Vagabond club members. Veterre would probably still be doing his thing in diamonds and robberies if he hadn't crossed another member of the Vagabonds, who wanted some money for drugs from Veterre and threatened him. Veterre wasn't the type to knuckle under. He shot the Vagabond in the kneecap and crippled him. A week later one of the Vagabonds and two of his Rounder friends got to Veterre. They grabbed him, and he's never been seen since.

Even though I was moving deals on the side with people like Yanover and the Colombians, I was still very active with the Commissos. In 1978 alone I handled seven arsons and bombings. Probably the most violent, and the one that was supposed to bring me the most money, was that of the Laramie Sports Store at 89 MacDonell Street in Guelph.

It was strictly an insurance blowout set up by the store owners,

Bruno Spizzichino and his partner, Armando DiCapua, with the help of another Italian friend, Rocco Mastrangelo. Mastrangelo was the connection to the Commissos for DiCapua and Spizzichino. He knew Remo Commisso very well.

Their plan was to bomb and set fire to the store, collect the insurance, and pay the Commissos $20,000 to do the job. Spizzichino and DiCapua went to Italy to borrow the $20,000 they needed. When they got the money, they flew to Las Vegas and then, after a short stay at one of the casinos, to Guelph. The idea was to make it look as though they had won the $20,000 they were bringing into Canada while they were in Las Vegas. Once in Guelph, they deposited the money in the Bank of Commerce and, after a short wait, took the money to Mastrangelo. He in turn paid the money to Remo and Cosimo Commisso.

I was working out in a gym in early June 1978 when Cosimo called me and told me it was important that I come to see him at the Casa Commisso. When I arrived, he told me he had a job for me.

"I got friends in Guelph," he said. "They got a business that's not good. They wanna burn it — blow it up and collect the insurance."

"How much is my end for doing the job, Cosimo?" I asked.

"Eight, maybe ten thousand dollars when the job is done," he said.

The next day we met at a pool hall on Dufferin Street, and Cosimo told me he wanted to drive to Guelph and introduce me to the owners. I didn't like the idea too much, but Cosimo said that the owners were friends of his family and that, for my protection, he would identify me only as "George," nothing more.

I finally agreed to go, but I said I'd drive, and so the following afternoon Cosimo and I drove to Guelph in my Corvette. When we got to town, I parked the car about a block from the store. Then we walked to the sporting goods shop, where Cosimo introduced me to DiCapua.

Once the introductions were out of the way, DiCapua gave me a tour of the store and the building it was in. He showed me a disco and an after-hours club on an upper floor and a karate club in the basement. Then he took me to the back of the store to a storage area and showed me a back door that led to an alleyway. While I was there, I studied some gas pipes that led downstairs. I told him I would probably place the bomb down-stairs near the pipes to set fire to the place.

"I'll be back in about a week with the materials I need," I said to DiCapua.

"Okay. I'll be waiting for you to return," he said.

On the way back to Toronto, Cosimo made a promise. When the job was done, when I had finished, I was to go to the Casa Commisso a few days later to collect my $10,000.

Before I returned to the sporting goods store, I ran into a problem. I'd gone to a cottage I owned to get the dynamite and blasting caps I needed. All told, I had twenty sticks of dynamite. But I had no fuse, and I knew it would be difficult to get the fuse, do the job, and not be identified later by inquisitive cops as someone who had bought a fuse at some store. My biker friends didn't have any fuses and neither did the Commissos. My alternative was to try using a sparkler, the kind you see at fireworks displays.

I went to a nearby novelty store and bought a large package of long sparklers, about two feet long. I had no way of being certain my idea would work without testing it, so I returned to the cottage, took out a blasting cap, and went out in the backyard. I took out a sparkler and put it in the blasting cap. It fit perfectly. Then I lit my makeshift fuse and watched, timing it to see how long it took for the sparkler to reach the cap and explode. It took about two minutes.

On the afternoon of June 20 I drove to Guelph. It was sunny and hot as I drove, and I was sweating as I looked at the package of dynamite lying beneath the glove compartment of my Corvette. I was also a little nervous when I arrived in Guelph, partially because of the heat and its effect on the dynamite. I drove around the block in which DiCapua's store was located. As I drove by, a police paddy wagon passed me. I pulled over to the side of the road a considerable distance from the store, parked in a parking lot next to a fire station, and waited to be sure the paddy wagon wouldn't return. At a little after 6:00 P.M. I walked back to the store with the dynamite in a gym bag. I was wearing my gym clothes — a gym suit, a sweat jacket, and driving gloves. The door of the store was locked, but as I turned the doorknob, DiCapua appeared and let me in. He was nervous, fidgety.

"I was expecting you last night," he said. "You never showed up, so I phoned this man, Rocco, to see what was keeping you."

"I had a problem getting some materials," I said, "that was all. This Rocco — I never heard from him."

As I talked to DiCapua, I unzipped the gym bag and showed him the contents. His eyes bulged out a bit, and he seemed to be shaking a little, but it didn't stop him from chattering like a magpie.

"Wait till late — till about one in the morning before you start the fire," he said. "I need plenty of time after I close the store to get home."

Then he walked me to the back door again, opening it to show me the main street behind the building.

"This isn't an alleyway like you told me before!" I snapped. I was angry — more mad at myself than anything for not casing the place better on my own the first time.

DiCapua was clearly afraid, but he kept his head. He gave me the telephone number of the karate club that was adjacent to his store basement.

"Please," he said, "phone them about ten, eleven tonight. Make sure no one's there."

"Don't worry about it," I said. "Of course I'll check. I don't want anyone in the building any more than you do. Nobody's gonna get hurt. Don't worry."

With that he left. I went to the basement of the building and sat in the storage area for nearly three hours, listening to the people at the karate school work out. I could hear them through the wall as they kicked the heavy pad, threw each other to the floor, and shouted their so-called battle cries. While I was listening to them, I carefully pulled the dynamite from my bag and taped it together. I also put in the blasting caps with the sparklers inserted in them. When I hadn't heard any noise for a while, I dialed the karate school's number to make sure no one was there. I let the phone ring and ring for a long time, hung up, and then phoned back again to be doubly sure everyone was gone.

Before I set the bomb, I walked quickly up the back stairway leading to the doorway and pulled one of the bars open to make certain that the door would open when I came running back up the stairs. I checked my watch and noticed it was about 12:30 A.M. DiCapua had had plenty of time to establish his alibi. I returned downstairs and started two fires in the storage room. As the fires burned, I went to the boiler room and placed the bomb inside the boiler. I wanted the cast-iron boiler to blow up and hit the gas main next to it. That would trigger still another explosion and blow the place sky high.

When I set the bomb in the boiler, I placed newspapers around one of the sparklers. As I left, I lit a match and touched it to the newspapers. They were burning as I dashed from that room, past the storage room where the other fire was now burning strongly, up the stairs, and out the back door. Just as I came out, I spotted the police paddy wagon I'd seen earlier. It was just pulling into a parking lot across the street, and two people were walking up the street toward me. I slammed the door with my right foot, uncertain whether it closed tight or not, put up the hood on my gym suit, and started jogging up the street as though I were a jogger working out.

I had used three sparklers to set the bomb off. That gave me six minutes to get out of the area. I jogged down the street, hurdled some guard rails, and ran across the railroad tracks and down the street to where my car was parked in the fire station parking lot. The alarm bells hadn't gone off by the time I reached my car, so the fire hadn't been spotted. It took me about a minute to reach the car. My palms were sweaty, and a chill ran along my spine as I started the car and drove off, deliberately unhurried, down some city streets to Highway 7 and then to Highway 401.

I went to see Cosimo two days later at the Casa Commisso to collect my money.

"You got the money you owe me, Cosimo?" I asked.

He shook his head. "I'm sorry, Cec," he said. "I gotta go to Guelph and get the money from these people. Come back in a few days."

So I did, and he handed me $2,500.

"Where's the rest you promised me?" I said angrily.

"That's all they gave me," he said. "They say the fire department came and put out the fire. The building — it didn't burn."

I didn't believe him. A few days later I drove to Guelph to check to see if the building hadn't burned as he claimed. I noticed as I drove by that a lot of the windows were all black, and those that weren't were all boarded up. I then drove around the side of the building to the other block where the hotel was located. I checked the outside wall and part of the sidewalk. I found they were intact. The bomb hadn't worked as planned. It had blown the boiler apart and destroyed the room it was in, but it had missed the gas line it was intended to set off. I didn't learn until later that I had just missed by a matter of a few feet the city's main gas line, which for some strange reason ran through that building. If I had hit that, I'd have taken a whole city block and probably killed a lot of people.

The building had burned all right, but not to the ground. The store was destroyed, and $100,000 worth of damage was done to other shops in the building, but the building wasn't levelled the way DiCapua and Spizzichino had planned. Fire investigators didn't realize the place had been bombed until years later, when I became a witness and gave them the details of the bombing. They thought all along that the fire had been caused by a gas explosion. No one had even suspected arson or a bomb.

It took me nearly four years to find out that the Commisso brothers had stiffed me on that job, just as they had stiffed me on a lot of jobs I'd done for them. They had collected the $20,000 from the store owners up front and pocketed all but the lousy $2,500 Cosimo gave me.

Among crooks on the street, there is supposed to be a code of honour of sorts. When it came to the Commissos, there was no honour. There was a greater code of honour among biker gang members than with the Commissos. In fact, two sixteen-year-olds breaking into a house have a greater code of honour than these mob men did. The only code they had was to look after their "family." I wasn't family, I wasn't Italian or Calabrian. I was an outsider, so they stuck it to me.

CHAPTER
13

SHAKING THE DISCO BEAT

Nightclubs, bars, and discotheques have long been the targets of shake-downs, extortions, and biker-run prostitution. When I was a biker, it didn't matter whether we were in Orlando or Fort Lauderdale, in Montreal, Toronto, or some small town on the outskirts — the bikers singled out nightspots and hotels for all sorts of money-making schemes.

Most of the strippers and topless dancers in Orlando and Fort Lauderdale were controlled by the Outlaws through "talent agencies" their members owned. The Pagans Motorcycle Club on Long Island and in New Jersey and Philadelphia had talent agencies run by bikers or biker associates, and these agencies supplied the topless clubs and strip joints that a lot of the young people flocked to. More often than not, those places where the bikers sent their women became centres of prostitution and muggings and frequently attracted violence between rival biker gangs. Since I "officially" left the street and biker clubs some years ago, nothing has changed except the names. Bikers still have talent agencies, still supply women, and still muscle clubs that don't want to do business with them.

In Ontario bikers control 80 per cent of the strippers who perform in clubs. They control them mostly through intimidation. The women get paid pretty well, and they are protected by the bikers, but they have to kick back part of their salary for that protection and for being placed in jobs by the agencies. The strippers and dancers who don't want to pay get hassled, beaten, and very often raped.

The Vagabonds had a guy named Steve in the mid- and late seventies who was a go-fer for the club president in Toronto. The president used Steve to drive him here, drive him there, take his sister shopping, pick up a pizza — you name it, Steve did it. Then suddenly Steve became a member. I never knew how or what qualified him, but they made him a member. A short time after becoming a member, he started a stripper talent agency that began supplying women to clubs throughout Toronto and other parts of Ontario.

The women who go to these agencies don't realize what they're getting into. Most of them are young, just out of high school, or they are hippy types. Some of them are girlfriends of bikers who are told to go to the agencies and work or else, and the "or else" can mean anything from a beating to a gang rape or even murder. Still others are starry-eyed kids who think these agencies are legitimate talent agencies, a stepping-stone to the stage or television or movies, and they go to them looking for work.

Once they start dealing with those running the agencies, they're hooked. They're told they have to pay an agent's fee and give a percentage of their salary to the agencies so they will provide them with protection while they strip or dance at various clubs. Most of the girls don't object. Those that do either get roughed up or find they can't get jobs. If they're dumb enough to land a job at a club that deals with these agencies or wants to keep peace with the bikers, they soon find themselves hassled by bikers, and very often they're roughed up and raped.

Some of the clubs that the girls dance and strip in are owned by bikers. The Outlaws and the Pagans owned a lot of topless bars, discos, and stripper joints in Long Island, Philadelphia, and Orlando. The ownership might be hidden behind corporate fronts, biker relatives, or biker associates, but the biker club members were the real owners.

The vast majority of clubs where bikers' women work, however, aren't owned by bikers. They are extorted and shaken down by bikers and forced to use biker women as their performers and entertainers.

It's a very, very profitable business. I had an opportunity to buy into an agency that had control of 125 girls, or so the owners claimed. A friend was going to buy in with me, but I had a bad feeling about the offer. It was too low—the owners wanted only $2,000 from each of us for control of the agency. They were bikers who said they were in a hurry to get out of the business. I suspected the coppers were breathing down their backs and the bikers figured they were about to lose everything anyhow, so they'd grab our four grand and leave us with all the headaches. So I didn't buy in.

What biker club members do is this. They go to a nightclub—a small bar or disco in Mississauga or Windsor in Ontario or Sept-Iles or Sherbrooke in Quebec. They go to the owners and promise them a kickback of the money they collect from the broads they supply. They also promise to look after the broads.

Now bar owners go for these tales, these promises, because they don't want bikers to come in and break up their place, and that possibility is implied when the bikers talk to them. You tell these owners that if they don't hire women who have the protection of the bikers, it's highly likely that some biker gangs may come in and cause trouble—wreck their place. When they hear a story like that, it's amazing how quickly they fall into line.

"Look, if you don't want my women in here, fine, but tomorrow night there may be twenty-five Vagabonds here having a r-e-a-l good party," the biker will say.

John the Bar Owner gets that message real fast. Twenty-five Vagabonds partying in a small bar or even a large nightclub can mean only one thing—trouble—and a very costly evening for him. So John the Bar Owner and hundreds like him all across Canada and the United States sign contracts to hire dancers, strippers, and entertainers supplied by the biker agencies. If it's a small club or bar, he is usually invited to use the shuffleboards, the pinball machines, and the video games that the bikers or their friends own or control.

The biker agencies, meanwhile, put ads in the papers for more dancers. But the talent search isn't limited to using girlfriends or advertising in newspapers and magazines. The bikers also muscle in on the talent that other agencies provide for the hotels, bars, and discos on both sides of the border.

What they are usually looking for are women between the ages of eighteen and thirty-two, generally not older than that. They offer them a good salary, even with the kickbacks. After the women join the biker agencies, many are eventually steered into prostitution as a sideline. Sometimes the bikers force them, sometimes they don't, but that fear is always planted in the women's minds — that if they don't do what they're told, they'll lose that protection from rowdy, violent customers, many of them bikers.

The girls who are hassled, beaten, and sometimes raped rarely report the incidents to police. The girls who dance at clubs are looked on as prostitutes anyhow by the cops, who have serious doubts about the truth of their stories when they say they've been raped. Others are afraid to talk because they fear retaliation by the bikers, who will intimidate them or their families, threatening to attack their mothers or sisters or burn down their homes. And some girls are too embarrassed to admit they've been raped, don't want publicity, and don't want to appear in court and be questioned by biker attorneys.

A good example of the kind of extortion I'm talking about involved the owner of a disco on Davenport Road in Toronto. The owner was a Greek who went by the name of Cosmo. I was introduced to him by Cosimo Commisso.

"Cosmo, he's having trouble with the bikers," Cosimo said. "They been causing trouble — fights, damage — in his club. They even raped his waitress and one of his customers."

"Which bikers?" I asked.

"The Paradise Riders," he answered. "They cause him lotsa trouble." Then he added, "You talk to them, get them to stay outta the place for a while. If they do, this guy, he'll pay. We'll all make some money."

"Okay," I said, "I'll see what I can do, but tell your friend it's probably going to cost him. Bikers don't do things for nothing, and you know I don't."

So I went to see a friend of mine at the Paradise Riders, one of the top club officers, and I talked to him about the problem and about the rapes by one of his biker members, a guy named Terry. I told him Terry and some of his friends had raped this waitress and one of the customers.

"Look," I told my friend, "stay out of the disco for a while. The guy, this Cosmo, is willing to pay me money if you do. We'll all make money."

At first my friend was against the idea. "Hell, no, Cec," he said, "we don't want any fucker tellin' us to stay outta his place. Nobody tells us where to go."

"Okay, okay, I understand what you're saying, but just stay out of there for a while — as a favour to me," I said. "I can make a few bucks. You know, one hand washes the other."

So he agreed. I offered him a kickback, a couple of hundred bucks for him and some of the boys to have a night on the town, but he refused. He was doing it as a favour, and you don't get paid for favours. I told him to tell his friend Terry that I'd get the girl off his back, stop her from testifying against him.

With the deal cut, I went back to Cosimo, and we sat down with the disco owner, Cosmo.

"My friend here," Cosimo said, "he talked to the bikers. They know him, and they're gonna stay outta your place. But it's gonna cost you. Nothing's for free."

Cosmo understood. He came up with several thousand dollars and paid for the protection that Cosimo was providing through me. He also had a long talk with the waitress. She agreed to forget what Terry and his friends looked like. Our success at the disco gave Cosimo some ideas about moving in on night-clubs and discos with an extortion racket that used the fear of bikers as a weapon for intimidation.

In May 1979 I set up the Superior Fitness Centre, a health club on Jane Street that I bought from a friend of mine who wanted to get out of the fitness business. I wanted in because I needed a business as a front and because I thought I could make some money out of it. It was a dumb move. It wasn't long before I was planning gun smuggling, bombings and arsons, and plots to shake down discos while running the health club. I didn't pay attention to business, and, as a result, I lost money operating it.

I soon found out that I wasn't a particularly good health club businessman. The club was in a poor location, and while I had good equipment, a pool, and a gym, when I bought the club I didn't buy much of a membership list, and to run a club like that profitably, you need a minimum of ten to fifteen members there every day. I also had problems with a landlord who kept raising the rent. By August 1980 I sold out and just about broke even on the deal. But in the more than a year that I operated the club, it provided a good front for my operations and for meetings with the Commissos and others with whom I had criminal dealings.

It was early in the summer of 1979, not long after we had straightened things out for the Greek disco owner, that the Commissos told me they were convinced there was gold to be mined in Toronto's discos.

Because I was an ex-biker with a lot of contacts among biker gangs and Rounders, I was the key to the Commissos' plan to shake down discos and nightclubs. The plan was simple: to use biker gangs to break up and muscle club owners and then promise them protection, for a fee, from biker intimidation. Of course, the bikers would get some of the profits, and they would be asked to stay away only *temporarily* from clubs that were paying protection. After a few weeks or months of staying out of a place, they could go back and terrorize it some more, and the Commissos would collect all over again. It was the first real semi-alliance to take place between some of the biker gangs and the Calabrian Mafia. But it was at best a shaky alliance, because no one trusted anyone, and for good reason.

The first test of the extortion alliance, as I'll call it, came when Cosimo came to see me at the health club. Cosimo knew a disco owner named Mike who ran an after-hours club on Yonge Street. The place had become a target of the Vagabonds, whom the owner had mistakenly tried to bar from his club and who kept coming back to break up the place and harass and frighten his customers.

"I got the idea when we did the job for Cosmo," he said. "You make the deals with your biker friends, we collect from the discos, and everybody makes money."

"I don't know, Cosimo," I said. "You don't tell bikers to stay out of places. They don't care about the money. It's a matter of pride."

"Try, Cec," he said. "See Mike. See what you can work out."

I set up the meeting with the disco owner at Harvey's Restaurant on Jane Street and talked to him about his problem.

"Maybe I can get the bikers to stop breaking up your joint, Mike, but it's going to cost you," I said.

"How much?" he asked.

"Two grand now . . . maybe some more later, but at least you'll be in business," I said. "The way things are now, you're just about shut down."

"Okay, see what you can arrange," he answered. Then he reached into his pocket and handed me $1,000. "Here's half on account."

I went to see a friend of mine at the Vagabonds and explained that I was rousting this disco owner for a quick buck.

"Look, get the guys to stay away from this joint for a few weeks, maybe a month," I said. "That'll give me a chance to make some money off this guy, and I'll look after you. Besides, we've helped each other before."

My biker friend agreed. "Seeing it's you, Cec, okay," he said. "This guy's an asshole. When you've gotten what you want outta him, let me know. Then we'll go back and break his lousy club up again."

I laughed, slapped him on the back, and left, and for the next two weeks I collected another $1,000 a week from Mike. I was supposed to split with Cosimo, but all he asked for was $500, so that's all I gave him. He figured I was splitting with the bikers. I gave my friend some, but I kept most of it.

There were other clubs we shook down the same way. Some worked, but one didn't — a disco called Peaches on Pears Avenue. It was owned by a guy named David Freedman, whom I knew through some friends. Cosimo knew about Peaches, and he knew about Freedman, who he said had plenty of money and would be an easy extortion.

Freedman had helped me a few times on a few deals, and I wasn't about to shake him down for Cosimo, so while I gave Cosimo a nodding agreement to handle the deal, I secretly called Freedman at his apartment in High Park to warn him.

"Look, Dave, some people want me to lean on you — you know," I said. "Remember that other place, that disco that burned down not far from your place? Be careful. You don't need their kind of trouble."

Freedman was quick to show he had no fear of the threat that I was trying, in my own way, to warn him about without actually saying who was involved.

"I don't know what you're saying to me, Cec," Freedman said, "but if anyone is trying to put the arm on me, they're gonna get nothing. If they burn my place down, they'll be doing me a favour."

"Dave, forget it," I said. "I'm just trying to give you a friendly warning, nothing more. Just make sure your insurance premiums are paid up."

I went back to Cosimo and said to him, "Forget about Freedman and his club. No way are you going to extort the guy. He's not going to pay up, so forget it."

Not all of the disco owners were targets for shake-downs by the bikers and the Commissos. At least one, Harold Arviv, had his own ideas about how to make money and get rid of business partners.

Arviv has pleaded guilty to his role in a conspiracy to blow up his disco on January 9, 1980. That's when Ji Shik Moon, the ex-Korean sergeant and partner of Chuck Yanover, took thirty sticks of dynamite and blew the disco sky-high, causing over $700,000 in damage. Yanover and Michael Gerol, who supplied the dynamite, were convicted when Moon testified against them. Moon said that Arviv had offered him $10,000 "front money" and 25 per cent of the insurance claim to blow up the place. Moon agreed to do the job after talking it over with Yanover, who was in prison at the time and who was to split the proceeds.

I first met Arviv in November 1977 through a Satan's Choice friend of mine, Frank Lenti, who frequently worked out at the same health club that I did. Lenti told me that he had set up a million-dollar burglary and that he wanted me to go in on it with him. He planned to rob a house owned by a Jack Mamann. Arviv and Mamann had been business partners in a place called the Hippopotamus Restaurant at Yonge and De Lisle streets. Lenti said that the information on the million-dollar set-up came from Arviv, who wanted us to rob Mamann's house and split the money we found with him. I agreed. The terms were that I would take 50 per cent of whatever we got, and Lenti and Arviv would split the other 50 per cent. I was taking the lion's share because I had the experience and I'd be doing most of the work, planning and executing the job.

I did a surveillance on the house, which was in North York on Coreydale Court, and kept track of the people who went in and out at different times. On the day I decided to break into the place, I telephoned to be sure there was no one in and then donned a mail carrier's uniform I had in the trunk of my car. I drove past the house again, making sure no one was around, parked a few blocks away, hoisted a mailbag over my shoulder with a crowbar inside, and walked to the house. I rang the doorbell, waited a minute or so for an answer, and when there was none, went to the rear of the house and broke in through a sliding glass door.

I searched the den, the bedrooms — the whole damned house — for about seven or eight minutes before the phone started ringing and ringing. I had a feeling I might have been spotted by a neighbour, who was calling to see if someone was in the house or if I was in there alone. So I left — empty-handed.

I was steamed over finding nothing, and a few days later I told Lenti. He went back to talk to Arviv, who claimed that there was money in the place and that he wanted me to go back and try to find it. I told Lenti the only way to do the job now was to stage an armed robbery, and in December 1977 I recruited a couple of friends who had just come out of jail to handle the job, Gary Barnes and another guy called Ray.

I took them to the house, showed them the layout, and told them what I wanted done. Then I supplied them with two balaclavas, handcuffs, and one revolver, a P-38, that I gave to Barnes. Ray had his own gun. I drove them to the house that evening. I parked about two blocks away while they went into the house to do the robbery.

They got inside and handcuffed one of Mamann's older sons. Mamann was not at home. They said the family was upset — the kids and wife were crying, and she denied that there was a big stash of money in the house. All they got was some jewellery and a few hundred bucks in cash. When they met me at the car, I drove off, checked the jewellery, and found a gold bracelet with Mamann's name engraved on it. There were also some rings. I told my friends to keep the money, but the jewellery I threw out over the roof of the car into a vacant lot.

When I saw Lenti again, he told me that Arviv had told him that Mamann had taken the money out of his house two days before the robbery and had had it deposited in an account in a Swiss bank.

I wasn't too happy about all the trouble I'd gone to for nothing, and I told Lenti that I wanted to see Arviv personally. A meeting was arranged, and I went to Arviv's disco, which was under construction at the time, and met with him. It was early January 1978. I went carrying a .22-calibre Hi-Standard automatic with a silencer concealed in the front of my pants and hidden by my coat. I was prepared for anything. Lenti had told me that Arviv was a former Israeli army commando, so I suspected that he could be violent and possibly armed too.

Arviv didn't know me as Cecil Kirby. Lenti had never told him or his contacts who I was. Arviv knew me only as "George," a name I used frequently when Cosimo introduced me to some of his "clients."

"You owe me some money, Mr. Arviv," I said. "You owe me for a B and E and a robbery — and I figure those two jobs were worth twenty thousand dollars."

He agreed that he owed me money for what I'd done for him and said he'd pay me $10,000. There was a problem, however. He said that because his expenses were running high at the disco he was building, he'd have to cover what he owed with several payments.

All the time he talked, I felt the gun cool and hard against my gut. Because of the way it was positioned in my pants, it was damned near impossible for me to sit down, so I stood and paced up and down slowly, keeping my jacket on to conceal what I had. If he'd made a move—tried anything—I was ready to blow him away right where he sat. But he didn't. He didn't give me a hard time at all.

The next day we met at the Hungarian Gourmet Restaurant on Hayden Street, where he paid me $2,000 in cash. Later, at another meeting, he paid me another $1,000. It was then that he told me about a friend of his who was the manager of an after-hours club. He said he would talk to this guy to arrange a fake robbery of the night deposits. He figured I'd get at least $10,000 from the job, and I could keep that plus the money he'd already given me.

On January 15, 1978, I held up Yvo Sajet, the manager of the Hippopotamus. I parked about a block away from the parking lot of the Hippopotamus and waited for a couple of hours. First some women who appeared to be waitresses got into a car and left. After they were gone, I walked cautiously back down the street and stood beside the edge of the parking lot, about seventy-five feet from the manager's sports car.

I saw a man come out of the club and walk to the car carrying some boxes, which he put on the car roof. I appeared out of the dark behind the guy. He was a big man, about six feet three, 210 pounds. As he opened the car door, I said, as Arviv had told me to, "You have something for me?"

Sajet hesitated for a minute, then answered, "Yes, I do." One box was still on the roof of the car. He pointed to it. "This is what you want."

"Turn around and bend down a little bit," I said, disguising my voice as best I could. As he did, I hit him with a blackjack I was carrying. The blackjack flew from my hand in front of the car. He was semi-conscious, lying on the ground. I grabbed the box, and as I walked around him, he said there was still something in the car. I looked inside, saw another box, grabbed it, and then walked to the front of the car and picked up my blackjack.

"Give me about ten minutes," I said to him, "then call the police." Then I jumped the fence and ran behind some apartment houses and down the street to my car. I opened the trunk and threw the boxes inside. Later, when I checked the boxes out, I found only $4,800 in cash and some charge receipts.

When I saw Arviv again, I told him he still owed me $2,000. His friend hadn't been carrying as much as he'd promised. Arviv said he realized that, but he couldn't pay me the $2,000 right away because he was short on cash. In the months that followed, Arviv kept his word and paid me what he owed. He seemed to be a gentleman among the criminals I knew.

There was an attempt to extort Mamann after that. One of my original contacts and some other guys, including one biker from Satan's Choice, tried to shake Mamann down. They didn't talk to me about it — it was something they did on their own, and they were caught by the cops.

I met with Arviv several times after that. He really hated Mamann. He never really explained why. He said he had started the Hippopotamus with Mamann and his brother, who had been his partners. There was a bitter separation. Arviv left and went into a clothing business that then went under. He said he tore the store down and started building the disco on money he borrowed from lawyers and other people. I couldn't figure out why he was having so much trouble getting money. His father-in-law was Louis (Lou) Chesler, a multi-million-dollar Canadian financier who was chairman of both General Development Corp., a company that sold Florida homes and lots through the mail, and Universal Controls Inc., a big electronics firm. Chesler had also worked in the Bahamas as part of a group that developed a gambling resort in Freeport.

Later, in October 1978, during a diamond-buying visit with Yanover, Chuckie asked me if I knew Arviv. I told him I did, and he said his friend, Ji Shik Moon, had lost a ring in a fight at Arviv's disco.

"You want me to see if I can get the ring back?" I asked.

Yanover nodded.

The next night Lenti and I picked up Yanover and went to the Oriental Palace on Bloor Street. There we met Moon, who told me what had happened during the fight. Leaving Moon behind, the three of us went to Arviv's disco and sat down with Arviv. I introduced Arviv to Yanover and told him about Moon losing the ring during the fight. Arviv said he had found the ring after the fight and had turned it over to police because no one had claimed it. While we sat there drinking his booze on the house, he sent one of his flunkies out, and within an hour Yanover had the $3,000 ring in his hand. It was an important meeting because it led to Moon's contract to blow up the disco for Arviv.

It was maybe ten months later that I took Cosimo to the disco. Arviv had told me he was tired of running the disco and wanted very badly to sell it. Because Cosimo wanted to get into the disco business and was using me to shake down most of the owners in town, I had told him that the disco was for sale and that it might be an opportunity for him to get into the business, using a front man to operate it.

Cosimo had other ideas. He tried to strong-arm Arviv and shake him down for the business. Arviv was too smart for that and suggested that if Cosimo wanted the place, he should come up with a million bucks or, lacking that, be a nice guy and sip the free champagne. Cosimo backed off from his extortion try after that. I was never certain why, but it could have been because of who Arviv's father-in-law was. Chesler had some heavy friends, people like Meyer Lansky, the American syndicate's financial wizard, and "Trigger" Mike Coppola. Those friendships and the respect the mob people had for Chesler probably made Cosimo think twice about muscling Arviv.

It was a couple of weeks after that, in the middle of August 1979, that I returned to the disco. Arviv told me that he couldn't sell the business, so he'd decided to blow it up.

"Can you do the job?" he asked.

"For fifteen thousand I can do it," I said.

"Make it ten thousand — after it's done," he said. "I'll get the money to pay you then."

"I'll need money for the dynamite," I said. "It'll take a big bomb here in this room." The room we were in, talking about the job, was at the rear of the bottom floor.

At first Arviv wanted to supply the explosives, but I told him no. I wanted to buy the dynamite myself and be sure of the stuff I got. He gave me $300 to make the buy. The bombing was to be done within a few months. I did buy some dynamite, but I never went back to see Arviv or deal with him. In 1981, after I had become an informer, I turned the dynamite over to the Ontario Provincial Police.

On January 9, 1980, Arviv's disco blew sky-high. Nobody was hurt. For a while I couldn't figure out who had done the job. I thought I was the only bomber in the city. In 1983 the truth came out. Moon pleaded guilty to bombing the disco and got a five-year sentence. He testified against Yanover, who got nine years, and Gerol, who got seven years.

Arviv fled the country and holed up in Miami. He was finally extradited to Canada, where he was freed on bail put up by his mother-in-law, Molly Chesler. She put up $250,000 cash bail, a $250,000 surety bond guaranteed by a condo. There were two more $100,000 bonds guaranteed by property owned by a popcorn company executive and a real estate executive. As an added guarantee Arviv had to surrender both his Canadian and Israeli passports. Moon and Yanover were convicted and jailed; even Sajet was jailed for thirty days for misleading police with the false robbery report. Arviv's trial was stalled for more than two years by his lawyers, and he is now free after pleading guilty. I've always wondered if that was part of a plan — delay and stall until killers could catch up with me so Arviv could walk free. There's still more than $100,000 on my head and a lot of people standing in line, waiting for an opportunity to get me out in the open once more.

There was one other club owner, a restaurateur really, whom Cosimo put the arm on. He wasn't trying to collect for himself on this one; he was trying to collect a debt that Willie O'Bront, the French-Jewish rackets friend and money launderer of crime boss Vincent Cotroni, said was owed him. O'Bront lives in Hallandale, Florida, where he was accused by American drug agents in 1983 of operating a $50-million-a-year narcotics-trafficking ring.

In early July 1980 I went to see Cosimo at the Casa Commisso. He had another job for me. The target was Maury Kalen, then the owner of the Mr. Greenjeans Emporium and Restaurant chain in Toronto.

"This Kalen, he owes money — a hundred thousand — to a friend of mine, Willie O'Bront," Cosimo said. "I want you to send the message to him with a bomb."

Now I knew who and what O'Bront was, but I knew nothing about Kalen, so I took Cosimo at his word. I also took his word that he knew where Kalen lived when he gave me the address of 123 Heath Street West. I also had a description of his car, the address of his office at Village by the Grange, and the location of the restaurants, one at Adelaide and Jarvis streets and the other in the crowded Eaton Centre.

Cosimo wanted me to set off a bomb either in Kalen's house or in his car, but on looking over his neighbourhood, I figured the best thing to do was to drop a couple of sticks of dynamite taped together, without a fuse, into his mailbox.

I ruled out bombing his car as being too dangerous, and the restaurants were out as far as I was concerned because there were too many people around the areas where they were located. I figured the bomb in the home mailbox was as good a message as any explosion, and that way no one would get hurt. If something more violent was needed later — well, that would be another story.

The job was worth $2,000, and Cosimo paid me the fee. Late on the night of July 7 I dropped the two sticks in the mailbox. I learned later that two guys in the room where Kalen was supposed to be saw the two sticks land inside their mail cage by the door. They called the cops, and early on the morning of July 8 the Metropolitan Toronto Police Explosives Disposal Unit was called out to remove the dynamite.

A week later I got a call from Cosimo and met him again at the banquet hall.

"Cec, this Kalen, he moved from Heath Street just before you put the dynamite there," he said. "I want you to go to his new home and bomb it. I give you two thousand more."

The new location was the Palace Pier on Lake Shore Boulevard, a place that was loaded with security.

"Cosimo, that place is crawling with security guards," I said. "It's too tough a place to hit."

Cosimo smiled broadly. "Don't worry, Cec," he said. "I take care of the guards. I know people there."

"You mean the security guard will let me in to place a bomb at the fuckin' door?" I asked.

"Well, maybe not," he said.

I told him I wouldn't handle the job, and later I learned from police that it wasn't even Kalen who owed O'Bront money. Cosimo was not only stupid in what he thought could be done, he also did lousy homework on the identities and addresses of his victims.

One other restaurant job that Cosimo asked me to handle in 1980 was an act of revenge, pure and simple. One day in May, as I entered the office at the Casa Commisso, Cosimo began pounding on a table and cursing in Italian.

"Hey, Cec," he said in his thickly accented English. "I gotta job for you."

"Whatcha want me to do, Cosimo?" I asked.

"I give you two grand to blow up this ristorante downtown," he said. "I want you to throw a bomb right through their fuckin' window — you understand?"

"Sure," I said, "through the window. But what place are we talking about?"

"It's this fuckin' Napoleon Ristorante!" he shouted.

While he was talking — his face flushed and his eyes flashing — he was counting out $2,000 on the table in front of me. That was unusual and gave me a hint of the depth of his anger. He almost never paid for a job up front. He was always making me wait for my money after I did a job for him. It was the nature of the man to keep you waiting. But not this time. This time he wanted a very well-known restaurant, located at 79 Grenville Street, blown up, and he wanted it done fast.

I asked him why he wanted the place hit, and he explained that the night before his wife and his mother-in-law had had to go to a nearby hospital and had stopped at the restaurant. While they were there, his wife had had an argument with the woman who owned the place.

"This woman," he shouted, "she threw my wife and the mother out, and my wife, she's very upset!" He pounded again on the table. "Throw the bomb right through the fuckin' window."

"Suppose there's people in there?" I asked.

"I don't care!" he snapped. "You do it Sunday night, when the owner's there. I don't care if there's anybody else inside at all. Fuck them. Just blow the inside of the place right out, you understand?"

"Okay, okay," I said. He was very agitated, building up a full head of steam, and it was no time to question him. "I'll do something similar to what you want," I said.

So I went up to my cottage and made up a bomb that consisted of two sticks of dynamite, a battery, and a timer and took it back down to Toronto that same night. I cased the restaurant and then parked my car at a nearby corner.

I slipped down the side of an alley on the east side of the restaurant and placed the bomb on a window ledge. For a split second, as I reached into my pocket to get something, I took my eye off the bomb. Then I saw it fall from the window ledge to the ground and felt I was suspended in time, watching my own death. The bomb took only seconds to fall, but it seemed to happen in slow motion, and I felt like my hands were frozen to my pants. As it hit the ground, my heart literally stopped. Something similar had happened to me while I was setting the bombs in the Wah Kew Chop Suey House in 1977. This time, if I had already wired the battery to the blasting cap and had the cap in the dynamite, I wouldn't be here to tell this story. They'd still be scraping pieces of me off the surrounding buildings.

After I caught my breath, I picked the bomb up slowly, put it back on the window ledge, made sure it was firmly in place, set the timer, and left. I was in the north end of Toronto, about twenty miles away, when it went off.

The next day I read in the paper that the bomb had gone off, injuring three women. Now that wasn't what I had intended. Despite Cosimo's orders, I had phoned the restaurant before I arrived to make sure nobody was inside. I had let the phone ring about thirty times, and when nobody answered, I'd figured it was safe. I remember that when I placed the bomb on the window ledge, I couldn't see inside the restaurant because the window was so thick and there were no lights on. But I guess the owner and two of her friends returned to the restaurant after I'd left and were sitting inside.

Police told me later that when the bomb went off, one of the vertical iron bars over the window next to the bomb was blasted loose and was thrown across the room to where the women were sitting. The police said it narrowly missed the owner's head and struck the wall. If it had hit her, it might have decapitated her. The bomb also sent glass flying through the air like razor-sharp missiles. The women were all hurt, cut up pretty badly, and they received awards for damages and injuries, but at least they survived. And Cosimo? He was pleased as hell with the results. He didn't give a damn about the women. The insult to his wife had to be avenged, and it was.

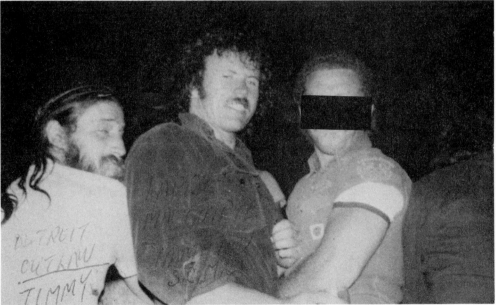

Top Satan's Choice bikers riding down Airport Road near Toronto, 1971, led by chapter president Larry Simmons *(left)* and road captain Cecil Kirby *(right)*.

Bottom, left to right "Timmy" of the Detroit Outlaws, Larry MacIntyre of the Satan's Choice, and Kirby in the Green Parrot bar in Key West, Florida, February 1974.

Top A Satan's Choice roadside conference at Airport Road and Highway 7, west of Toronto, 1971.

Centre Kirby's pride and joy — his bike. 1973.

Bottom A field day at Rice Lake, 1973. The photo on the right shows Kirby.

Top The Wah Kew Chop Suey House after it was blown up by Kirby in May 1977. *(Toronto Star Syndicate)*

Bottom The funeral of Antonio Macri, Reggio Calabria, Italy, 1979.

Paul Volpe in the late seventies. *(Canada Wide/ Toronto Sun)*

Remo Commisso at the funeral of Mike Racco, 1980. *(Canada Wide/Toronto Sun)*

The funeral of Mike Racco, 1980. *(Globe and Mail)*

Top left Helen Nafpliotis. *(Hartford Courant)*

Top right Peter Scarcella *(right)* meeting with two associates from Philadelphia, March 1981.

Bottom Antonio Rocco Romeo.

Michele Commisso getting into a car driven by an unidentified man in front of Howard Johnson's after meeting with Kirby, April 21, 1981.

Opposite Police examining Volpe's body in the trunk of his wife's car at Toronto International Airport, November 14, 1983. *(Globe and Mail)*

Kirby *(driving)* and Cosimo Commisso leaving Howard Johnson's in Kirby's bugged car, April 23, 1981.

Opposite The Volpes' former home. This photo was taken just after Paul Volpe's murder. *(Toronto Star Syndicate)*

Top Cosimo Commisso *(left)* and Kirby *(right)* meeting in front of Faces discotheque, February 27, 1981.

Centre Kirby *(back to camera)* and Cosimo *(facing camera)* at this meeting.

Bottom Cosimo and Kirby after the meeting.

CHAPTER
14

FALSE HOPES, FALSE STARTS

Montreal's Mafia is supposedly run by a Sicilian "Man of Respect" called Nicholas Rizzuto. He divides his time between Canada and Venezuela, where he has a business. I don't know Rizzuto personally, but I do know that he and the Commissos were close. I also know that for many years before Rizzuto took over, Montreal's Mafia was ruled by Vincent Cotroni and the three Violi brothers, Paolo, Rocco, and Francesco. All of them had two things in common: they were Calabrians, and they had gotten to where they were in Montreal because of Carmine (Lillo) Galante.

Before he was killed in July 1979, Galante was Joseph Bonanno's underboss in New York. While he was with Bonanno, he was sent to Montreal to organize a branch of the New York crime family in Montreal. That move, and a few other things, caused Buffalo mob boss Stefano Magaddino to complain that Bonanno was ignoring other mafiosi to plant his "flags" all over the world. Those who helped Galante plant Bonanno's flags in Montreal were the Cotroni brothers and the Violi brothers, who were, like Galante, among the most vicious killers and mob men ever to walk the streets of Montreal.

At first Galante's top men in Montreal were Giuseppe and Vincent Cotroni. The youngest brother, Francesco or Frank Cotroni, moved up later. At the same time the Cotronis' closest supporter and enforcer was another Calabrian, Paolo Violi. The only guy who wasn't a Calabrian was Galante, and he was born in the States. His father was supposed to have been an immigrant fisherman from Castellammare del Golfo, the same Sicilian village that Bonanno came from. The alliance between the Cotronis and the Violis resulted in a Bonanno family branch that ruled Montreal and provided a smuggling route into the United States for heroin imported from Sicily and Marseilles, France.

The Montreal Bonanno branch then became a full-fledged Canadian crime family run by Vincent Cotroni. Galante eventually became Bonanno's successor, but he got greedy. He tried to take over the narcotics supply routes of some other bosses of the American Cosa Nostra, so they had him knocked off by his own people and replaced him with Philip Rastelli, who had a lot of friends in Montreal and Toronto. Before Galante was killed, Cotroni went to jail for a while, and Paolo Violi became the acting boss of the Montreal family.

I first became aware that there were problems between the Commissos and the Violis on February 11, 1977. That was a couple of days after Francesco Violi, the youngest of the Violi brothers, had been killed at the headquarters of a Violi importing and distributing company. Violi was supposed to have been backed against a wall and shot in the face with a shotgun. Another killer made sure he was dead by pumping some bullets into him with a handgun.

Cosimo Commisso called me and told me it was very important that I come as quickly as possible to the Casa Commisso. When I arrived, Cosimo was pacing up and down. Remo was nowhere to be seen.

"So I'm here," I said. "What's the big hurry?"

"I need some guns, some pistols and shotguns, and I need them fast," Cosimo said.

"How many?" I asked.

"I need five, six, maybe more if you can get them," he said. He was very agitated, pacing back and forth.

"What the hell you need them so fast for?" I asked.

"You ask a lotta questions, Cec. Maybe too many!" he snapped.

He looked at me, his eyes flashing a bit. I was starting to get pissed off myself now, and I made sure he knew how I felt.

"Oh, for chrissake, Cosimo. You want guns? I'll get you guns!" I said sharply. "I don't really give a damn why you want them."

His voice softened, and for the first time he sat down. "I'm sorry, Cec," he said. "You see the stories about Frank Violi?"

"Yeah, sure," I said.

"Well, the people in Montreal, they think me and my brother, Remo, killed him," he said. He paused and lowered his voice. "We may have to go to Montreal to kill the rest of the family . . . like we got this guy."

Had he and Remo killed Francesco Violi? I had only what he was saying and the way he was acting to go on. Just because he said they got Francesco didn't mean they did, but he was desperate for guns at that moment. I didn't press him any more on what had happened. I just left, and within a day or two I had acquired all the guns he wanted. When I was ready to deliver them, I called the Casa Commisso and asked for Cosimo. He wasn't there, but Remo was. I talked to him.

"I got that package ready that you need," I told him.

"Forget it, Cec," he said. "We're not going to need them."

Almost a year went by before the Violis made headlines again. This time it was Paolo Violi who made the front page.

"Blood Spilling Is Feared after Mafia Boss Killed," was the headline of the January 24, 1978, Toronto *Sun*. The story described in depth the slaying of Paolo Violi. He had been shot and killed in his Jean Talon bar and restaurant on January 22 by two masked men who had burst in from the street and gunned him down while he was playing cards. Both of the killers had used shotguns, a favourite mob weapon. Four men, Sicilians, were arrested and later convicted of conspiracy to murder Violi.

Were the Commissos involved? I remember going to their banquet hall the day after the murder. We were meeting constantly at that time, handling hijacked cigarettes, arsons, extortions, and assaults that the Commissos were assigning me to work on.

"Where's Remo?" I asked Cosimo.

"He's in Montreal."

"Wasn't that where Violi was killed in his restaurant?"

"Yeah, isn't that funny," he said with a smirk on his face.

It was funny all right, but there was something else I found strange too. Both Violi brothers had been gunned down with shotguns. Remo's favourite weapon was the shotgun. He loved skeet shooting, and he said it had been his favourite weapon in Italy. The Commissos were also close friends of Nicholas Rizzuto, the guy who took over the Montreal mob from the Violis.

On October 19, 1980, the last of the Violi brothers, Rocco, was gunned down by a single shot in the heart while he sat at his kitchen table with his wife and two children in his home in the east end of Montreal. The cops said the shooting was the work of a professional killer. I remember wondering at the time if the Commissos were involved in that shooting as well. It was their style. They wouldn't hesitate to kill a guy in front of his wife and kids. Anyone who would kill whole families in Italy, including a baby in a crib, would kill a rival in front of his family. They had no ethics, no honour about murder when it came to wielding power.

For some reason, during 1978 and 1979 a lot of the Commissos' extortions and arsons went wrong. It had to do with their lack of planning, their rush to act without checking things thoroughly. They'd hand me a job to do and say, "Go do it" without even looking the plan over to see if there were any flaws in it. And if someone got hurt or killed because they were careless, they didn't care.

The Avala Tavern job was typical of the carelessness I'm talking about. The tavern was located on Eglinton Avenue West in Toronto. Remo just handed me a key to the back door and told me to use garbage bags filled with gasoline to start the fire. I'd never been in the place before, never had a chance to check it out and see where things were. So when I got there on the night of July 6 and let myself in with the key, it was like groping around in a dark, unfamiliar closet.

I was carrying a jerry-can filled with a mixture of kerosene and oil, and wherever I went in the damned place, I kept banging into things. I finally found my way to the basement, where Remo wanted me to start the fire, but I couldn't find a light switch. There was none. I tried to find a door to the upstairs, but I couldn't find the damned thing. I left the can on the floor and was lighting matches, trying to see where I was going. Like a dope, I hadn't brought a flashlight with me because I thought there would be light switches I could use when I got into the basement. No matter where I looked, I couldn't find that upstairs door. This arson assignment was a disaster from the beginning because it hadn't been properly planned. I didn't have a layout and hadn't even had a look at what I was supposed to torch.

I finally found a couch downstairs, so I took the jerry-can and poured the contents all over the couch. Now Remo wanted me to shut the back door to the basement behind me and lock it. But because I couldn't find the upstairs door so the fire could spread to the upper floor of the tavern, shutting the back door cut off all the air. After I lit it, this fire had nowhere to go but out.

At 4:38 A.M. the fire department was called to the scene by a police constable who had spotted the fire. The damage was limited to the couch, and the fire had virtually gone out by the time the firemen arrived.

The Commissos paid me only about $100 because the place hadn't burned down. Even if I'd burned the place to the ground, I would have gotten only a few hundred bucks. Later on someone hired a young Italian kid to go back to the tavern and torch it. The kid burned himself when he got caught in the fire he set. He was convicted, but he needed a lot of medical treatment first.

A month later the Commissos had another arson scheme that was almost as bad. This time the place was a restaurant and banquet hall in Niagara Falls, a place called Vaccaro's Italian Gardens, which Cosimo said was owned by a friend. This time I went to the restaurant with Cosimo. He drove while his driver, Vince, sat in the back seat. It gave me an uneasy feeling, like it was a set-up, but I shrugged it off as my imagination. It was. I went with Cosimo because I wanted to see what I was supposed to handle so I could plan accordingly. I wasn't going to get caught again groping in a dark basement without a light switch.

When we got to the restaurant, we all took a tour of it, outside and inside. I went up to the roof and looked around, noticing a giant Ferris wheel nearby, and checked other buildings in the area. When I was through, we all sat down to a dinner with wine that the owner had prepared. While we ate, we talked first in general terms, then more specifically, about the arson. Even then I felt uncomfortable because stragglers and wise guys were coming in and wandering around while we talked.

What bothered me most was the way the man Cosimo said was the owner wanted it done. He wanted me to bomb the building next door in such a way that his place would catch fire by mistake.

"That's too damned dangerous, Cosimo," I complained. "It'll take too damned much dynamite to do what he wants. If I put dynamite between the buildings, I can't guarantee that it'll work properly. And somebody could get hurt."

"Don't worry," Cosimo said. "It's worth ten, fifteen thousand dollars if you do the job right."

"I'm telling you, Cosimo, it's too risky to do it the way he wants it," I said. "I can take this place down good if I put the bomb in the kitchen — and there's less chance of somebody getting hurt."

Then the owner wasn't sure he could pay the price. He wanted time to check his insurance policy and told me to come back again at a later time. A couple of weeks went by, and I didn't hear from Cosimo about the Italian restaurant. Finally I asked him about it.

"Forget it, Cec," he said. "It's all been taken care of."

I learned later that the restaurant had burned to the ground. I never did find out how it was done, and I didn't care.

Sometimes I think carelessness was the Commissos' middle name. They were forever making mistakes — mistakes that caused injury to innocent people or damage to the wrong location. They were reckless. They were like Brooklyn's gang that couldn't shoot straight. The only difference was, they just shot or beat up the wrong people. But as careless and reckless and stupid as they seemed to be even to me, they were still making millions, whether they did nickel and dime extortions or rattled the cages of a whole industry, like construction. For them there was nothing too big or too small to make money from.

Typical of the nickel and dime jobs they managed to screw up was one involving a business called Cook-O-Matic, a pots and pans distributor that operated on Lawrence Avenue about three miles from the Casa Commisso. The owner of the business was a man named Frank Mauro, whom Cosimo and Remo had tried a number of times to extort without much success. So they turned to me to handle Mauro, and I in turn went to a friend of mine, a kid I'll call Jimmy Tires.

Jimmy was a young hustler and tough who wanted to make some money on the side, so I told him I'd pay him a few bucks if he hassled Mauro for me while I handled some other work. Jimmy did what he was told. He went to Mauro's business location, flattened all the tires on the guy's car, and then poured paint over it. Then he made some threatening calls to Mauro. It wasn't enough.

Cosimo reached out for me again and complained that Mauro still wasn't paying. Finally, one night in December, Cosimo and I drove by Mauro's business. Two men were standing in front of the office loading boxes into a parked car.

"That's him!" Cosimo shouted. "That's the fuck that refuses to pay."

"Which one?" I asked.

He pointed to one guy holding a box. "That's him," he said. "I want you to break his arms like this." He angrily snapped a toothpick between his fingers.

"Screw it," I said. "I'll do it right now." With that I parked the car around the corner, got out, and walked toward the man Cosimo had identified as Mauro. My head was down so neither man could make out my face. As I reached him, I caught him cold turkey on the chin. He was bleeding as he fell back and hit his head against the wall. I took off in a dead run around the corner, jumped in the car, and drove off.

It wasn't until years later that I found out I'd hit the wrong guy. The guy I'd banged around was the warehouse manager of Cook-O-Matic, Peter Antonucci. I'd hit the guy Cosimo had pointed out to me, but he'd pointed out the wrong one. Cosimo couldn't even get straight the identity of the guy he wanted done in.

In its June 21, 1982, issue, *Maclean's* magazine described Carmelo Gallo as a key figure in what it called "the Italian Connection," a multi-million-dollar, international opium-, heroin-, and cocaine-smuggling scheme that stretched from Italy and the Middle East to Southeast Asia and Vancouver. It also described him as a thirty-five-year-old "cheerful grocer" who had single-handedly extended his narcotics trial by four months when he escaped from a Vancouver hospital bathroom in 1981 while the trial was still going on. He was sentenced to life imprisonment for conspiracy to traffic in heroin and another twenty years for conspiring to deal in cocaine. The cops didn't see him again until January 1983, when he gave himself up to appeal his conviction.

I knew Gallo by a different standard and a different name.

When I met him in March 1979 with Cosimo at the Casa Commisso, he was introduced to me as Carmen Gallo, their "family" man in Vancouver. He was not only their main West Coast connection for heroin; he had also been, since 1976, their primary source for counterfeit money. It was the same counterfeit American money that caused so much trouble for the Calabrians and my biker friends. Gallo was nicer than most of the Calabrians I met at the banquet hall or in meetings with Cosimo. He was a little guy, sort of quiet, always smiling, with a sense of humour and the kind of laugh that made others laugh too. He was only about thirty-two years old with wavy brown hair and brown eyes. That was one thing about the Commissos' Mafia family. They were almost all of them young. There weren't any old-timers, any of what they call the "Mustache Pete" types.

When Cosimo introduced me to Gallo, he told me that after Gallo left Toronto and returned to Vancouver, he would be calling to arrange to have me join him on the West Coast.

"Carmen, he's gonna phone us," he said. "He's gonna give us information for a big robbery that you gonna handle."

Cosimo went on to describe the robbery they had in mind. It involved a courier who left an underground location in downtown Vancouver carrying a bag full of money — $200,000 to $500,000.

"They been doin' this for years," he explained. "They got no security — no guards, no cops, no gun, nothin'. This courier, he just takes the bag of money, he brings it out to the docks, and he pays the fishermen. They do it for one week steady, every day, and that's it. We get only one shot at the jackpot."

"Okay," I said, "I'm ready to leave anytime. Just get ahold of me the usual way."

A week or so later I got the call and flew out to Vancouver, where I met Gallo again, this time at an Italian restaurant on Hastings Street. He took me to a twelve-dollar-a-night hotel in the Jewish section of town and got me a room there.

"I'll be back in the morning to take you down to the place we want to hit," he said. "I'll have a driver to get you there. You'll have a gun, handcuffs — everything you need for the job."

I should have known right then to case the courier and the location on my own. The Commissos hadn't given me details on the location, what route the courier followed, the time he left and arrived—nothing. Past experience should have told me that when it comes to getting information screwed up, the Calabrian Mafia has no peers.

The next morning Gallo showed up at the hotel. There was no driver with him, no gun or handcuffs, and he wasn't smiling as he usually was.

"We missed it—we missed the last payroll yesterday," he said dejectedly. "I tried to call Remo, but it was ridiculous. He wouldn't listen—you can't talk to him."

With the right information and the right time, it could have been a simple job. I would have just flattened the tire on the courier's car, and when he changed the tire, knocked him out, thrown him in the trunk, and left with the bag of money. I'd have been back in Toronto by the time he got out of the trunk to report the heist.

I was supposed to get one-third of whatever was in that bag. Gallo was to get a third, and the Commissos would have gotten a third. But the truth is, I'd planned to take half to make up for all the money they still owed me. It was just another false hope, a false start on another plot that failed because the Commissos didn't do their homework.

Probably the worst arson plan of all was the one carried out at the Dominion Hotel in Acton, Ontario. I was supposed to blow it up, but like the Vaccaro's Italian Gardens job, I insisted on certain preconditions, so in the end I didn't handle it.

I was upset by the plan from the beginning because Cosimo had brought the client, the owner of the hotel, to the Casa Commisso to meet me. It was unusual, and it made me nervous. I didn't like meeting the people who were hiring me through him to do jobs, even though Cosimo always introduced me to them as "George." It gave him a two-on-one edge if any arrests should result from the crimes. The worst part of it was, I always had the feeling that I was being set up or used. I never knew if these so-called clients were who Cosimo said they were or some Calabrians getting ready to do me in.

As "George" I met Cosimo Mercuri in early August, just before going to Niagara Falls. Cosimo identified him as Cosimo Val-Currie, not Mercuri. They talked some in Italian first, which I didn't understand, then the hotel owner said he wanted me to burn his hotel down.

"I'll come up and look at it and tell you the best way to do the job," I said. "Maybe it can be bombed, maybe burning is best." Then I added a word of caution. "There's one thing I want to be sure of. I want to be sure there are no people inside, and I want ten thousand dollars up front before I do any planning on this job."

Mercuri admitted there were people living in the hotel, but he didn't seem concerned about it.

"Then they have to be taken out somehow," I said. "You got to make some arrangement so there's no one inside when it goes up — maybe a phone call saying there's a bomb in the building to get them the hell out of there."

"I don't know," Mercuri said. "I do not have the money right now. I will get back to you. Give me a week to get the money."

I never heard from him again, but on August 19, 1979, the Dominion Hotel burned to the ground. A fifty-nine-year-old hotel guest named Howard Gibbons was trapped in the fire and died. Mercuri and two others, Michael McCrystal, a hotel employee, and Leonard Cripps, were arrested. Cripps was acquitted, but Mercuri and McCrystal were convicted after I testified that Mercuri had approached me with Cosimo to have me burn down his hotel. Mercuri was sentenced to life imprisonment, while McCrystal got two years.

The Vaccaro's Italian Gardens and Dominion Hotel jobs and a dozen other plots that I never got paid to do — they were all part of an increasing mistrust that was developing between me and the Commissos. I had been screwed out of more than $30,000 in promised fees in 1979 alone. Up to then I had pretty much trusted the Commissos. I knew they had been chiselling me out of money, but that wasn't all that unusual in the underworld. Everybody chisels. Everybody's hustling. That's the way of the street. Even so, there was always a nagging question at the back of my mind — why had they chosen me as their chief enforcer? I wasn't Calabrian. I wasn't a sworn member of their Honoured Society. I played by *my* rules, not theirs.

I had always figured that the Commissos had gone outside their group because there was no one within it who was straight enough, who had the capabilities and experience I had, to handle their jobs. Yet I knew that there was a possibility, a likelihood, that they would eventually kill me because I knew too much about their operations and had handled too many of their jobs.

While that nagging feeling in the back of my head bothered me, it didn't concern me enough to make me fear for my life. In truth, I didn't really worry that much about living or dying. The day I started working for the Commissos, I was divorced by my wife. It was my own fault for fooling around with other women, but because of it I had lost her and my daughter, and I really didn't have a handle on where my life was going at the time.

I remember asking Cosimo when I started working for him in 1976 about my predecessor.

"I know you had to have somebody working for you, doing what I'm going to be doing," I said. "What happened to him?"

"Oh, he went back to Italy," Cosimo said. "He didn't wanna stay in Canada."

I didn't really believe him then, and in 1979 I still didn't believe him. I figured the guy had been killed and that sooner or later that was what was in store for me. The plan to kill Piromalli was what really made me start thinking about it. I think what made it jell more for me mentally was seeing one deal after another go down the tubes as well as fewer and fewer jobs being offered. But the uneasiness became worse when I saw how Cosimo dealt with other people who worked for him—like Anthony Carnevale.

Carnevale was a drug dealer, a street punk, a guy who robbed card games and pool halls with other street hoods, and he did it for the Commissos. The Commissos would set up the games and promise to provide protection for them, and then they would turn Carnevale and his thugs loose to hold up the games. They would take $3,000 to $20,000 or more from people who were so-called friends of the Commissos. Carnevale and his men would take the piece allotted to them and give the rest to the Commissos, who planned the jobs for them. The Commissos made hundreds of thousands of dollars from holdups like that, many of them never reported to police, all of them handled by their stick-up men.

On January 1, 1980, Carnevale was killed by a shotgun blast through the window of his parents' home. His girlfriend, who was with him, was badly wounded, but she survived. I heard that Cosimo had been tipped that Carnevale was a police informer, yet he'd done nothing to hurt the Commissos or anyone involved in the dozens of robberies they were involved in. It took a couple of years before the link between the Carnevale murder and Cosimo was firmly established in my mind, although I had

had information that he had ordered Carnevale wasted. The link that confirmed it for me was the arrest of another street stick-up man whom I knew Cosimo controlled, a guy named Joseph John Imperiale of Vancouver. Imperiale had shot a Toronto man during a card-game holdup. With him on that robbery was Carnevale.

CHAPTER
15

LET'S MAKE A DEAL

I liked Cpl. Mark Murphy from the first moment I met him. He was tall and gangling, and there was something that reminded me of Jimmy Stewart in the way he walked and talked. Beneath his cap was a shock of dark brown hair and a mischievous Irish face. His eyes sort of sparkled with excitement when he talked, and when he had something to say, I knew I was listening to the voice of an honest man. There was nothing devious about him. He was what he said he was—a tough, dedicated Royal Canadian Mounted Police officer who wanted to fight organized crime in Canada more than he wanted to eat — almost more than he wanted to be with his wife and children, to whom he was really devoted.

He had been an important investigator in "Operation Oblong," a big RCMP intelligence-gathering mission aimed at the crime organization of Paul Volpe. He was familiar with and had worked on Nate Klegerman, Volpe's top lieutenant in the loan-shark rackets, and he knew Chuck Yanover and what he was up to almost as well as I did.

Murphy and the investigators he worked with had spent thousands of hours looking at Volpe's rackets — loan-sharking, diamond smuggling, casino investments, arson, you name it. Their investigation had led them to Las Vegas, to New Jersey and Atlantic City, and finally to convictions for extortion of some of Volpe's flunkies — Yanover, Murray Feldberg, and Jimmy Bass. The fact that he knew all this and more about organized crime made my meeting with Murphy all the more important. It was a freak, a stroke of luck that changed my life and is probably the reason I am still alive today.

By November 1980 I knew it was only a matter of time before I would become one of the Commissos' victims. The jobs they were assigning me were fewer and farther between, and each seemed to be more reckless than the other. It was almost as if they were handing me assignments that they hoped would get me killed or caught by the police.

My suspicions were first raised when they wanted me to go to Italy to murder Piromalli, the Calabrian Mafia boss. The Commissos swore they had a plan for my escape, but in the back of my mind I knew they didn't. I knew I was going to be wasted by some grubby little roadside in Italy and buried in some field where I'd never be found, and I would only be listed as a missing person.

In May 1980 Cosimo insisted that I bomb the Napoleon Restaurant, a stupid act of pure vengeance that nearly resulted in the deaths of three women, simply because Cosimo's wife had been insulted. There was nothing professional about that. Just bomb them, and if someone gets killed, so what? They shouldn't insult my wife. Only crazy people do things like that for those kinds of reasons, and that bothered me. Only crazy people wipe out entire families, including a baby in a crib, because they think the kid will grow up and kill them. And then in October there was what I considered his reckless order to bomb Maury Kalen's apartment despite heavy security. If I'd carried out that plan the way he wanted me to, I'd have been killed by one of the security guards the moment the bomb went off.

There were also a lot of little things, things I couldn't put a handle on, that made me uncertain and insecure. I would enter a room at the Casa Commisso, and the talk would stop. Cosimo, Remo, and I would be talking about something in English, and when a friend of theirs entered the room, someone who spoke and understood English, the language would suddenly turn to Italian. Remo was using cousins and relatives to contact me at the health club for meetings or to deliver messages and money to me. I had the feeling he and Cosimo didn't trust me, and yet I'd never, up to then, talked to a cop or done anything that was suspicious.

I was also being cheated out of money I had coming to me, and it was causing friction and arguments. I knew it wasn't healthy for me to protest so loudly about the money they owed me or refuse to handle the extortions, beatings, and arsons they assigned me to. There was no room for a rebel in the Commissos' Calabrian organization. Rebels might give younger, impressionable members ideas about discipline and leadership and whether Cosimo should be a boss. But then I wasn't a member of the family.

Along with all these insecurities, I was also facing the likelihood of a long jail sentence for an old break and entry that also involved an assault and extortion. The Commissos had always seemed suspicious about the delays my lawyers got in the case. There was something about their questions that made me think they thought I was whispering in some cop's ear. There was also no better place for the Commissos to have me wasted than in jail. A prisoner with a shiv, a prison fight — suddenly I'm history, and they've got no one to worry about.

I had to find a way out, protect myself, cut a deal, and work something out with someone in law enforcement. If I could trade important information for some help in getting my sentence reduced or even dropped to probation, I'd have breathing space and maybe a chance to survive.

My first attempt had been with Terry Hall of the Ontario Provincial Police. I had told him back in 1978 that his life was in danger, that the Vagabonds had a contract to kill him. He didn't even say thanks, let alone talk about what he could do for me on the charges I was facing, charges in which he and Ron Tavenor of the Metro Toronto Police biker squad were the key figures. So there was little chance I would get anywhere with them. They'd take whatever I gave them, but they wouldn't help me make a deal. If I couldn't talk to them, who could I talk to? I had to be careful — very, very careful.

On October 11 I picked up the telephone and dialed the number of the Royal Canadian Mounted Police National Crime Intelligence Section (NCIS).

"RCMP . . . can I help you," the voice at the other end said smartly.

"Who am I talking to?" I asked.

"Corporal Murphy . . . Corporal Mark Murphy," was the reply.

"Look, Corporal Murphy — we don't know each other, but I

can help you," I said. "I can solve a lot of cases for you, maybe even some murders."

"I'm listening," Murphy said, "but you haven't told me anything yet."

I told Murphy that I was a former member of the Satan's Choice and that I could give him information on robberies that had and were about to take place. I also told him that if he played it straight with me, I could give him information about organized crime, particularly the Commissos.

"All I want is someone to put in a good word for me when I'm sentenced on a B and E. For that you get a lot of heavy stuff." Then I added, "If you're interested, meet me in half an hour in the parking lot of the Casa Loma. Come alone — and no wires, or we don't talk."

"What's your name?" he asked.

"No names for now," I said. "Just be there."

Casa Loma is a tourist attraction in downtown Toronto. It was built in 1911 and took three years to complete. It's advertised in magazines as North America's "most famous castle," and I admit I can't remember ever seeing a castle anywhere else that has gold-plated bathroom fixtures and porcelain troughs for horses. But it wasn't those or its ninety-eight rooms that made me select it as a meeting place.

Casa Loma is situated in such a way that it's easy to spot people in the parking lot or approaching it from various vantage points. It's also not the kind of place that mafiosi or bikers come to very often. By getting there before Murphy, I could check to see if he was being followed or if there was anyone else there who looked like a cop or a hood.

I watched Murphy come up the driveway from Austin Terrace and pull into the Casa Loma parking lot. He parked where I had told him to, climbed out of his car, and stood up, towering over the roof of his unmarked police vehicle. I jotted down his licence plate number so I could check it out through a friend later. When I was sure there was no one following him, I walked up behind him.

"You Corporal Murphy?" I asked.

"That's right," he said. "What do I call you?"

"Call me Jack — Jack Ryan for now," I said. "When we know each other better, I'll give you my real name."

As we talked, my eyes tracked the entire parking lot and the overhead terraces of the castle for anyone, anything out of the ordinary. I saw no one. I patted him down to see if he was wearing anything. He wasn't.

"It's not that I don't trust you," I said, "but cops aren't my favourite people, and so far the ones I've dealt with haven't been too trustworthy."

"Let's get on with it," Murphy said, a little bit annoyed by all my precautions.

"One more thing before we talk," I said. "I've already supplied good information to Terry Hall of the OPP. He double-crossed me on a case in court. I don't want to deal with him any more. That understood?"

Murphy nodded.

"I'm not asking to have charges against me dropped," I said. "I just want you to assist me at my sentencing . . . put in a good word for me. I can't beat the B and E — I'm looking at two to four years. I just want to minimize the sentence."

Murphy understood, but he guaranteed nothing. "I can't promise you anything," he said. "If what you tell me is useful, I'll talk to my superiors, see what can be done for you. But you've got to produce."

"Good enough," I answered. With that I began to supply him with information on some drug deals, some armed robberies, and some burglaries. We talked about bikers, about the Mafia, and about guns.

"I'm in the business of guns," I said. "I sell them. I sell them to bikers, to Rounders, I sell them to the Commissos. Some are handguns, some are rifles, some are machine guns, and I know where they are. Sometimes when I sell these guns to them, people are shot." Then I added, "Maybe if things check out the way you want, I can give you some unsolved murders."

With that I left, telling Murphy to take some time checking out things I had told him. "I'll get back to you in a few days, and then we'll see where we go from there," I said. "Just don't double-cross me. I won't forget it. I may even have to come after you."

When we separated that October day, there were problems, some of which I was unaware of. I had by then given Murphy my true name, but when I called him, I used the name "Jack Ryan" so that no one else knew that it was Cecil Kirby who was talking to him. The veiled threat made an impression on Murphy. So too did the relationship that developed between us in the year that followed. He considered me dangerous, and he said so in a confidential RCMP report dated November 2, 1982, two years after our first meeting.

"Kirby, in my view, if examined by a psychoanalyst, would best be described as a schizophrenic. His dual personality ranges from a very kind person to a vicious, hot-tempered, violent individual who is quite capable of killing. He might also be described as an opportunist. I quickly perceived Kirby to be an experienced criminal who had tremendous potential as an informer."

Murphy was cautiously optimistic that I could be helpful to him, but Hall and Tavenor and some of their superiors didn't see it that way. Hall and Tavenor put me under surveillance and tailed me to another meeting with Murphy on November 26. They secretly watched me, and they recognized Murphy. Tavenor and his superiors at Metro called Murphy at the RCMP office and arranged a meeting. They demanded to know what I had been talking to Murphy about. Murphy told them but warned Tavenor not to say anything because I had made a veiled threat to him if he told Tavenor and Hall I was talking.

At that meeting with Murphy I had given him information I'd just received from a Rounder friend about a stash of 100 pounds of hash that was hidden in a store on Osborne Avenue.

"If you want," my friend had said, "we can hit this place—rip them off. All we have to do is pull our guns, tell them we're cops, tie them up, and leave with the load of hash."

I had told him it was a great idea, then I went to the meeting with Murphy to tell him about it. He said I would have to talk to a narcotics sergeant of the RCMP about it. I talked to the narcotics sergeant and told him I'd stall my friend as long as possible to give the RCMP time to confiscate the hash.

"If you hit it in the morning," I said, "be sure you have a cop outside and that he's visible."

"How the hell do you know it's there?" the sergeant asked, a little testily.

"Look, it's there—I guarantee it," I said. "If you don't go, I'm going to fuckin' go and take it with someone else for myself!"

On November 28 my friend and I drove down to Osborne Avenue to hold up the store and the drug dealers. As we approached the store, I pointed to a uniformed cop standing in front.

"We better get the hell out of here," I said. "There's a cop there." We drove off as my friend cursed our bad luck.

The RCMP wasn't so unlucky. They seized forty-two pounds of hash, 900 hits of LSD, some pornographic film, and a stolen stereo. The haul was worth over $150,000, and they arrested three people to boot. Murphy suggested I be paid $2,000 for supplying the information. It wasn't unusual to be paid for giving such good information. It was done all the time. His request was turned down. I got nothing, and the narco squad took all the credit.

Less than a week later Hall pulled me out of court during my trial.

"You're talking to the Horsemen," Hall said. "Get this straight, Kirby. You'll get no help on these charges unless you talk to us."

"I don't trust you, Hall," I said. "I'm not dealing with you."

It wasn't that I thought Hall or his superiors were dishonest. As far as I knew, they weren't. I just felt that Hall wouldn't help, particularly after I'd warned him about the plot to kill him and he'd done nothing to help me. Telling him how I felt didn't improve matters. For the next month or more Hall, Tavenor, and the brass they worked with did everything they could to stop Murphy from helping me.

I was caught in a tug-of-war between rival police forces. Local forces hate the RCMP — and maybe for good reason — and the RCMP don't trust local forces. They don't like sharing their information with the locals — they want the glory. The RCMP like to operate on a one-way street. They like to take information from other police forces, but they don't give information unless they have to because they either don't want to share the credit for a big arrest or don't trust the local force they're supposed to be working with. The result of all these rivalries and the mistrust between police forces is that organized crime profits by it. Members of different mobs learn to work together because it means saving their own skins and making big money. That's something police at national levels haven't learned to do yet, and until they do, the mobs will always slip through those cracks of rivalries and mistrust.

In this case, though, the big hang-up was with the locals. They didn't want the RCMP in the form of Murphy coming in and taking over a case or a possible informant, and they threw up every roadblock possible. It seemed to me it was more jealousy than anything else. As far as Murphy was concerned, I had proved to him I could be a valuable informer, but it wasn't enough for his bosses or for Sgt. Robert Silverton of the Metro Toronto Police, the supervisor of Hall and Tavenor. Then on January 20, 1981, I dropped information on another important case in Murphy's lap.

There had been a robbery of a jewellery store, the Dolly Jewellers on Weston Road in Toronto, on January 15. On the day of the robbery I was maybe half a block away from the store when I bumped into the two guys who'd held it up — Nicolino Pallotta and Richard Cucman. I knew them both from the street, and they told me they'd just held up Dolly's and had a bag full of jewellery.

"Sounds like you got a lot," I said, after listening to them brag about the job. "Look, if you have any trouble getting rid of the stuff, let me know. Maybe I can help out."

As I talked, my mind was spinning with possibilities. I could use what I knew about the robbery as a bargaining chip with Murphy and those he worked for, and maybe I could make myself some money by recovering the jewellery and selling it. Less than a week after I'd seen them, on the 20th, I called Murphy.

"You know that Dolly Jewellers robbery?" I asked.

"Yeah, what about it?" asked Murphy.

"If I can get some help at the court, if someone will speak to the Crown for me, I'll solve their robbery for them," I said. "I'll give them the names of the hold-up men on a silver platter."

"I'll see what I can do," he said.

Murphy tried. He talked to Silverton, who he said wouldn't even consider speaking to the Crown for me. He then talked to two inspectors he reported to and asked them to intercede with Silverton's boss, Staff Insp. Don Banks of Metro. According to Murphy they refused. When he told me that none of the coppers involved with him or with my case were willing to go to bat for me, I was furious — not at Murphy, but at the people he worked for who were so goddamned narrow-minded.

"Maybe if you give me the names, some proof, I can get them to agree," Murphy said.

"I'll have to think about it," I said.

A few days later Pallotta and Cucman came to me with the bag of jewellery and asked me to sell it. I took it, but I couldn't sell it because they were asking too much money for it. So I returned it to them. It was mostly junk jewellery anyway, about 100 diamond rings, gold chains, and knick-knacks. They had also grabbed about 100 used watches, which I told them to throw down the incinerator of the apartment we met at, or the police would track it back to them. I didn't know it then, but I found out later that they had tried to sell the jewellery to the Commissos.

Finally I decided to give Murphy the names of the hold-up men. The cops arrested them both, and they were later convicted, but that didn't impress Murphy's two superiors, particularly Insp. James McIlvenna, the boss of the Joint Forces Special Enforcement Unit (SEU) that was later to provide protection for me. Murphy said that McIlvenna had told him he wouldn't touch my case "with a hundred-foot pole."

"McIlvenna and Inspector [J.] Wylie said I should let you go to jail, Cecil," Murphy said. "I just want you to know I'm not giving up. So don't *you* give up."

I didn't and he didn't, but a year later Pallotta and Cucman pleaded guilty to the robbery in court. Their attorney, Earl Levy, in a grandstand play to the press outside the courtroom, charged that I had "ripped off" $140,000 worth of stolen jewellery from them. Cucman, who got three years because he was carrying the gun during the robbery, made the charge because the Commissos had told him to. They were trying to show I had lied as a witness. It didn't take McIlvenna long to jump on the bandwagon after the charge by Levy appeared in the press.

"Did you keep $140,000 worth of jewellery from those two?" he roared.

"If I had $100,000 in stolen jewellery, I damned sure wouldn't be here talking to you!" I snapped back. "I'd be in Florida, where I wouldn't have to listen to your shit."

Pallotta, who got two years as an accomplice in the robbery, wouldn't back up Cucman's story. He told the cops that I gave all the jewellery back, and he took a lie detector test to back up his claim.

McIlvenna never once said he was sorry for suspecting me, but then he had never wanted Murphy or the Crown or anyone to deal with me. He wanted me in jail, and if he had had his way, I'm certain I would never have become a witness. But because of

Murphy, he and some other short-sighted brass hats didn't get their way. The trouble is that in the end Murphy paid a terrible price for being as supportive as he was.

When I took the step of calling Murphy to provide him with information on robberies, burglaries, and later assaults and murders, I never considered the possibility of becoming a witness. It also never dawned on me that the Commissos would call me in to have me handle a murder in the United States. Just after I told Murphy that I knew who had held up the jewellery store in January, I was summoned to the Casa Commisso for a meeting with Cosimo.

"I gotta job for you, Cec," Cosimo said. "It's very important."

Cosimo seemed nervous and edgy as he spoke. He paced from one side of the empty banquet hall kitchen to the other and, for a while, seemed to be avoiding looking directly at me. Suddenly he stopped in front of the table where I was sitting and looked squarely into my face, his eyes searching mine as if what he saw would tell him something he didn't know.

"There's this woman in Connecticut," he said. "She's a big problem to some friends of ours. She's gotta be done, and I want you to handle the job."

"Why me, Cosimo?" I asked. "Why don't your friends have an American handle the job? Why don't they do the job?"

"Because it's a family matter. It's gotta be handled by an outsider who knows what he's doing and who can do the job right," he said. "That's you, and it's worth fifteen, maybe twenty thousand to you."

"I don't know . . ." I started to answer.

"We take care of everything," he said. "Your expenses, the gun, everything you need to know about the girl we give you."

"Let me think about it, Cosimo," I said. "I need the money for the lawyers on the case that's before the court, but I don't know if there's time. Let me think about it."

We didn't talk much more about it after that for a while, and for nearly two weeks I didn't say anything to Murphy. I was worried. I'd never killed a woman before, and I didn't like the idea. Suppose the whole deal was a plot to get rid of me? What better way? I go to the States, I blast this broad, and then I get wasted. There's no witness to the conspiracy, they get rid of the broad, and they unload me — an outsider who knows too much about their Honoured Society and its members.

Over and over something kept clicking in my head. "They're gonna waste you any day now. They're gonna bury you with this job. Do yourself and the broad some good. Call Murphy." Still I waited.

I guess I knew from the start that if I didn't handle the job, they'd get someone else to kill the woman. And in fact, they tried. While I stalled, Cosimo went to Ken Goobie and offered him $25,000 to kill the woman. Goobie then went to Gary Barnes to discuss whether or not to handle the job, and Barnes told me about it later. For some reason Cosimo never got Goobie to handle the job.

Finally, on February 17, I called Murphy to tell him about the contract. I didn't want to see the woman killed, but I didn't know how to prevent it without Murphy's help, so I called him.

"I've got a contract, Murf," I said, "and I don't know how to handle it. We've got to talk."

We met again in the Casa Loma parking lot. This time Sgt. Norman Ross was with him.

"Take the contract, Cec," Murphy said. "Find out who the woman is. I'll get office approval. We'll go to the States, see the woman, and remove her from danger. You can then return to Canada and tell them there was just too much heat and police around, so you couldn't handle the murder."

I didn't want to follow Murphy's orders, but I figured I had no choice.

"Okay, but don't hang me out to dry on this, Murf," I said. "I got to meet Cosimo and someone else at two P.M."

Murphy told me to go ahead with the meeting, and he would go to his office to get expense money to pay for the trip to the States to save the woman.

"How about wearing a tape machine to that meeting?" Murphy asked.

I was taken aback at first, and then I refused. "Look, Murf, it's too dangerous right now," I explained. "They got a habit of touching you, putting their arms around you, and here I'll be meeting with some strange guy. He may want to check me out, pat me down. It's too risky."

"Where are you meeting?" he asked.

"On Dixon Road, near Faces discotheque, at Howard Johnson's," I answered. "One other thing, Murf. I'm broke. I haven't enough change to buy a drink right now."

Murphy had repeatedly asked his superiors for expense money for me. Each time they refused, although I had by this time given them information that had helped them solve dozens of burglaries and robberies, and I had supplied them with inside information on a number of murders.

"Here, Cec," he said, reaching into his pocket, "here's ten bucks. It's all I can swing right now."

So I left with Murphy's personal ten dollars to finance what was probably one of the most significant meetings I ever had. I felt like a complete jerk. Here I was, about to deal with a mafioso on a $20,000 murder contract, and all I had in my pocket was a lousy ten bucks — enough to buy maybe one round of drinks. It was crazy. Murphy was crazy, and so was I. Only crazy people try to beat the Mafia this way. What kind of coppers was I dealing with anyway?

At 2:00 P.M. I met Cosimo at Howard Johnson's. With him was Antonio Rocco Romeo. We sat down at an isolated table, and Cosimo began talking in low monotones.

"Cec, this here's Antonio Romeo," he said. "He's the man who's gonna put you together with a friend named Vince in the States. It's Vince who wants this woman done. Vince will take care of everything. He'll show you the woman, he'll get what you need to do the job."

While I was having no problems negotiating with Cosimo about final instructions and expense money to fly to LaGuardia in New York, Murphy was running into one roadblock after another. He asked for backup to accompany us to the States. He told the brass that he had no way of knowing how I would act. He said he didn't know how reliable I would be and pointed out that I was an ex-biker with a reputation for violence. His request for support people to go with us was turned down.

But Murphy's troubles were only just beginning. Nobody told him it was illegal or against RCMP regulations, so he decided to take his service revolver along for self-protection. He declared the gun at U.S. customs. He didn't know it then, but by doing that he sealed his fate. Those who opposed him used this as one of the charges they later brought against him for what they called "conduct unbecoming an officer of the RCMP." When he tried to explain that he took the gun because he felt the need for protection since he had no backup, his excuse was brushed aside.

He didn't realize it then, but powerful forces in the RCMP were at work to get him for defying past suggestions that he let me rot in jail rather than put in a good word for me. If I had known that then, I would have told them all to go to hell.

On February 19 Cosimo and I met again. He advanced me $300 and said that when I got to New York, I was to get transportation to Stamford, Connecticut. There I was to meet Romeo and the man who had ordered the hit contract, Vince, at the Marriott Hotel the next evening at 9 P.M.

"When you meet Vince there," he said, "you get the gun, expense money, and five thousand dollars advance. You get the other ten thousand when you finish the job."

I just nodded and left to meet Murphy and buy my airline tickets. The next day we left. The tickets cost me $260, and Murphy had to give me $50 more out of his pocket so I'd have some money for expenses. And I knew that when I returned, unless something happened, I would be going to jail. I was beginning to wonder whether I had been stupid in trying to make a deal with the RCMP and save this woman's life.

CHAPTER
16

THE CONNECTICUT CAPER

I felt the American Airlines jet engines roar to life as we hurtled down the runway of Toronto International Airport. I looked across the aisle and to the rear. From the corner of my eye I could see Murphy looking past me as if I didn't exist. Not the slightest sign of recognition passed between us as the jet roared skyward toward LaGuardia Airport in New York.

My hands felt clammy and cold as I leaned back and watched the flight attendant pass out coffee and drinks. I ordered juice, and as I looked out the window at the clouds, I wondered how in the hell I had been talked into taking this trip.

Nothing had been resolved about my sentence before we left. I was still looking at from two to four years, and no one but Murphy was in favour of suggesting to the Crown or a judge that I be given a break for helping the police. Yet here I was, without the promise of anything, flying to New York with an RCMP officer, preparing to meet with Calabrian Mafia hoods who wanted me to kill a woman I'd never seen before in my life.

I had boarded the plane using my true name, but once I hit New York, I would be operating under a fictitious name with phony identification in a strange country among people I didn't know. I thought to myself, "Cecil Kirby, you've got to be crazy doing this." Even as I wondered if I'd lost my marbles, the warn-ing words of Murphy kept echoing over and over again in my head.

"You know too much, Cecil," he said. "Sooner or later the Commissos have got to dispose of you. They can't let you live."

"You're just working on my head!" I remember snapping as we talked about what he expected me to do after I had taken the contract from Cosimo to kill the woman.

"Be realistic," Murphy said. "First, they owe you forty thou-sand dollars by your own estimate. Why should they pay that much if they don't have to? Second, you've become a liability to them. You're a non-Italian working for the Honoured Society. You're not one of them. You don't live by their codes. You could put them in jail for a long, long time. So you're a liability." Then Murphy struck a chord that made even more sense to me.

"Remember Ian Rosenberg?" he asked. "He became a liability to the Volpe crime group. So what did they do? They bailed him out of jail and killed him and his girlfriend. If you don't work with us, that's what could happen to you."

"You mean you think they might be setting me up for a hit on this Connecticut caper, don't you?"

"It's a possibility. It's something to think about," he said. "What better way to get rid of you? They have you enter the United States and take an assumed name. They get you to a small place like Stamford, and after you do in the woman, or even if you don't do her, they kill you. Who would really be concerned about an ex–Satan's Choice biker if, in fact, they ever found your body?"

The dangers that we'd talked about were still ringing in my ears as the plane dipped down toward New York and the "Fasten Seat Belts" sign flashed on.

When we touched down, I quickly passed through customs and caught a cab for the Holiday Inn near the airport. Once there, I took out the telephone number of a detective at the New York City Police Criminal Intelligence Bureau and called, leaving him my phone number and room number as Murphy had instructed me to. The name I used was Jack Ryan, the same name that I used to check into the hotel.

It couldn't have been more than an hour before Murphy was knocking on my door. With him were two FBI agents. Within minutes we were in a Bureau car and on our way to Connecticut. When we arrived in Darien, Connecticut, I was introduced to several other agents, including John Schiman, Donnie Brutnell, and David Cotton, all from Connecticut. I was taken to a room at the Holiday Inn in Darien, where I briefed the agents on what I was supposed to do there. I told them I was supposed to meet Romeo, who was coming in from Toronto, at the Marriott Hotel in Stamford at 9 P.M. He was supposed to be with someone named Vince who would provide me with the money, keys to the apartment of the victim, photographs, and a gun to kill her.

Just before 8:30 P.M. I took a cab from Darien to Stamford. I got out at the corner near the hotel and was met by Schiman and Murphy. With barely a word passing between us, I walked to the hotel entrance, entered the lobby, and sat down in a chair to wait for Romeo to appear. I sat there for several hours. Nothing happened. Finally I got up, hailed a cab, and went back to the Holiday Inn.

I couldn't figure out what had happened, but I had to find out. There was a problem, though. How was I going to find out? I had no idea how to reach Romeo or his boss, Vince, and I hadn't brought my phone book, so I didn't have Cosimo's home number. I was stymied, but I told the agents to give Romeo until the next day.

"Something must have held him up, eh?" I said.

At that point a light went on in my head. There *was* a way to reach Cosimo. I called an ex-girlfriend and asked her to go to Cosimo's home.

"Have him call me at this number," I said. "Have him call me as soon as possible."

Cosimo didn't call, but he gave Linda a message to relay to me when I called her back early the next morning.

"He said to tell you that the guy you were supposed to meet with was delayed by weather," she said. "He said he'll be there today, and he'll meet you at the same place and at the same time."

As soon as she got off the phone, I called Murphy, who was in the same hotel. But I didn't realize that he was in a room next to mine.

"He got held up in Toronto by fog," I said to Murphy. "He's coming into LaGuardia today. I'm supposed to meet him tonight — same time, same place."

While I stewed in my hotel room, waiting for something to happen, Murphy was busy with the agents and New York City detectives at LaGuardia Airport, looking for Romeo. When they spotted him, he was moving from phone booth to phone booth, making calls.

When I saw Murphy later, he was upset. He said the driver had almost blown the surveillance of Romeo by pulling the Bureau's car to within fifty feet of Romeo as he stood by the curb, waiting to get a taxi to Stamford. Murphy said he had had to insist that the guy get out of the car and open the trunk as if he were unloading luggage to avoid having Romeo spot them.

Things sometimes have a way of getting worse before they get better, and Murphy said that was what happened as they tried to tail Romeo. He said that a bad identification had been made on the taxi that Romeo drove away in, and the assisting surveillance cars had lost him as he'd left the airport. They'd finally spotted him on Route 95, ten miles out of New York, heading toward Stamford and had this time kept the tail tight with other surveillance cars from the Bureau and New York City police, playing leapfrog so Romeo and his cabbie wouldn't know they were being tailed.

It was early afternoon when my phone rang.

"This George?" the voice on the phone asked.

"Yeah. Who's this?"

"This is Vince. We meet the same time, same place, tonight."

"Okay. I'll be there."

After hanging up, I called Murphy again and told him that I'd gotten a call from a man who called himself Vince.

"I think it's the guy who gave Cosimo the contract," I said. "He must have gotten my phone number from him."

"I've got to get you out of that room — now," Murphy said. "I don't want them to be able to watch you, set up a counter-surveillance. Understand?"

Within minutes Murphy was at my door, and we left the area. At 9 P.M. I entered the lobby of the Marriott Hotel in Stamford for the second time. There were agents everywhere, but they blended into the scenery. They were impossible to spot.

Vincenzo (Vincent) Melia didn't look all that impressive to me as he stood there with Romeo in the hotel lobby. Romeo clearly treated him as though he were very important. Romeo was about twenty-four, and Melia was more than twice his age. Romeo treated him like the mob treated Don Corleone in *The Godfather* — with a great deal of respect.

"Please, Mr. Kirby," he said, "I like you to meet Vince Melia. He's the man you're supposed to meet."

I stood up and shook hands with Melia. He was medium in height, with dark brown, wavy hair, a thin, clean-shaven face, and piercing brown eyes. In Connecticut Melia was as important as Cosimo Commisso was in Toronto. He was the boss of a family, and he didn't take a back seat to many people. He was very close to Michele Racco, the old man who had been the senior boss for the Calabrian Honoured Society families in Canada and the United States until he died in January 1980.

Melia was an Italian citizen who had moved to Toronto from Siderno and then to Stamford, where he operated a construction business. No one, not the community, not his neighbours, not the FBI, knew what he really was. But in Canada his name had surfaced as early as 1972 in conversations of Honoured Society members recorded by police. In the lobby of the Marriott he was quiet, but careful. The lobby wasn't a good place to talk, so we went to a bar in the hotel, ordered some drinks, and sat down at a table.

"Look, before I do anything," I said, "I want five thousand dollars up front."

"Tomorrow. I'll have it for you tomorrow," he said.

"What about the gun?" I asked.

"You get that tomorrow too," he said.

"I'm going to need a picture so I know what she looks like," I said. "Who is this broad anyhow?"

"Her name is Helen," he said. "A relative, he lives with this woman. He's not to be harmed, remember that. I don't want him killed. He's family. The woman, she's blond — a good-looking hairdresser."

He was somewhat nervous as he spoke. His eyes shifted from table to table in the darkened bar, searching, looking for someone he might recognize. We couldn't have been there more than ten minutes when Melia leaned over the table to me and whispered, "That guy at the table over there — he looks like he's a cop."

"Nah," I said, glancing at the guy he had motioned to. "There's no cops in here."

Melia was nervous now. He was suspicious about everyone in the bar, and he wanted to leave.

"Let's go outside," he said. "I got someone I want you to meet."

We left the table and began to walk outside. I knew the FBI was watching. So was Murphy. But I didn't see any of them. Before I got outside, Romeo stopped me and took me aside as Melia continued on ahead.

"Look," he said, "I don't want these guys to tell you what to do. You do what you gotta do. You do your own thing, and we'll look after you." He spoke in clear English, with only a trace of the broken Italian. Later, when he had to appear in court, he and his attorney said he couldn't speak English.

Outside Romeo and I caught up with Melia, who walked me to the hotel parking lot and a Cadillac driven by another of their paisans.

"This is Jerry Russo," Melia said. "He's going to drive you to the house of the woman you are to take care of. He'll show you her house and her car. Then he'll take you to a hotel and a room we got for you. We also got a car for you."

"Don't want any of that," I said. "You keep the room and the car. I got my own equipment, and no one knows where I stay. I do things my way. Incidentally, I'm not too happy about taking a ride with your chauffeur."

"Don't worry, don't worry," he said. "He's all right. But you can tell him to forget he ever saw you. He'll know what you mean."

He looked around, reached into his pocket, and handed me some keys. "Here," he said, "here's the keys to her house and her car." He fumbled in his pocket for something else. "Here's three hundred dollars for expenses and my phone number," he said. "Before you kill her, call me so we can be sure the relative's not there. Okay?"

I nodded. "Okay. And the five thousand?"

"We meet here tomorrow, two o'clock," he said. "You get everything then."

So I climbed into Russo's Caddy. I had noticed it as I walked into the hotel before meeting with Romeo and Melia. At the time it had looked like there was a connection, and I felt a sense of satisfaction knowing that I had spotted it and made that connection. They — Melia, Romeo, and Russo — had all come early in that Caddy to check me out as I arrived and see if anyone was tailing me before they met with me. Obviously they'd spotted nothing, or the meeting and our conversation wouldn't have taken place.

As I drove off with Russo, Melia and Romeo climbed into Melia's yellow Ford and drove off in another direction. I noticed a Bureau tail car following them at a discreet distance. We drove to the woman's home at 98 McMullen Street in Stamford. As we drove slowly by, Russo pointed out which side of the house she lived in and which room she slept in. He pointed to her car, a Toyota. We continued past the house, a small bungalow, for about half a block. Then I asked him to stop. He pulled over to the sidewalk, and I got out.

"Stay here," I said sharply. "I'm gonna take a quick look around. I'll be right back."

While Russo watched me, as did some unseen eyes of the FBI, I walked back toward the house and jotted down the licence plate number of the car. As I turned to go back, one of those unseen eyes came roaring up the street past me. I waved — keep going, don't stay around. Luckily Russo didn't spot anything. The over-protective surveillance was understandable. The FBI was worried and keeping a tight watch. Overall they were super — concerned, professional, and tough.

The FBI had cautioned me about staying out of the house and yard before I met with Melia. None of us knew the address at the time, but they were afraid that if I went into the yard or house, I might be setting myself up for a hit. Murphy had told them there was a possibility that the Commissos might be setting *me* up as well as the woman.

"Stay away from that house," one of the agents said. "Don't go in that house, wherever it is — you could get blown away. This could be a set-up even with the cops. There could be a cop in there waiting to blow you away because they've been tipped off you'll be breaking into the house." The message was clear enough. The Melias could have friends with the local coppers, and the FBI didn't want to take any chances. In fact, they took no chances. Every step I took, every place I went, I was watched, and those I was with were photographed.

As Russo and I returned to the hotel, I took some black driving gloves from my pocket and pulled them carefully over my hands.

"Word to the wise," I said menacingly to Russo. "You better forget who I am, and you better forget what I look like." I watched his face twitch slightly around the jawbone in the subdued light from the dashboard. Then for emphasis I added, "I don't want to have to make another trip back down here."

I could see Russo's right arm and hand start to tremble slightly after I said that. Later on Murphy and others told me I'd put the fear of God into Russo that night. He was convinced that I would come back and kill him if he remembered anything.

When Russo dropped me off at the Marriott, I stood at the entrance for several minutes watching him go. I then hailed a taxi and, after a few side trips downtown to be sure Russo hadn't the balls to track me, I headed back to the Holiday Inn in Darien to meet with Murphy and the agents. I turned over Melia's phone number, the licence plate number of the woman's car, her keys, and her address. The money I kept. Nobody said I shouldn't. I was tired of living off the nickels and dimes that Murphy had to scrape up out of his pocket because the RCMP refused to provide support money on the grounds that I was only an informant with a case still pending in court. I briefed the FBI and Murphy on what had happened and what I had to do the next day. Then I went to bed.

It was 2 P.M. on Sunday when I got to the Marriott Hotel lobby. Melia was waiting.

"The girl will be back tonight," he said. "You'll have to kill her tomorrow, not today. Kill her tomorrow after ten A.M. Somebody is with her up to ten. Wait till he leaves, and kill her after that."

"What?" I said, registering surprise. "You don't want me to kill the guy she's with?"

"No, no, no, no! He's family!" Melia said excitedly. "Don't kill him."

"Why do you want her hit?" I asked.

"She's caused trouble, a lot of trouble, and the guy she's going with is messing up," he answered.

He said nothing more but motioned for me to follow him outside to the parking lot. We stood in the lot by Melia's yellow Ford waiting for Russo to show up with the $5,000 and the gun.

"You know, if you want to come back down here," Melia said, "I got other work for you to do — places to burn. I got lots of work here."

"Well, I'll have to think about that," I answered. "You'll have to talk to Cosimo about that."

"I know Remo many years, longer than Cosimo," he said. "I talk to them both."

"When do I get the other ten thousand?" I asked as we waited.

"What other ten thousand?" he said with a look of surprise. "You're supposed to get another five after you get this five."

"Hell, no!" I snapped. "Cosimo said the job was worth fifteen to twenty thousand. Now you're telling me ten!"

"It's ten thousand," he said, his face darkening a bit with anger. "If you make sure she disappears and isn't found, I give you a bonus — an extra thousand. That's it."

"Okay," I said. "I'll see what I can do, but the deal was for more."

Just as things started to get a little heated, Russo drove up in a silver Capri. He got into Melia's car. Out of the corner of my eye I could see agent John Schiman in a telephone booth maybe twenty-five to fifty feet away from me. There were agents hidden all over the place, snapping pictures of everything that was happening. Russo handed me $4,000, and Melia reached in his pocket and pulled out an additional $1,000. Russo then pulled a bag out from beneath his shirt that was tucked under his belt. The gun was in the bag. I took the gun out and examined it.

"This isn't a fuckin' thirty-eight, it's a lousy twenty-two!" I said angrily.

"Well, that's all we got," Melia answered.

I took the clip out to make sure it was loaded, and I checked to see if there was a bullet in the chamber as well as in the clip. There was. It was a .22-calibre, Sturm Ruger nine-shot automatic. I noticed a long, thin silencer at the end of the barrel. I tried to remove it, but I couldn't. It was handmade and would probably work, but it wasn't the kind of silencer I felt comfortable with. Silencers usually screw into the barrel; they're usually custom-made for the weapon. A bad silencer can screw up a weapon, cause all kinds of problems. I made Melia know that I wasn't happy with the kind of weapon they had supplied me with. I thought to myself, "Some Mafia bunch this is."

Along with the gun, they handed me a picture of two women. One was a blond. Melia pointed to her. "That's the one I want killed," he said. "Remember — if she disappears, there's a bonus."

"Consider it done," I said.

With that we shook hands and I walked off, watching them as they drove away in Melia's Ford. When they were out of sight, I grabbed a taxi for the Ramada Inn up the street, where I thought I was supposed to meet some agents and be picked up. I wasn't. I stood there with the gun and the money for almost half an hour. I felt exposed, naked, in a dangerous spot. A local cop might check me out and find the gun. Finally I hailed another taxi and returned to the Holiday Inn in Darien. I sat down in the lobby and waited. Sooner or later, I figured, the agents and Murphy would find me there. The best thing to do was wait.

It was a little after 3 P.M. when a couple of agents spotted me in the lobby and escorted me to a room on the second floor. Murphy was there; so was agent Schiman. I drew the gun from my belt and threw it on the bed. Schiman jumped up and grabbed it. I removed my jacket, dropped the $5,000, and threw it on the side of the bed. Nobody touched it as I sat on the bed next to it. As far as I was concerned, the money was mine, and nobody was contesting that. I didn't say a word. I just scooped up the money, put it in my pants pocket, and waited for them to debrief me.

Murphy was later reprimanded by his bosses for not seizing the money. He couldn't. I'd warned him that if the RCMP wasn't going to pay my bills, then the Commissos were. They owed me more than $30,000. Besides, I was helping save a woman's life, and Murphy's people weren't doing a damned thing to help me with my court problems.

After more than an hour of debriefing by the agents, I was asked to go with them to the woman's house. By now I knew she was a Greek hairdresser and the mother of a six-year-old girl. They wanted to set up a surveillance of the house the next morning and familiarize themselves with the neighbourhood. Beyond that, no one was really sure of what was going to be done the next day.

When Murphy and I returned to my room, he asked me to take out the money. "Let me record the serial numbers and take some sample bills," he said. I agreed, and we spent more than an hour recording the numbers and carefully placing bill samples from four different stacks of the money in a special evidence envelope that Murphy had with him. He had $150 in sample bills, some of which I suppose had Melia's and Russo's fingerprints on them.

It wasn't until the next day that I knew what the FBI was going to do with the woman. They were going to keep her under surveillance, and when she and her boyfriend separated, they were going to snatch her.

"Can I come along on the surveillance?" I asked.

"Sure, why not," Schiman said.

They put me in a van they had equipped with cameras, and I sat there with a couple of agents, waiting and watching the house while other agents were parked in the area in other cars.

I guess it was a little after 10 A.M. when Helen Nafpliotis opened the door of the house and walked to the car. I was looking at her through the telephoto lens of the camera, and I snapped the first picture of her. She started the car, went back into the house, and came back out. This time the agent was doing the picture taking. I watched from a van window.

A minute or two later a man about six feet tall and in his mid-forties came out and climbed into her car. He was Nick Melia, the brother of Vincent Melia. I sat in the van as agents in other cars followed the couple at a discreet distance.

I was sitting outside the Holiday Inn in a car with two agents when the agents returned with Helen Nafpliotis. They had waited until she dropped Nick Melia off in downtown Stamford. When the agents were convinced that Melia was not around, they flagged down the woman's car on the highway, flashed their identification, and told her it was urgent that she come with them to Darien. Meanwhile a Bureau agent took her car and hid it. For the next three hours the agents and Murphy questioned her while I sat in the car outside. I later read a statement that Murphy compiled of what she had to say.

Helen Nafpliotis was born in Greece on July 26, 1947, and she had lived in the United States for about ten years. For all but six months of that time she had been living on and off with Melia, and out of that relationship came their six-year-old daughter, Christina. She also had three other children by a husband with whom she'd split up in 1977. He'd gone back to Greece and taken her three kids with him without her knowing it. She said that Melia had gotten into trouble with police for shooting Antonio Ianniello, a Stamford hairdresser she had worked for for several years. She was working for him when Melia shot him.

For a while, Helen told Murphy and Bureau agents, she had worked in Melia's hairdresser shop, Continental Coiffures of High Ridge Road, Stamford. That lasted until Melia's wife found out, called her at work, and threatened her. There were other incidents after that. The tires of her car were slashed. After they were replaced, new tires blew out as she was driving, causing her to lose control and almost roll her car over just before Christmas 1980. A year earlier, on November 3, 1979, her car had almost rolled over because of slashed tires that blew. She said she finally couldn't take any more threats and flew off to Greece, where she stayed for five months. She said Melia's brother, Vincent, had told her it would be smart for her to leave.

She returned in 1979 and went to work for Ianniello until August, when he was shot. She said Ianniello's brother had told her one day not to go in to work, that Melia had shot Ianniello. Apparently, she said, Melia was jealous of Ianniello, who had never so much as dated her. She said she was even afraid to dance with Ianniello because of Melia's jealousy. She also said that Ianniello owed Melia money. She said she had tried, unsuccessfully, to break her relationship with Melia several times, but each time he found her and made her return. She said she supported herself by working at a $300-a-week job and renting two apartments in her house for $450 a month each. She had no other place to go.

"Where can I hide?" she asked the FBI. "Even if I go to God, Nick will find me."

She was really afraid of this Melia. He'd moved to Canada from Italy when he was nineteen and to Connecticut when he was in his twenties. She said she never saw him work. She knew he'd been accused of having stolen jewellery and of shooting Ianniello, but she didn't know anything about his "family" connections. They had been to Atlantic City the weekend before I arrived, and on the weekend I had been provided with the money to kill her, they had been in Astoria, Queens, in New York.

When the interview ended, Murphy, Schiman, and I had another meeting. The FBI were going to provide protection for

Helen, but they couldn't hide her forever. And if the Commisso mob and the Melias found out she was still alive, I'd be a dead man.

"You're going to have to become a witness," Murphy said. "It's the only way we can save her — and you."

I sat there for a while, thinking about it, looking for a way out. There wasn't one, and we had to return to Toronto. It was Monday, and as things stood, I was supposed to go to jail on Thursday. Without some sort of agreement, some deal with Murphy and the Crown prosecutors, I was a dead man.

"Look, Murf," I said, "I'll be your witness. I'll help you get the evidence you want on other cases, but I can't do it without protection. If I talk to you about everything I know, if I help you, I want immunity from prosecution for past crimes. The Crown's got to support my family and me, relocate us, and give us something to live on when it's all over, when I'm through testifying."

"I can't promise that, Cec," he said. "I can't promise anything. I'll do all I can to help, but that's all I can promise."

"You get me what I want, and I'll give you what you want," I said. "One thing more. I work with you, not somebody else."

Before we boarded our plane for Toronto at LaGuardia, Murphy took a big gamble. He called Crown attorney Al Cooper, told him the whole story, and held out the chance that they could wipe out the leadership of the Commisso crime family in Toronto.

"We could do a lot of damage to organized crime in Toronto, Al," I heard him say. "Without Kirby we have nothing. With him we can do a lot, but not if they make him go to jail on Thursday."

Unlike Murphy's superior officers, Cooper saw the dangers and the possibilities. He made no promises, but he agreed to meet with Murphy the next morning to see what could be arranged.

Even as they spoke, the FBI was busy in Stamford. They took Helen Nafpliotis back to her house, let her gather her jewellery and a few belongings, and then staged a kidnapping that witnesses reported to police. They secretly sent her back to Greece, but it wasn't the last I was to hear of Helen Nafpliotis. Although I never saw her again, she and the FBI almost got me killed.

CHAPTER
17

THE INFORMER

C pl. Mark Murphy's superiors at the RCMP were clearly not happy. By going to Crown prosecutor Al Cooper, Murphy had leapfrogged the chain of command and the people who wanted me in jail, not running around gathering evidence against organized crime. Instead of being praised for saving a woman's life and doing a hellava good job with me, Murphy was in deep trouble. His bosses were furious that I had been permitted to keep the $5,300 Melia had given me, even though they had always refused to provide for my living costs and those of my family. They were angry that I hadn't been forced to wear a body recorder. And they were critical of Murphy for going to Cooper.

Trouble or no, Murphy met with Cooper as promised. They then went to see two prosecutors familiar with my B and E case — Steve Leggit, chief Crown prosecutor in Toronto, and Frank Armstrong. Leggit and Armstrong were as inflexible as were Murphy's bosses and biker squad officers Hall and Tavenor. It looked hopeless.

Sometime after 6 P.M. on February 24, 1981, Cooper and Murphy were called to meet with the Deputy Attorney General of Ontario, Rod McLeod. At that meeting Murphy told McLeod that in addition to putting the Commissos behind bars for conspiracy to murder the Connecticut woman, the Crown could also clear up most of the bombings that had taken place in Toronto over the last seven years as well as extortions, arsons, and bombings in Guelph, Hamilton, and Montreal. All told, there were more than twenty-three major criminal acts that could be solved and more than a dozen people arrested.

McLeod wasn't as short-sighted as the others; he saw the potential. He assured both Murphy and Cooper that I wouldn't go to jail on Thursday and that I would be made available to meet the Commissos and gather further evidence. The next day McLeod ordered Leggit to hold my case over. A deal was in the works.

"You're going to have to wear a body mike," Murphy said as we talked about the promise McLeod had made. "You're going to have to wear a mike and get evidence to nail these guys."

I wasn't at all happy at the prospect. Becoming an informer for Murphy had been difficult, a gut-wrenching experience. It was against everything I had grown up to believe in. Up to that point I had justified it by not fingering friends and not testifying as a witness against anyone. I could even excuse the Connecticut deal. I had helped save a woman's life, and I had stiffed the Commissos and their mob for a change.

"There's no way around it, Cec, you're going to have to testify," Murphy said again.

I wanted to puke. It sucked, it really sucked. I was faced with doing what I had been willing to kill others for doing. I tried to find a way out.

"Christ, I don't know, Mark," I said. "It'll never work. The Commissos — their friends — they're always putting arms around me, touching me, poking at me. They're sure to find any tape I'm wearing."

"They won't. I guarantee it," Murphy said. "Besides, I'll be close by."

"I don't know," I stalled.

"There's no other way!" he said harshly. "Either you play the game, or you go to jail. And you know what will happen when they find out that the girl isn't dead, that the FBI grabbed her and you took their five thousand dollars."

"Sure. I'll be another unsolved homicide," I said. "I should never have come to you people. You've got me between a rock and a hard place." I paced up and down, shaking my head. I felt sick to my stomach. I was certain I was a dead man — I just wasn't in the box yet.

"What guarantees have I got?" I said.

"Only my word," Murphy said, "and these consent forms I want you to sign."

The consent forms were my ace in the hole, the protection for my backside. Under the consent agreement, I promised to wear a body mike and record conversations I had with the Commissos. Murphy had added a clause that held that the Crown and police could not use the tapes or any conversations on them without my consent, and if I consented, I would be protected against self-incrimination for any crimes discussed on the tapes or in testimony I gave later.

"Okay, Mark," I said. "But get that agreement drawn up and approved as fast as you can."

We both agreed that meetings with the Commissos should be arranged, as much as possible, away from the Casa Commisso. It was too difficult a place to surveil and record conversations in. The industrial nature of the area could cause interference in transmissions, and, if I needed help, it would be difficult for Murphy and whoever was with him to get to me once I was inside the banquet hall.

I called Cosimo to arrange a meeting. He wanted it to take place at the Casa Commisso, but I convinced him to meet me at the Howard Johnson's hotel. I was nervous as they taped the body pack on me, and I was cautious. I had put on extra clothing — a heavy sweater — to conceal the taping device and anything I thought might be bulging.

"Calm down," Murphy said. "He isn't going to spot anything. You'll do just fine."

I nodded, but I wasn't convinced. I was also worried about whether the body pack would break down. I felt clammy and cold as I parked my car and walked toward the hotel. Driplets of cold sweat trickled down from my armpits, and I checked behind my jacket, under my belt, to see if I could reach the gun that I had slipped in there. Although I had not yet signed an agreement, I wasn't supposed to carry a gun. But what the hell. I felt more secure with it.

At 1:15 P.M. Cosimo and I met outside the hotel. Parked nearby were Murphy and his immediate superior officer, Sgt. Norm Ross. They snapped pictures as Cosimo and I greeted each other. Almost immediately Cosimo noticed the extra clothing. "Why you got so many clothes on?" he asked.

"I'm cold as hell," I said. "I've been living up north, and I'm

just cold." I clapped my gloved hands together and stamped my
feet. A sort of involuntary shiver went through my body.

He didn't poke me or put his hand on me or his arm around
me as I had expected, and I felt a sense of relief. I wasn't sure
how I would have reacted if he had.

"How are you?" Cosimo asked.

"You told me fifteen thousand!" I snapped, catching him off
guard, letting him know I was unhappy with what had happened
in Connecticut. My purpose was to put him on the defensive,
make him talk about the murder conspiracy so Murphy and the
Crown would have evidence to prosecute with.

"Vince — he give you the money?" Cosimo asked.

"He paid me five. He didn't give me ten," I said.

"Five thousand?"

"Yeah."

"You do the job? When you did it — Tuesday?"

"Hell, no, Monday."

"Monday night?"

"I don't want to get into details, okay?" I said. "Vince said to
me, he said he'd pay me extra if she was a missing person. He's
something else, that fellow. That's why I want the fifteen thousand."

Cosimo was surprised and somewhat puzzled. He didn't understand what had happened. My mind was working like a computer now. Set up an alibi, I thought. Protect yourself in case
someone saw Murphy or an FBI agent with you. I was in high
gear now, and my nerves were steady. I was in a game of cat and
mouse, and I was enjoying it.

"I'll tell you why, okay?" I said. "I took another guy down
there. They didn't see him, okay? He didn't see them. I figured
maybe I'd want an extra guy with me in case, you know, I got
any static. We got the broad out okay. She's gone — they'll never
find her again. There's a lotta lakes around there. They got a
big fuckin', you know, strait there, or sound — Long Island
Sound . . ."

"There's a lotta things to be done over there," Cosimo said,
indicating he had other jobs in mind, that Melia wanted me to
handle other jobs for him. "Never mind this — you gonna get it.
I make sure he give it to you — the five, right away."

"I want it," I said. "I'm going to Vegas, leaving at noon tomorrow."

"I'll try, whatever I can get now for tomorrow, Cec," he said.

"Look, I told him, I said, 'You want her missing?' I said, 'I want an extra thousand.' Six thousand, okay?"

He nodded his head. "Okay. Six thousand."

The discussion then turned to my case in court, and I explained that everything had been postponed until April 10. Cosimo seemed to understand. He was appealing a conviction of his own. We agreed to meet again on March 10, at which time he said he'd pay me $5,000 more.

"We meet March ten," he said.

"All right, March tenth. Here, at twelve o'clock," I said. "I don't want to go near the banquet hall, okay?"

"I come — I come and see you at your house," he suggested.

"No, no, I'm never home," I said. "I tell you, I got this other broad, okay, up in Barrie. I don't want to be seen around too much — you know. When the court case is over with, okay, fine, but for now I'm keeping low. I don't want to go near the Casa any more."

"All right," Cosimo answered.

"I always worry about cops every time I go around there," I said, showing my concern. "I don't want the heat."

Cosimo didn't like the idea of returning to where we were standing. He didn't have control there. His friends and family weren't there.

"Stop by my house," he said. "Nobody else comes to my house. You understand what I mean."

"Sure, I know that," I said, "but you never know, you might have the cops watching. I don't need the heat."

"All right," he said with resignation.

"March tenth, here, at twelve o'clock," I said. "I want the fifteen — I want the six thousand."

"All right," he said again.

"And the rest later — a month later, okay?" I asked.

"Okay," he said with a shrug. "Have a nice time."

The recording session had gone well, but there was still no agreement with the Crown. Murphy had outlined what I wanted at a special meeting of police brass representing the RCMP, OPP, and Metropolitan Toronto Police. He also said, as I had told him to say, that I would not work with anyone but him while I was on the street, acting as their agent. I agreed to talk to others after an agreement was signed, but not before.

By now I was desperate for money. I owed more than $4,000 in legal fees, some $2,000 in credit card charges, another $2,000 to my father, and I had a bank loan, alimony, and other bills to take care of. March 10 loomed on the horizon, and Cosimo was scheduled to pay me $5,000. Murphy said I had to turn that money in for evidence.

"Look, Mark," I said, "all I've gotten from your outfit up to now are two hundred-dollar expense payments. That don't pay the bills. You tell them they'd better pony up the money so I can pay the bills."

We met again on March 10.

"You got the money?" I asked.

Murphy shook his head. "Inspector McIlvenna said he'd have the five thousand in my hands before the meeting, but I haven't gotten anything. Look, Cec — you can't keep the money Cosimo gives you. I'll have to seize it as evidence."

"The hell you say!" I shouted. I was fuming, and I let Murphy have both barrels. "You can tell the RCMP, McIlvenna, Sergeant John Simpson, and all the rest of them that they can go fuck themselves. The deal is off. I'll meet Cosimo later tonight and get the money when you're not around."

Murphy pleaded with me to be reasonable, but for me there was nothing reasonable about the jam I was in, the bills I was facing, and the way his bosses were dancing me around. I knew they didn't have enough to make a case without another recording and without me. Murphy got out of my car and walked back over to the car of Sergeant Ross. He told Ross what I had told him. Then he came back to my car and again tried to change my mind.

"Mark, I'm tired of getting fucked! I'm tired of their fuckin' promises that they never keep!" I said angrily. "The only way I go through with that meeting is for you to promise, right now, that you don't take that money."

Murphy threw up his hands. He really didn't have much choice, and it was almost time for me to meet with Cosimo. "All right, Cec," he said with a sigh, "you have my word. I won't seize the money."

The meeting went down as planned.

"You look sick, Cosimo," I said.

"Feel sick," he said.

I smiled, made light of his problem. "And me—all sunburned. I went to Florida instead."

Cosimo was mildly surprised.

"Yeah, I couldn't get to Vegas."

"By yourself you went?"

"Nah, with a friend of mine," I said. "We went down the Keys —the only place it was warm. It was just freezing everywhere else."

"It was freezin' there?" he said with surprise.

"Oh, it was cold near the top of Florida," I said, "so I went down the Keys, went fishing for a couple of days. I got sunburned out on the boat. I still don't feel well."

"I'm tired," Cosimo answered.

"You got the money?"

"Don't worry 'bout. I went and borrowed it for you."

"So how much is here?"

"Five."

I shook my head. "All right. But you know I told you Melia said he'd give me an extra thousand."

"Yeah, because you kill her, eh?" Cosimo asked. "The car— she's disappeared too? Her car?"

"Yeah, in a roundabout way," I said. "They'll never find it. She'll be a missing person sooner or later. That's it. It's better for everyone."

Cosimo was happy, and he promised to get the additional six thousand from Melia. I told him I had to pay my accomplice for helping me dump the woman and the car in Long Island Sound where it would never be found. Then he dropped the bombshell. He had a new contract for me, and he wanted it done before he went to jail on counterfeiting charges. He didn't identify the target then, and he didn't say how much it would be worth to me. All that he would tell me later.

"When am I gonna see you?" he asked. "How can I get in touch with you?"

"It's hard," I said. "I'm with this broad, and she didn't even get a phone where we're at—out in the country."

"Still things to be done," Cosimo said.

Meanwhile Murphy had to hold off the wolves. He went to Cooper, the prosecutor, and told him what had happened—that the RCMP hadn't come up with the money as promised and that he'd had to let me keep the money Cosimo paid me, because otherwise I would have shut down the investigation and taken the money without any photos or tape. Cooper took the problem to Howard Morton, the Crown attorney who had been assigned to handle the Commisso case. Morton wasn't that upset. "It doesn't really matter a row of beans if the money was seized or not," he said. "The fact it was paid by the Commissos to Kirby is what really matters."

By now my car, a Chevrolet, had been carefully bugged by Murphy's people. They had also rigged a transmitter inside a belt buckle and given it to me to wear as a backup in case the body pack failed. But it was sometimes difficult to get Cosimo into the car. Cosimo was by nature suspicious. He was suspicious of cars, clothing, telephone pagers, and strange buildings. He was constantly afraid of being bugged by the police. I always had to be creative, fast on my feet, with my thinking cap screwed on right at all times.

On one occasion Murphy complained about the poor recording of our conversations, which often took place outside the Faces discotheque and Howard Johnson's. These recordings were sometimes difficult to understand because of the roar of overhead planes and nearby trucks. One conversation Murphy had difficulty recording took place when Cosimo told me he needed a gun and asked me to get him one.

"You mean one like this?" I asked as I pulled out a .32 automatic from the small of my back.

"Yeah, something like that," he said, surprise registering on his face. "Why you carry the gun?"

"I got some problems," I explained, "so I carry a gun." Then I put it back.

From that point on Cosimo and his brothers knew I carried a gun. They knew I carried it either behind my back or in a pocket or behind my belt buckle in the front of my pants. Knowing that, I think, has something to do with the fact that Cosimo did not pat me down, check to see if I was carrying anything unusual on me. I think he was always a little afraid of me because I had the balls to carry the gun and show him I was carrying it when we met.

The gun gave me a sense of security, but I wouldn't have been so secure if I'd known what the RCMP learned when I turned in the gun after all the meetings with the Commissos had ended. I had borrowed that gun from two Rounders who were friends of the Commissos, but I had never had the chance to test it because I was always in the city working with Murphy and other investigators. When I finally turned it in, Murphy sent it to the RCMP laboratory to be checked, to see if it had been used before to commit a crime. What he found was that the gun had a faulty firing pin. If I had ever tried to use it to protect myself, I'd have been hung out to dry. A cap pistol would have been more effective.

Losing most of that conversation and the lack of clarity on some others concerned Murphy. He was also worried about my safety and about the evidence they collected on the recordings. To allay those fears, one day I showed up for a meeting with Murphy at the Skyline parking lot equipped in an unusual way. As he stood by the car, I took off my shoe and sock and pulled out an elastic bandage from my jogging suit pocket. I wrapped the bandage around my ankle and looked up at him with a smile on my face.

"Guaranteed I get Cosimo in the car today," I said with a chuckle. Murphy was smiling from ear to ear as I drove off to meet Cosimo.

Cosimo spotted me and walked over as I pulled into the Faces parking lot.

"Get in," I said to him.

"Cec, you know I no like to talk in the car," he said. "The cops — they could have bugged your car."

"No chance, Cosimo," I said. "The people I send over to your place to do the debugging check the car out all the time. I never take chances. Besides, I can't walk — I can't get out of the car."

"What's the matter?" he asked.

I opened the door and pointed to the bandaged ankle and foot.

"Your foot — what's the matter with it?" he asked.

"I went jogging this morning," I said, "and I sprained — maybe broke — my ankle when I fell."

"Ah, that's a shame," Cosimo said, climbing into the car. The conversation that followed was clearly recorded by Murphy and his team without any feedback.

There were instances when the bug, the transmitter that they'd hidden behind the dash, caused some problems. On the last day before the cops wrapped up the Commisso conspiracy investigation, I had to meet with Michele Commisso in the car. Michele wasn't as reluctant to get in the car as his brother was. He'd generally just jump in no problem and start talking. On this occasion, just minutes before he was due to meet with me, I turned on the radio. It started buzzing, giving off static noise right through the radio. The noise was interference given off by the transmitter, which had been hidden inside the radio. I had to make sure the radio stayed off as we talked. I just told him that the radio wasn't working right, and he never suspected a thing.

There was one time that Cosimo didn't even hesitate about getting into my car. I still get a chuckle out of that when I remember the circumstances. I was at Howard Johnson's, waiting for him, when he arrived in a taxi instead of his car. He paid the driver and walked over to my car with a slight limp and climbed in.

"Where's your car?" I asked him. "Why are you riding a taxi?"

"I was a passenger in a car driving down the street, and I was just in a car accident," he said as his hands flailed at the air in frustration. "I hurt the leg, banged my leg against the dash."

When our meeting ended and he had paid me some money, $1,000, I drove him to the Cambridge Hotel parking lot. As he got out of the car, I said to him, "Hey — limp down the street. The cops are out there. You'll have witnesses, and you can put in for an insurance claim."

He turned and looked at me with a smirk on his face. "Yeah, yeah, you're right, Cec. Good idea. The leg. It's swollen, and I got whiplash."

"Got another idea, Cosimo," I said. "Better than that. Put your fuckin' leg in front of the car, and I'll run over it. Then you'll really collect."

Cosimo looked back, shaking a fist at me. "Fuck off, Cec," he said, laughing. He slammed the door behind him, started to walk over to a car in the lot, then remembered and started limping again while the surveillance cameras snapped and recorded the whole event.

All these transmitters and body packs gave added security to Murphy and those who sometimes helped him as they monitored and recorded the conversations in a specially equipped van. The van was a three-quarter-ton, blue vehicle with a big square box in the back and dual wheels on either side. It had glass windows in the back with a one-way, mirror-like window. The coppers could look out, but nobody could look in and see anything while they were looking out, taking pictures.

The van was my security blanket — and then some. It was a rolling recording and movie studio. It was loaded with sensitive electronic recording equipment and cameras of all types with special telephoto lenses, and there were pictures all around of Cosimo and me together. There were other vehicles that could pick up the conversations and record them, but the van was usually the one Murphy used, particularly when he was alone. There were at least five occasions that he had to cover me alone, without any backup, because of problems in his office. I look back now at some of the things that happened, the shortages of equipment and personnel and the bickering that took place while I was out meeting these Calabrian mafiosi, and I marvel at the fact that I lived through it.

It was a little after noon on St. Patrick's Day 1981 when I drove up to Cosimo's house at 477 Ellerslie Avenue, North York. It was a nice home — a little on the conservative side, but comfortable. Cosimo was smart enough to know that if he lived too high off the hog, he'd attract attention. He tried, not too successfully, to keep a low profile with the police.

I knocked on the door. There was no answer. I knocked again. Still no answer. I began to wonder if Cosimo had forgotten our meeting. I started to walk up the street toward Remo's house, talking as I went so that Murphy could record and understand what I was doing without becoming too concerned.

"Just going up the street here to Remo's house for a second," I said as I walked. The recorder picked it up. Within a minute or two I ran into Remo.

"How you doing?" I asked.

"Going," he said, without elaborating.

"Where's Cosimo? He's supposed to be here at eleven-thirty."

"He's home."

"I knocked on the door. There's no answer."

"He's home for sure. I just called."

"Jesus, he must be deaf then. Must be sleeping."

I returned to Cosimo's house and banged on the door. Just then his wife drove up with the kids.

"Is Cosimo sleeping?" I asked. She shook her head. "He must be deaf."

"Deaf?"

"Deaf. I rang the doorbell and banged on the door about ten times."

She opened the door wide to let me in. I shouted inside. "You getting up, Cosimo?"

"Yeah, I'm ready," he answered.

As I started to walk inside, his wife cautioned me to take off my boots. Before I pulled them off, I turned to her and said, "I got my car running. If he's not going to be too long, I'll just leave it running."

Cosimo entered the room then, and I showed him I was a little agitated at the delay. "I was out there half an hour waiting for you," I said. He appeared surprised. Before he could say anything else, I put my boots back on and started out the door. "I'll wait for you outside. I got the car parked out there, and I don't want to get a ticket or anything, you know. Where we gonna go? Where do we have to go — north, south? Have I got enough gas?"

"South a little bit."

"South of what? I only got a half tank of gas. Is that enough?"

"Yeah."

I got into the car. While I waited, I talked into the transmitter, telling Murphy that we were going south on a particular road. I had to wait another twenty minutes before Cosimo finally climbed into the car. As we drove, we talked small talk about my upcoming sentencing, which I said was set for April 10 but would be postponed again. He asked if I'd seen Ken Goobie recently, and then the purpose of all the driving came into focus. The purpose was to show me where Peter (Pietro) Scarcella hung out. Peter Scarcella was the new contract, the target Cosimo wanted me to hit.

Scarcella was only thirty, but he had become one of Toronto crime boss Paul Volpe's most trusted associates. He chauffeured Volpe to meetings, he was frequently seen at Volpe's home, and he seemed to be one of the bright young stars in the Volpe crime organization. Scarcella walked both sides of the fence: he was close to Volpe, and he was close to the Commissos.

Now Cosimo wanted him hit, and he was laying out the floor plan of Scarcella's lifestyle — the places where he lived and hung out. Cosimo was directing me to an apartment that Scarcella used, and I let him give the directions while I played the role of tourist. He reeled off the names of this street and that in an area where I grew up, but I played dumb, repeating each street name so the surveillance teams could keep up.

"Turn right here," Cosimo said. "It's hard to get that guy."

"Hard to get him?"

"Over here, yes."

"Why is it hard to get him there?"

"He lives with his family there."

"What is it, a house or an apartment?"

"No, it's an apartment."

"You got his name and everything?" Up to this point he hadn't given me a name that I could record on the tape.

"Yeah, but first I wanna show you another two, three places where he usually goes."

Cosimo showed me Scarcella's father's place and a location where Scarcella went to play cards two nights a week.

"He goes to poker games," he said.

"Poker games — what, around here?"

"No, they move it every night. There is a restaurant he goes to almost every night."

"Around here?"

"No, no, at Dufferin and Castlefield — where Canadian Tire is. There's a restaurant on the corner — it's open twenty-four hours. He goes there every day."

He asked me how I was going to handle it and when I'd do it.

"I'll come back. I'll just keep watching this guy," I said. "There's no hurry for this, eh?"

"No, no," he answered quietly. "One other thing. I wanna give you, when it's another time — I give you more, you know — particular details."

"Oh, I'll just watch," I told him. "I'll look around here, then I'll go to this restaurant. Does he drive his car by himself?"

"Most times, yes," Cosimo said. Then as we drove from one location to another, he added that Scarcella parked his car outside his parents' apartment at Winston House.

"You got the licence number?" I asked.

"Yes," he said. "Last three numbers are seven, four, seven."

"Open this darn page," I said, "and write it in. Write his name down here so I can check it out myself, eh? Then the number where he lives with his mother and father."

I figured that if I got Cosimo to write down the information, it would be another nail of evidence to hammer in his coffin.

"You got his first name?" I asked.

"It's Peter," he replied.

"Peter?"

"S-A-R-C-E-L-L-A," he said, spelling it wrong at first and then correcting himself.

I tried to pry out of Cosimo why he wanted Scarcella eliminated. It came slowly, with great difficulty.

"He did something, the bastard."

"What, is he a stool pigeon?"

"Looks that way."

We got to the restaurant where Scarcella went every day to meet gamblers and a girlfriend who was a waitress. Then Cosimo dropped another nugget of information. Scarcella was going to be at the Casa Commisso to see him the next day at 1 P.M.

"All right," I said. "I'll get a look at him. I won't come in, but I'll be around there, okay? I'll park across the street or something."

Cosimo nodded. "Just between twelve-thirty and one o'clock."

"Between twelve-thirty and one o'clock he's gonna meet you, eh?" I said. "And he'll be driving that car?"

While Cosimo thought I'd be there watching, I wasn't. The members of the surveillance team were, and what they discovered was important. They spotted Scarcella at the Casa Commisso the day Cosimo and I met, and they tailed him that afternoon to the Four Seasons Hotel in downtown Toronto, where he met with Paul Volpe and two other people. We didn't know it then, but the Commissos were worried—worried about facing a gang war with Volpe and his people. They were busy plotting to strike first.

CHAPTER
18

ON THE DOTTED LINE

I was still working for Murphy, the Combined Forces Special Enforcement Unit (SEU), the RCMP, and the Crown prosecutor without any kind of agreement or any immunity, and I was getting nervous about it. All that was supposed to change with a meeting between me and members of a special steering committee representing the agencies involved in the Commisso investigation. It was supposed to, but it didn't.

We met at the Holiday Inn in Toronto just two days after Cosimo had given me the contract to kill Scarcella. As we started to sit down, Inspector Wylie of the SEU told Murphy to leave while they talked to me. When I saw Murphy walk toward the door, I stood up. "If Murphy goes, I go!" I snapped.

"Wait," Wylie said. He motioned to both of us to return to our seats and sit down. "Corporal Murphy can stay."

"Mr. Kirby, we'd like you to work with Sergeant Al Cooke of Metro and Sergeant John Simpson of SEU," Wylie said. "They're better equipped to handle this case."

I shook my head. I knew Cooke. He was all right, I had nothing against him. But he wasn't Murphy. I also knew Simpson. I didn't like him. Besides, I knew and trusted Murphy.

"It's Murphy or no one," I said. "I've said that from the start, and that's the way it is. I trust him — period. If I don't work with him, I don't work."

I could see a lot of unhappy inspectors in the room. They were going to be even more unhappy before the meeting ended. First I rejected the agreement they had signed and asked me to sign. It generally met all my conditions except the one most important to me — immunity from prosecution for all past crimes.

"Can't sign that," I said. "Not till I get immunity. Without immunity I don't testify — and you can't use the tapes."

That really upset them. They had tapes and admissions on those tapes that represented solid evidence of two conspiracies to murder. And there was the promise of more to come at future meetings. But the admissions weren't worth a dime unless I testified and agreed to the use of the tapes. Stalemate.

"One other thing, gentlemen," I said. "I've got another payment of seven thousand dollars or so coming from the Commissos. I intend to keep it unless you people come up with money to pay my expenses and living costs."

They all agreed to pay my expenses, but when I left, the agreement was still unsigned. I said I'd continue to work with Murphy as long as they took care of my expenses, but unless I had immunity, I was still a "confidential informant" of the RCMP and wouldn't have to testify. Murphy had given his word, and his bosses didn't like it.

For the next few days there were additional meetings, including one with Simpson, all designed to get me to work with other investigators instead of Murphy. None of them worked. Then Cosimo arranged another meeting with me at his house, and events started to move rapidly — a lot faster and in a lot more directions than was expected.

Cosimo was awake and waiting for me when I arrived on the morning of March 27, 1981. The last thing I expected him to talk about was that he thought a Mafia war was developing, but that's what he ended up talking about before the morning ended. And as he talked, the transmitter in my belt buckle and the body pack near my hip recorded it all.

"Listen, I got a few things to talk to you about this Scarcella," I said. "Want to go outside? Let's go outside. Few problems I've had."

Cosimo wasn't in any hurry to go outside to the car. He was comfortable where he was as I talked, so I didn't press it. I didn't want him getting suspicious. I did, however, want to pick up the conversation where we had left off the last time we met. The Mounties needed more on his plan to kill Scarcella. As a prod, I used information the Mounties had pulled together by watching

Scarcella from the moment he left his apartment to the time he went to the Casa Commisso.

"You know the day you told me he was going to be at the hall there?" I asked.

Cosimo nodded. "We were there."

"All right," I said. "I went over to the apartment about nine o'clock, and I sat there. I saw him come out. I got the licence number of his car and everything, eh?"

"Yeah."

"Now I followed him from there. I had a different car, a broad's car. I followed him right down to the Four Seasons Hotel downtown."

"Yeah, and?"

"In the morning, okay? I parked the car, I went in there, and you know who he's standing there talking to?"

"Who?" asked Cosimo, his interest raised.

"Paul Volpe. How come? What's he doing talking to Volpe?"

"He's close to him. That's okay. Forget it for now."

"He's close?"

"You don't have to worry 'bout anything."

"But who wants him killed?" I asked, really puzzled by the events and his answers. "Is it Volpe who wants him killed, or you, or what?"

"No, no, no, I'm — " he started to say.

I interrupted. "You know, I saw Volpe, and I said, 'What the fuck's going on here?' "

"I'm wondering that he wants to do it to me," answered Cosimo, obviously concerned. "Him and this fellow."

"It — it's you that wants this done? Or Volpe?"

"It's me, not Volpe."

"Volpe doesn't know nothing about this?"

"No, no. Why?"

"You know, I didn't want to stick around the lobby too long 'cause I've seen Volpe before. I don't know if he's seen me."

"You ever meet him before?"

"Oh, I've seen him before — with Chuck Yanover."

"Recently?" he asked nervously.

"No, 'bout a year ago," I said. "Year or so ago."

"Nobody saw you?" he asked with concern.

"No."

"You tell anybody 'bout this thing?"

"No, nobody knows about it," I reassured him.

"Things — they're bad over here," he said, deep worry showing on his face. "I don't know why these guys — I don't know. They wanna do me and my brother."

"They what?" I asked with real surprise.

"They wanna do — to do me and my brother," he repeated. "Maybe I can't trust any one of them."

Cosimo was talking gang warfare without saying it. He was telling me that he and Remo were targets of possible mob hits and that Volpe and his organization were behind the plot. Scarcella was some kind of double agent, playing both sides for his own interests.

"Who, Volpe does?" I asked. "You think Volpe wants to kill you and your brother?"

"This guy," he said, meaning Scarcella.

"What, with this guy?" I asked to be sure I was getting his story straight.

"Yeah, it's the two of them."

"What — this Scarcella's playing both sides? He's telling Volpe everything about you and him?"

Cosimo shook his head. "No, nothing about me and him. It's just that I don't know what's going to happen next year, you know. We just don't know."

"So what do you want to do?" I asked. "You want to kill Volpe in the future?"

"No, not for now . . ." he said, his voice trailing off, not finishing what he was saying.

"Not for now?"

"Like wait for this guy [Scarcella] for another week or so, okay?"

"Pass on him for a week?"

"Yes."

"All right — a week."

" 'Cause I'm waiting for an answer. I wanna be sure it's him." Then Cosimo switched back to questions about Yanover, who obviously concerned him. "You talk to Chuck about these things?"

"About this?"

"Yeah."

"No. He's on the run, Chuck. People are looking for him."

"For what?"

"He ripped somebody off. He sold somebody a kilo of coke or

something. All right, so wait a week or so on this guy, eh?"

Cosimo nodded.

"Now what do you want?" I asked to try and get more details out of him. "Do you want his body left lying around? Do you want him disposed of or what?"

"Which way you can do it?"

"I can do it whatever way you want."

"Gonna do it. You with me," Cosimo said, looking at me with a smile.

"That's right," I said. "I just did this Connecticut broad with no problem."

"You were with me," he said, staring at me, trying to read what I was thinking. "You be with me because there's lotsa things will go on with this fuckin' town. You see what I mean?"

The message was loud and clear to me. As far as Cosimo was concerned, a gang war was coming, and he wanted to be certain I was going to be there to help him.

"I don't know. I stay away from this shit now, you know," I answered.

"Yeah, you stay away, but be sure you are with me," he said sharply, "not with those other people."

"That's right, that's right," I said. "You know that."

Still he was worried—worried about betrayal in his own camp, worried about being stabbed in the back by people he trusted, including me, particularly because I was broke and needed the money he owed me. He probably wondered if I would sell him out for money. He didn't know it, but I'd already sold him out —for my life.

"You won't betray me, eh?" he asked. "You wouldn't go against me?"

"Never."

"Thank you, Cec."

"Never, Cosimo."

A feeling of exhilaration gripped me as I left. If the recording equipment worked — and it did — the surveillance teams had some strong evidence from that meeting. I was certain that Cosimo was convinced he could trust me, at least for the moment. I was equally certain that if I actually handled any of the hits he had planned—whether it be Scarcella or Volpe—I would be wasted eventually myself.

Cosimo was a very suspicious man. He had been very close to

Scarcella, had trusted him. Now he was ready to sink that knife into him once he was certain that whoever was whispering in his ear about Scarcella was whispering truth. True or no, the seed had been planted, and it was festering like an open sore.

For the next few weeks Cosimo stalled. He stalled on paying the money he and Melia owed me. He stalled on setting a date to hit Scarcella. But on April 8 he came close to making a commitment on Scarcella.

Cosimo was nervous as we sat in my car talking. I had enticed him into the car by showing him my foot and ankle wrapped in bandages. He had seemed to accept my explanation that I'd injured it when I fell while jogging. Then he noticed a small telephone pager I was wearing on my belt. Immediately his suspicions reached an almost fever pitch. He appeared convinced that it was a tape recorder until I told him I had gotten the pager so that he could reach me when he needed me. I gave him a number.

"Here it is," I said. "R, eight, nine, four, seven."

"Just call and give the message?"

"Right, and just leave a number. Don't say a name."

"By tomorrow night they gonna page you, okay? If you can, grab more information on the guy — Peter."

Cosimo's voice dropped to a whisper as he mentioned Scarcella's name. He was still nervous about the car and the pager I was wearing. I repeated the last name, Scarcella, then I tried to ease his suspicions again.

"It's all right, this car. I check this car all the time, every week."

"Then next week Michele gonna call you. And without mentioning the name, he gonna say yes or no, okay? If it's yes, go ahead, okay?"

"If he says yes, go ahead."

"Yes," Cosimo said without hesitation.

"All right, what about Volpe?"

"No, no. For now forget about him," he answered excitedly.

"You're gonna have to get rid of him sooner or later, aren't you?" I asked.

Cosimo looked at me for a long minute before answering, shaking his head slowly. "You talk with anybody about him?"

"No, I don't," I said sharply. "I don't talk to fuckin' nobody. I don't even talk to anybody, okay?"

"About anything?" he pressed.

"Nobody," I said. Then I hit him with some information I'd gotten.

"I could tell you things that people around this fuckin' city are shooting their mouth off about, okay? I just don't pay any attention to them. And Goobie's one of them. He's got a big mouth. You don't tell him nothing. Okay?"

"No, no, no."

"All right." 'Cause everything you tell him he repeats, you know."

"That's right," Cosimo said in agreement.

"Goobie told Gary Barnes about this thing down in Connecticut."

I watched as Cosimo's eyes widened in surprise.

"Yeah?" he said in shock.

"Yeah. I didn't tell him, so you must have told him."

"Well, he didn't know you went. He didn't know that it was done."

"He said to Gary, he said, 'You wanna make twenty-five thousand?' " I watched Cosimo's reaction. "He says, 'There's a broad down in Connecticut that they wanna get rid of.' "

Cosimo was flustered, upset. He had gone to Goobie and told him he would pay him $25,000 to kill Nafpliotis as added insurance in case I failed to do the job. He was going to pay this bastard more than he'd offered me. Goobie had gone to Barnes to get him to help him kill her. The last thing Cosimo expected was that I would find out about it. Finally he admitted talking to Goobie. His suspicions that I might be talking were sidetracked now by a much deeper suspicion about Goobie, and I played on that.

A couple of weeks later, on April 21, I met with Michele at Howard Johnson's. He didn't have the money that Cosimo had promised, but he had information that jolted me. I felt cold driplets of sweat under my arms, and the palms of my hands were clammy as Michele hit me with the bombshell. He had been to the States two weeks earlier to see Vince Melia and collect the money that was owed to me for killing Helen Nafpliotis. Melia had stalled, and the Commissos were having trouble raising the cash. Cosimo's legal fees on a case were over $15,000, and they had other commitments. With all the problems, Michele said he'd have $2,000 for me in a few days, but I'd have to wait until

Melia came to Toronto for a wedding later in the month to collect all the rest.

"Vince — he gave me the runaround," Michele said. "He says there was some money missing in the apartment, some jewellery . . ."

I was stunned. I didn't know it at the time, but the FBI had let Helen Nafpliotis take all her money and jewellery with her when they staged the fake kidnapping. Vince Melia and his crew had apparently gone into the apartment to search for the money and take back the jewellery, because Nick Melia had given her most of it. When they didn't find it, they tried to convince the Commissos I'd gotten enough with the jewellery and cash and the initial payment.

"Yeah, well, I made it look good," I said to Michele.

"You know what happened to Vince," Michele said. "I've checked it, and it's true. His brother Nick is into some trouble down in Kentucky. And he's out on $150,000 bail. He's waiting for his brother to beat the case and come up with the money."

"That could be another two years from now," I said angrily.

"No, in May," he said. "He's either in or out. But this week he's bringing some money, that's for sure."

When I threatened to turn up at the wedding, which was to be held at the Casa Commisso, grab Melia, and shake the money out of him, Michele excitedly told me to stay away and guaranteed I'd be paid. Two days later Cosimo and I met. He handed me $1,000 and promised to pay me $500 a week from a business he was taking over so that I wouldn't be broke any more.

"You know, we' gonna put you on the payroll," he said. "So much a week. Then when things are done, you gonna have a bonus for it. You see what I mean?"

I nodded my head in agreement. Then without explanation he added, "Ah, Scarcella — forget about it for now."

"What?" I asked in surprise. "For how long?"

"I don't know," he said. "A month, two months. There's another guy I wanna take care of."

"So you don't want me to kill Scarcella," I said, making sure that his orders to kill another man could be heard and were being recorded clearly. "You want to do another guy? What's his name?" I was trying to squeeze more information out of him without arousing his suspicions. "Maybe I know him."

"I tell you, but you don't worry about the name. You see him, okay?"

"What is he, a gambler? Another gambler."

"Ah, you know," he said with a shrug. "Next week. Next week you gonna have two thousand."

While I was busy working for the police on the Commissos, I saw Chuck Yanover one night at a discotheque. Meeting with Yanover gave me an edge at my meetings with the Commissos, who were afraid I would defect to Yanover's boss, Paul Volpe. Yanover was always a braggart and loved to talk about other people. As a sometime Rounder, he was in a position to get information off the street about different Rounders and hoods, including the Commissos. So I made a point of listening when Chuck talked, because he could be a fountain of useful information when he wanted to. But the last thing I expected him to talk about was a plot to seize the island of Dominica.

"Want a job, Cec?" he asked.

"Maybe," I said. "What have you got in mind?"

"How'd you like to go to the Caribbean with me, to an island called Dominica?" he asked. "We're going to take it over."

Yanover said that he had been hired by Wolfgang Droege, Toronto leader of the Klu Klux Klan, and James Alexander McQuirter, Canadian director of the KKK. Droege was about thirty-four and McQuirter twenty-three, and the two of them were planning to take over the island and set up their own government. Yanover planned to become one of their top government officials, set up a casino with Volpe's help, and become very, very rich. The island had all kinds of potential as far as he was concerned. It could be used for gambling, as a jumping-off point and storage warehouse for narcotics, a place to hide felons, and a sanctuary for mob money through offshore banks they would set up. There was just no limit to Chuckie's dreams of riches.

Yanover and one of his buddies, Michael Gerol, had gone to Dominica on what was supposed to be a Caribbean vacation. They had photographed all the island's important locations, including its police station, its small military post, and the best approaches from the sea. The information and photos that he and Gerol had gathered, he said, he'd turned over to the two Klansmen so they could prepare for the invasion.

"Join us," Chuck said. "You'll make a fortune."

I shook my head. "Thanks, Chuck, but that's not for me. I got too many problems here to take care of."

I told everything I knew to Murphy, and he reported it to the SEU, the RCMP, and the OPP, all of whom launched an investigation. At the same time, I was told, they notified the FBI, who with other agencies had already infiltrated the "invasion force." If they hadn't stopped the plot when they did, a lot of people might have been killed.

The plot, I learned later, was to team up on the island with some Rastafarians, called "Dreads" on Dominica, who grew pot, kidnapped and killed island residents, and threatened officials who stood in their way. That would have been some crazy team —Klansmen, who think whites and blacks should be separated, and Rastas, who hate whites and extort and terrorize their own people to push drugs and what they call a religion.

On May 15, shortly after the Dominica story broke in the papers, Cosimo mentioned that the island had been offered to his crime group some time before.

"Looks like the police are after Yanover," I remarked. "Those people in that Dominica plot, they got pinched. They're looking at about fifty years."

"You know that the first people they talked to was us," said Cosimo. "They came to us two years ago."

"What?" I was dumbfounded. The last thing I expected him to say was that he and his brothers were somehow involved in Dominica. I was really stunned. "They approached you on it?"

"Sure — before anybody else," he said with a smile.

"What, the people down there?" I asked, still startled by what he'd told me.

"The people down there, from Dominica," he said. "I was down there. It's a nice, beautiful island, beautiful island. Well, first it was too much money. Then at the time when they approached me, the people in power were the right people."

I was fascinated by what he had to say, and for the most part all I did was listen with little more comment that an occasional "Yeah."

"Then there was an election, and they lost it," he continued.

"Then it changed," I suggested.

"You understand," he said with a smile.

"And now it's the same people from before?"

"Ah, no, but now they've changed, okay? So that's why we dropped the idea. You know, we had people interested. Everybody was ready to go in. But then the people, they lost the election. These other people, they want nothing to do with it. The deal was, twenty-five years we run a casino — twenty-five years tax-free."

"Is that right, eh? Jesus. That would have been nice."

"What they wanted was for us to build them a runway and airport."

"An airport?"

He nodded his head vigorously. "Yeah, because they got no airport. There's no airport there at all."

"So you can't land a plane there," I said.

"Not a jet," he explained. "Just a small plane. So there was two million dollars' wortha work on the airport. They would give us the best site of land, five hundred acres farmland. For nothing. Just free. That way we could build on it."

"Yeah."

"Okay. So much per cent was to go to the prime minister there. That's all it was. Then this thing changed."

"Yeah, that's too bad."

Cosimo was upset by the change of government, that was pretty obvious. The people he'd depended on were out, and there were new people trying to take over Dominica who had approached other people in Toronto after the Commissos dropped out. The new people wanted to overthrow the government and seize the island. Cosimo called that approach a waste of time.

He rambled on about the place, about the lost opportunity. Cosimo saw it as a gold mine for his group and a great place to spend his time.

"Like I said, that was no more than two, four, five years ago when we were approached," he recalled. "Then that thing in Vancouver happened [the counterfeiting bust], and then we lay around a little bit. A lotta things happened."

Cosimo was disappointed that his group hadn't been able to take over the island on the terms he'd originally agreed to. But he was disgusted that Yanover had somehow gotten involved and blown the deal forever with the ridiculous invasion plot. The island paradise would never be a casino plum Cosimo could pluck.

CHAPTER
19
THE LAST CONTRACT

When I went to meet Cosimo on April 29, 1981, I felt a lot more secure than I had in all the months I had worked for Murphy as a confidential informant. For the first time I had a written agreement, signed the day they grabbed the Dominica "invaders," that guaranteed me immunity as a witness and protection and support for my family. I should have known then that all that glitters is not gold and that things written on paper can always be altered. Promises made are not always promises kept by men or their governments.

But when I saw Cosimo at Howard Johnson's that day, I was concerned only with getting the evidence needed to wrap this thing up. I was tired and tense, and Murphy was stretched to the limits of endurance, providing surveillance and protection for me and working extra-long hours to check out the information I brought in. In his spare waking moments, he was fighting with his brass, trying to get added physical and financial support for me. I have to say now that I will always admire Murphy for his honesty, his integrity, and his guts. I'm alive today because of him.

Cosimo complained that he was still in pain from the injury he had received in the accident. The leg still bothered him, and he was limping slightly. He looked terrible. His eyes were bloodshot, his round face looked drawn, and he was unusually nervous and suspicious.

"I've got something I wanna talk to you about," he said. "We get outta the car for a second. I don't trust cars."

"All right," I answered. "Looks like you got a lot on your mind. Looks like you haven't been sleeping too good. You can tell when your eyes are all red."

His tone was sharp, and there was an edge of suspicion to his questions.

"Why you want my brother Remo here for?" he asked.

"Well, look. You told me last week that you're going to put me on the payroll," I said, trying to explain why I had asked him to bring Remo to the meeting. Remo had not come, and Cosimo was annoyed and suspicious about this request.

"Now I just wanted to confirm it with him in case something happens to you," I added.

"Nothing will happen to us," he said. "What could happen to me?"

"Well, suppose you get picked up?" I asked. "Get another charge. Then I won't see you any more."

"Don't you worry about that," he said. "If you don't see me any more, you think I'm gonna die? I wouldn't die." He stopped and pointed to my hip. "What's that?"

I looked down and smiled. "The pager. It's off now. If I turn it on, it starts beeping." To demonstrate and put him at ease, I turned it on, and it began beeping.

Cosimo then switched to problems with his people in Connecticut. It was out in the open — Melia and his friends didn't believe that the Nafpliotis woman was dead.

"They still don't believe that it's okay because even her suitcase is missing," he said, with just a trace of suspicion reflecting from his narrowing eyes.

"Yeah, well, I took care of all that, okay?" I said.

"Melia said that all the jewellery is missing," he complained. "It was his."

Think fast, Kirby. Come up with a story he'll understand. My mind was in high gear, and my mouth was about to catch up.

"Well, my partner took some jewellery and some other stuff!" I snapped, grateful that early on I had established that I had had to take someone with me to help me dispose of the body. "We took the stuff out to make it look like she more or less went on a vacation."

The FBI hadn't given me or Murphy or the SEU a clue as to what they had done with Nafpliotis. They never told us they'd taken her back to the house to get her jewellery and her clothes. They didn't tell us she was back in Greece, trying to sell her home and other property from there. I knew they'd staged a kidnapping because it was reported in the papers. But a kidnapping required two men. If I hadn't created a fictional hit man helper, the Commissos would have been certain things were phony, and I'd have been dead. As it was, the FBI's action was endangering me and the undercover operation, perhaps not intentionally, but it made me scramble and raised unnecessary suspicions with the Melias and the Commissos.

Then Cosimo dropped another hot rock in my lap.

"Just a minute," he said. "You know, the radio says that she's living in Italy, in Greece, or in Toronto."

A little bell went off in my head. This could be trouble — real trouble — unless I played hard and fast with Cosimo, kept him offbalance with my questions and answers. They say the best defence is a tough offence.

"Who said that?" I snapped heatedly.

"The radio, not me . . ." Cosimo said defensively, afraid I was about to come after him.

"Radio? What radio?" I asked. "Jesus Christ," I thought to myself. "Why the hell didn't the FBI tell us what was going on?"

"Back there," he explained. "They haven't found the car yet. Where's the car? In the lake too?"

"Yeah."

"That where she died?"

"Yeah."

"Far away or nearby?"

"About thirty miles from there. How fuckin' far do you want me to drive the car? Back to Canada?"

"No, no, no, no. That's good," he said nervously. "You know, probably they just made those stories up."

"Lookit, she's dead."

"I know it." Sweat glistened on Cosimo's brow.

"You got my guarantee on it, okay? Do you want me to go show you where she's dead?"

He waved his hands in the air and then wiped his brow. "No, no, no."

"Well, why doesn't he fuckin' pay us? I told Michele the other day I was gonna go out in that parking lot and wait for him and give him a kick in the ass. You know, I still might."

Cosimo shook his head vigorously. "I know, but don't you worry about this money."

"If you can't trust me after this long . . ."

"I trust you now. Just tell me one thing. Was she dead when you . . ."

"Knocked her out," I answered, finishing his sentence. "I didn't use the gun. I threw the gun away somewhere else. I didn't know where this gun had been, all right? They hand me a fuckin' gun, and first of all it's supposed to be a .38, only it wasn't." I paused, looking at him, knowing he was on the defensive, convinced I had done the job despite what his friends from Connecticut were saying. "You figure they're making this up so they won't have to pay you?"

"That's what I think, but don't you worry about it for now, okay?"

I didn't. I knew he was convinced by what I'd said that Melia was trying to cheat him with a phony story, and he was sore. He'd go back and collect now from Melia. It was time to turn the conversation to other important things, to Scarcella and Volpe.

Cosimo was filled with surprises that afternoon. The plot to kill the other man was off. There was no longer a need, as he had told me there was at a previous meeting, for him to take me to various locations and show me the victim's routine. The hit was off, pure and simple, and he had no name to give me. Then he dropped the other shoe. The plan to kill Scarcella was also definitely off.

"You're in no rush to get rid of Scarcella?" I asked.

"No, no. We're gonna get him with us," he said, shrugging his shoulders and gesturing with his hands in the air.

"You're going to *what*?" I asked. I was floored by the turn of events, but I tried not to show it.

"I think we're gonna get him on this side now," Cosimo said with a smile.

"You're going to have him on your side now?" I asked to be sure those listening in understood. Scarcella, the cheese company owner, Volpe's former union organizer, his trusted companion, was now on the side of the Commissos! If only Volpe knew . . .

There was no such change of heart when he turned his attention toward the fate of Volpe.

"Kill him," he said heatedly. "You understand what I mean?"

"I do," I said. "I know where he's at. Yanover told me where he lives, okay? You know where he lives?"

Cosimo shook his head vigorously. "Nothing," he said. "I have nothing."

"I do," I said confidently. "You want me to get him, kill him tonight?"

"All right," he said.

I knew I needed more time to get things arranged, to talk to Murphy and other SEU investigators. So I changed tactics and stalled a bit.

"I'll go," I said. "I'll see what I can do, okay? I'll work on it in the next week or two. I guarantee you, he'll be dead in the next two weeks."

"All right, fine," he said with a smile.

For more than twenty years Volpe had been the mob power in Toronto. He'd had connections with the old Joe Bonanno mob in New York City, and then he teamed up with the Stefano Magaddino family of Buffalo, who were involved in the distribution of narcotics. According to the newspapers, he'd gotten heavily involved in property in Atlantic City, he and Vincent Cotroni were close, and he had built his own crime organization in Toronto. But for some reason I knew nothing about at the time, he hated the Calabrian Honoured Society, and they hated him. Now they were going to do something about their hatred.

Cosimo was worried about my having seen and talked to Yanover. He was particularly concerned that I might have tipped my hand on the Volpe hit. I denied it, told him I hadn't talked to Yanover about Volpe. In fact, I noted, Yanover had invited me out to see Volpe's heavily guarded, fenced-in estate in Nobleton.

"You ask Yanover about this guy?" he asked.

"Did I ask anybody about him?" I repeated. "No, no, no, I didn't ask anybody. I can find out on my own. Yanover said, 'You want to go up to Volpe's place?' I said, 'Yeah, I wouldn't mind going up.' He told me where he lives, in Nobleton."

"Where's Yanover gone?"

"He's downtown."

"But he was to have been on the run, they told me. He was on the run for something."

Since I was the one who had orginally told him abut Yanover being on the run for a drug rip-off, I had to come up with a plausible story for his not being in hiding.

"Oh, yeah," I recalled. "He's always fuckin' somebody. That's why I think he wanted me to meet Volpe. He said, you know, 'You want to meet him?' I said, 'Well, yes, maybe.' And he told me where he lives. He told me almost exactly where he lives. His name's on a mailbox out there."

"You still walk round with the gun on you?" Cosimo asked with concern.

"Yeah," I said with a half smile, knowing it worried him that I carried a gun when I met with him. We agreed to meet at the Howard Johnson's again on May 15 if I didn't go to jail on May 5. I told him that's when I was scheduled to appear for sentencing on the B and E case after pleading guilty to the charge.

"I'll see you in here May fifteenth, two o'clock, all right? Read the papers," I said.

"Ah, don't you worry about it," Cosimo said. "You shouldn't be going in."

"I'm worried about you," I answered. "Those accidents you're getting into."

Cosimo was smiling as we split, but I was worried. How was I going to show him that I had taken Volpe out without doing it? Did we have enough for a case? And if we didn't, what would I have to do? All those questions and more were to be answered by Murphy, but not without some hassles from the people who gave him his orders.

Murphy was upset when we met later that day.

"What the hell are you doing carrying a gun?" Murphy shouted. "Are you crazy?"

"I feel safe with it!" I snapped. "Besides, Cosimo knows. It keeps him honest."

"It's against the fuckin' law, Cec!" he roared. "You could be in a whole lot of trouble, and so could I because of a stupid thing like that. Jesus! Where the hell are your brains?"

I shrugged, reached under my belt, pulled out the gun, and handed it to him. "Okay, okay," I said apologetically, "but with the kind of support you're getting, what the hell do you expect me to do? You got one guy with you now; other times you're doing the fuckin' surveillance by yourself. Who's going to help me in time if things go wrong? Me, that's who. But here's the gun."

There had been references to the gun in previous conversations, but Murphy and the others listening in hadn't picked them up, and it wasn't until months later that they transcribed all the tapes. They had all assumed that Cosimo was referring to the telephone pager I carried when he asked me if I was carrying a gun or when I told him I was carrying one. That didn't cut any ice with Murphy's superiors. They were convinced that Murphy had known all along that I was carrying a gun when I met with Cosimo. This was one of the charges they levelled against him when they reprimanded him.

I felt naked without the gun, and I was going to feel even worse when I had to step into the pressure cooker again on May 15 and explain to Cosimo why I hadn't called to say I was ready to kill Volpe. I needed time to get a good rundown on Volpe and his way of life. I didn't know it until later, but there was no better source for that information than my friend Murphy.

Volpe took his orders from the Stefano Magaddino mob in Buffalo, which also gave orders to the crime family in Hamilton run by Giacomo Luppino. Murphy told me that Jimmy Luppino, the son of Giacomo, used to visit Volpe every day in Toronto until I was given the contract to kill him by the Commissos. No one has ever said publicly who gave the Commissos the contract to kill Volpe. I had information from some mob friends that it was Vincent Cotroni of Montreal. He was a former member of the Joseph Bonanno crime family, but more important, he was from Reggio Calabria, and his Calabrian ties and associations were strong. A lot of contracts for the Commissos, who were called "Canada's Murder Inc.," came from Cotroni.

Everything was about to come to a head when I met with Cosimo at Howard Johnson's on May 15. All those months of undercover work were going to end, at least temporarily, although I had no evidence of that when we met in my car.

"This thing with Volpe," I said. "How much you gonna give me for that? I want to know. I don't want no payroll or five hundred bucks—I want it all in one lump. I want to know how much you're gonna give me and then how much you can give me after that."

Cosimo hesitated. He didn't want to set a figure, and in the back of my head I knew he didn't really plan on paying me. My payoff if I killed Volpe was going to be two in the head, burial in a shallow grave, or my body dumped in the Bayview Ghost.

"Ah, Cec, I don't like — " he started to say. I cut him off.

"I want out — I want to fuck off out of the country," I said. "I've been out in the rain for the last two nights watching the guy's place, for chrissakes."

Cosimo was edgy, nervous about the car, afraid we were being bugged and overheard. He was always afraid of being bugged, yet he still talked. When I reassured him, he appeared satisfied that the car had been debugged and checked out. He stopped looking at everything in the car and began talking again.

"Listen, let's move this way. You see, I don't want to promise you any more to put up until I'm a hundred per cent sure."

"All right. Your word's good with me. Your credit's good with me, okay? You owe me five thousand dollars still, from before."

"Yes."

"All right. I just want enough money to get around in, and I want it after Volpe's killed. He'll be killed soon. I've been up there ten times. Do you know where this place is?"

"No, Cec."

"It's out in the country, okay? You can't park like here, like you do in the city. It's hard. I gotta park at least a mile away where I got a good spot. I got a mile to go through the bush. I tell you, I've been fuckin' soaked the last coupla times. I'm gonna end up with pneumonia."

"In the morning, Cec — how it look in the morning?"

"Ah, I must have got there too late. I usually get there at nightime, eh? He's got "Fox Hill" on the mailbox with TV towers and a tennis court back there. He drives a maroon Cadillac, burgundy, and he's got a station wagon too."

"He drives one of those Audis — you know, the car," Cosimo added.

I shook my head. RCMP and SEU intelligence wasn't all it was cracked up to be. They didn't tell me about an Audi, probably because they didn't know about it. Think fast.

"Haven't seen it up there," I answered. "Unless he's got it put somewhere else. He's not bringing it home. Maybe he's switching cars in between, you know? I've done that before. You go out, switch a car, and go in another car."

"You know him?"

"I know him to see him — Christ, yeah!" I said sharply. "Couldn't miss him. I saw him come home one night in the Cadillac, and I didn't have anything with me at that time. I wasn't even expecting to see him, but I got a good idea when he comes home. I have a very good idea, and it's beautiful. Nobody'd hear it out there."

"There's no people?" Cosimo asked.

"There's no neighbours beside him," I said. "There's a house next door, but it's up for sale, and there's nobody in it. He won't be much of a problem. Just catching him at the right time is all I have to do."

"But you know him," Cosimo repeated, making sure I had the right man to hit, that there would be no mistakes.

"I know him," I said, showing my annoyance at his continued line of questioning on this point. "Tall, but sorta bald, hair on the sides. He's had three-piece suits on sometimes. I saw him down at the Four Seasons with Scarcella. I've seen him around before. I saw him talking to Yanover one day, but I was off in the car, you know. He doesn't know me to see me."

"I wanna — I wanna make sure, you know, Cec," Cosimo said. "It's very important. You know what I mean, Cec. I wanna make no — "

"There won't be no mistakes in this, okay?" I said, finishing his sentence.

"All right."

"Definitely okay," I emphasized. "All right now, how much? You're not talking about some idiot on the street or some dope hustler, you know."

"Cec, I know."

"You know — this guy gets knocked off — how about twenty thousand?"

"I couldn't give it all at once, not that much money."

"All right, twenty thousand over a period of time."

"All right."

"All right. Soon after it's — the next day after it's done, I'm going to come and see you."

Cosimo shook his head. "Four days after."

"Four days? Okay. Make sure you have at least five thousand on you."

He nodded his approval. "Okay, Cec."

"Either you or your brothers or somebody — make sure you have five thousand," I emphasized.

"All right, all right," he said impatiently. "And then I pay you after two months."

"All right, no problem. I'm waiting now. You know I've been patient about this other five thousand bucks for the thing in the States."

"I know, Cec. It's just the wrong time. We mortgage ourselves over our heads — four, five property. Buy here, buy there — see what I mean? If we don't pay the mortgage, we lose the property."

"What — you got your house mortgaged too now?"

"No, no, no. What I mean, I have property in Richmond Hill. It's four thousand dollars a month. Property in Mississauga, it's few thousand dollars a month. Property in Burlington, it's four thousand a month. Property in King City — it's all property."

"You own that much land?" I was surprised by the amounts he said he was paying out.

"Yeah," he said. "I'm no broke. I have no cash, okay, but we have lotsa property. We have maybe ten million dollars' worth of property."

I let out a low whistle. "Ten million?"

"Maybe. You see what I mean?"

I smiled. I had a solution to his cash flow. "Well, give me a lot," I said. "Give me a piece of property."

Cosimo shook his head. Most of the land was in large lots and couldn't be subdivided. One section of land was worth two million dollars alone. There was also a ten-acre section of land in King City, and I registered my interest in that.

"You know how much I paid for that, Cec?" he asked with a smile.

"How much?"

"Half a million dollars I paid for it."

I whistled low. Cosimo and his mob were heavily into real estate investments. One of the sections they owned was a large piece of land north of Kingcross Estates, luxury estates where a lot of rich people lived. He said he planned to subdivide it in a year, and then maybe he'd have some land for me. But I'd have to be patient.

He said that the land he wanted to subdivide cost more than $100,000 just to service. "That's what happen," he said. "We mortgage ourselves right up to here [pointing to his throat]. We talk maybe twenty-two thousand a month in mortgages. It's a lotta fuckin' money."

Before we split up, I had one more question for him. Normally there are rules about how you hit a Mafia man. Wives are almost always left out, not harmed. That sometimes complicates the planning of a murder. It's got to be timed so that only the target is hit, not the wife or children. I knew that Cosimo and his brothers wouldn't care. They didn't live by the rules, and they didn't kill by the rules, but I wanted others to know it. I wanted their ruthlessness on the tape so that others would understand how they thought and operated.

"What if his wife's with him?" I asked. "I'm getting impatient, you know."

"I leave it to you," Cosimo said.

"I'll do the wife," I said coldly.

"Very hardly that they go out together," he replied.

The next twenty-four hours turned out to be critical. One of the big holes in the investigation was Remo Commisso. The SEU and Crown attorney Howard Morton were convinced that the evidence against Cosimo and Michele was sufficient for murder conspiracy charges, but the evidence against Remo was thin. He had said very little to me on tape. They had to get him out into the open on tape. But how? It was Sgt. Lyle McCharles of the OPP who came up with the idea. Why not stage a phony Volpe hit? Why not get Volpe to lend me his wallet and have me take it to Remo while Cosimo was doing weekend jail time for the smuggling of aliens?

McCharles and Murphy had floated the idea at a meeting of the SEU staff and Morton on April 30. Everybody had laughed except Insp. Wilf Steferak, who was assigned temporarily as officer in charge of the SEU. Murphy had said he knew Volpe well enough to ask him. (Murphy later told me that he'd met Volpe in 1975 after starting a project that had turned into "Operation Oblong," an RCMP investigation that severely damaged Volpe's gambling empire.) Steferak had said it was worth a try. The whole ball game was to go down on May 16, and that morning Murphy called Volpe and told him it was urgent that he see him.

Murphy and Sgt. Al Cooke of Metro Intelligence went to see Volpe at his home. They told him that there was a contract on his life and that there was one person involved on whom they lacked sufficient evidence to make an arrest. Would he help? Volpe said he would, provided he had Murphy's word that there would be no double cross. He got that, and Murphy took Volpe's wallet complete with his driver's licence, credit cards, and other identification.

Murphy and Cooke also got Volpe to agree to drive into Toronto with his wife and stay inside the RCMP headquarters on Jarvis Street for the entire day without talking to anyone. Murphy later told me he had been surprised when Volpe agreed. Volpe had a condition, however. No one was to tell his wife, Lisa, why they were going there. He would invent a story to tell her. Murphy and Cooke agreed, and they drove Volpe and his wife to RCMP headquarters.

It was just after 11 A.M. when I met Murphy at Bathurst and Steeles Plaza. He told me what had happened with Volpe and handed me Volpe's wallet. By 11:15 I was at Remo's home at 484 Ellerslie Avenue, knocking on his door. A woman answered. In the background I could hear a radio playing and a child's voice. I asked the woman if I could see Remo, identifying myself only as "George." Remo came out, and Michele was with him.

"I gotta talk to you," I told Remo. "Can I talk to you, outside? I got something in the car I want to show you."

"You have something in the car?" he asked. "You want to take me to your car?"

"Yeah. Not in the house," I said. "There's something I got to show you."

Remo was suspicious. There was no way he was going to go to my car and sit and talk. "Bring it to the house," he said. "We go downstairs to talk. I don't trust a car."

"I'll get it all right," I answered. "I know you don't trust cars. I don't trust houses."

"No, we go in the washroom," he said.

As I returned to the car to get the wallet, I talked into the recorder to let those conducting the surveillance know what was going on. We wouldn't be able to use the car recorder, but there was my body pack and the belt buckle transmitter. I knew we'd get whatever he had to say on tape.

When I re-entered the house, I saw Michele Commisso playing with the kids and asked him if he was babysitting. He shook his head. Weekends, he said, he stayed at the house to play with the kids. "At'sa nice mafioso," I thought to myself.

Remo was standing nearby and motioned for me to follow. We went downstairs, through his recreation room to a washroom. He put his finger to his mouth to indicate quiet. Then he turned the cold water tap on just in case there were bugs in the house. He signalled that we could talk.

"Volpe, he's dead," I said.

He looked surprised, almost at a loss for words. "How come?"

"I just killed him, an hour ago," I said matter-of-factly.

"What happened?"

"Well, Cosimo told me you and him wanted it. Want to go outside? Wanna talk in here?"

"George, you should never come here." Remo was very upset, annoyed that I was in his house telling him this, apparently fearful that police might be watching and following me and that I'd lead them to his house.

"Well, lookit. He's dead. So's his wife too, okay? They're both dead, about an hour ago."

His face was clouded, and he was getting more and more upset. "You should never come here."

"Well, listen," I continued, "I need some money and I'm broke. I told Cosimo yesterday when I saw him. I said, 'I'm broke. I need some money, and I wanna get the fuck out of the country now.' Okay, I want some money today."

"Tell me when I'm gonna get it to you, George."

"Well, a thousand or something just to get me out of here." I reached into my pocket and pulled out Volpe's wallet. "I took this right out of his back pocket."

"You should have thrown it away!" he said excitedly as he looked it over and checked the identification.

"Well, listen, you people have doubted me in the past," I reminded him.

"All right, don't worry. We'll take care of you. You know we respect you like a brother. Don't worry about it."

"Yeah, but look at before. You've told me — Cosimo still owes me five thousand."

"You know you'll get the money from him."

"All right, but there's two people dead now."

"I don't even want to talk about these things." He shook his head.

"All right. I got this thing from him partly just to prove to you."

"That's all right." He returned the wallet to me after he'd looked it over. "Throw it away. Don't leave it."

"No, I'll get rid of it," I promised him. "I'll drop it down the sewer when I go out, far away from here."

"Where you wanna meet?" he asked. "When? Maybe tomorrow up here or Monday?"

"I need some money now, I wanna leave today," I said urgently. "I'll meet you down at the hall."

"Where I'm gonna get the fuckin' money today?"

"A thousand bucks."

"All right, but it's not good to come by the hall."

"Then where? Get Michele to meet me down at Howard Johnson's again, okay? At five o'clock. A thousand dollars."

"Okay."

"I'll be taking off for a week or two. I'll be back in two weeks. I want the rest of the money then. Cosimo — I told Cosimo yesterday twenty thousand bucks, eh? I want at least five thousand."

"I know nothing about this. I didn't know that he told you to do it."

"But he told me a long time ago that you and him wanted this done."

"Me?" he exclaimed. "I never said that."

"That's what he told me," I replied.

"Did you ever talk to me about this thing?"

"No, but hey, you know what's going on. You didn't know this?"

"No." Remo shook his head. "What's the difference, so what? All right. You come. Michele will meet you at five."

"All right. I got to be back in two weeks. What about this other guy, this Scarcella?"

"Forget about him. This fella, we don't want to do nothing no more. No problem."

So I left, taking the wallet with me, returned to the car, and drove to the location where all the cops had been recording the conversation. A security detail that had been assigned two weeks earlier to take me off the street and protect me was waiting to escort me out of the area, back to an apartment I was staying in.

I handed the wallet to Cpl. Danielle Bouchard, who was supervising the case. One of the supervising sergeants piped up, "That cinches it. You're finished."

"Are you sure?" I asked. "Don't you want me to meet Michele

at Howard Johnson's and get the money off of him?"

"No, no," he said, smiling, "we don't need it. We're finished. We've got them all."

I shrugged and walked off with my security guards. I said to them, "You know what? I think they're going to want me to meet him." We went to a bar, had a couple of drinks and about three or four beers, and then went up to my room at the Holiday Inn. Murphy was on the phone, and he was upset.

"Cec, you don't have to — you don't have to do this," he said.

"I know what you're going to fuckin' ask," I said. "You want me to go back there with Michele."

He laughed nervously. "You're right, Cec. You gotta go back and pick up that payment from Michele."

They had followed Michele after I left Remo's house and had seen him go to the home of Domenic Racco, the son of the old Calabrian Mafia boss and the man everyone was saying was going to succeed his father. They speculated that at the house Michele got the money to pay me.

Murphy arrived at the Holiday Inn, where I was staying with my security detail, and I got into the bugged car with him. We drove like we were at the Indianapolis 500 to get to the meeting on time. We must have been doing ninety miles an hour or more. When we got there, I had to urinate in the worst way but I couldn't — I didn't have time. They had body-packed me. I had to pull in my stomach for the body pack, and I damned near pissed in my pants.

In spite of all the problems, I got to Howard Johnson's and parked in front of Faces discotheque before Michele arrived in his Oldsmobile. Murphy and his surveillance van were perfectly situated to get pictures and recordings. There was another special team of sharpshooters nearby ready to gun down anyone who tried to hit me. I waited maybe ten minutes, and Michele pulled up. There were four in the car. Michele got out of his car, walked to mine, and handed me what he thought was $1,000. He hadn't counted right. It was $1,100.

"Who's with you?" I asked.

"My kid cousins — Claudio, Remo, and Johnny," he said. "We got to go to a wedding in Niagara Falls."

"Yeah, well, I'm going to Miami in about another hour," I said.

"Take care of yourself," Michele said.

"I will for sure," I answered as I watched him leave.

Michele didn't realize it, and I didn't find out until hours later, but when Murphy and the special marksmen team spotted his car with four inside, everyone got their rifles ready and sighted in. If someone had gotten out of the car with Michele, the marksmen were all prepared to waste them on the spot to prevent them from killing me.

I remember saying to Murphy, "But they were just kids on the way to a wedding in Niagara Falls."

"You're right, Cec, but at that moment we didn't know that, and we damned sure weren't going to take chances with your life," he said.

In the hours ahead Michele would be stopped for speeding and arrested on the conspiracy-to-murder charge. Remo was arrested at the home of his girlfriend and charged, and Cosimo was charged in jail. It was a clean sweep.

CHAPTER
20

BYE, BYE, PAULIE

Two weeks before the arrest of the Commissos, I was placed under the protection of the RCMP. I had bodyguards with me day and night. I was living in hotels and getting a $250-a-week allowance to pay for my hotel room and my meals. It was worse than living in prison. In prison what you can't see you don't miss, and you forget about it. The way I had to live, I could see all the goodies of life, but I couldn't touch. There was very little wine, women, and song — the high road that the news media and lawyers said I was strolling down — to enjoy. There were four walls, the faces of my protectors, some card games, and an occasional drive in a Chrysler leased for me by the government. Those drives were never alone. There were always a couple of bodyguards along.

The leased car drew a lot of criticism from the media later on, but to me it was a necessity. I needed wheels, I needed to feel a breath of fresh air on my face, I needed to get out of the confinement of my room if I was to retain my sanity. Unless you've lived in an undercover posture as I have, you can't know what it's like.

When the investigation of the Commissos began, the Mounties and the SEU had to use my car. If I had suddenly changed to a new car, Cosimo and Remo would have immediately become suspicious. So they decided to use mine. They bugged it, they photographed it — wherever I went to meetings, that car was with me. Only it wasn't really my car. It was my dad's.

Once the Commissos were arrested, the car had to be stripped of its equipment and returned to my dad. I couldn't use it again. It would be the first thing the Commissos and their associates would look for—Cecil Kirby and his Chevrolet. The alternative was the leased car, and that was only for a short time. Eventually it became impractical for protective purposes. I was too hot a property to be allowed out in the open, even with bodyguards at my side. Not only was I in danger, but they were also in danger should some crazy Calabrian decide to take me out.

Picture the circumstances. What I'd done was about to end, at least for a decade or more, the criminal careers of some of Canada's most powerful crime leaders. They were naturally furious, mad enough to kill, mad enough to make it worth anywhere from $100,000 to $250,000 for someone to kill me. Of course, if anyone had succeeded, the chances of their living to collect that contract money were about one in a billion. Dead men can't tell tales. They can't be arrested and later forced to testify in court.

With all that money on my head, the mission of the SEU and the Crown was to keep me alive at any cost, so round-the-clock protection was a must. It wasn't always successful, but it was a must, and when it wasn't successful, it was *my* fault, not that of those assigned to protect me. For a street criminal, life in confinement is hell. I was a jogger. So I jogged, and my protectors jogged with me. Some weren't in good enough physical shape to jog, so they followed in a car. I was a socializer. I loved to hit bars and clubs where my Rounder friends were. Now I couldn't, or I wasn't supposed to.

It would be safe to say that I wasn't exactly a model protected witness. It would also be safe to say that the art of handling protected witnesses in Canada hadn't been perfected. It still hasn't. The model the SEU were using was the Witness Protection Program of the U.S. marshals in the States, and that is one of the most criticized programs there. It's funny—the criticism comes not so much from the press, but from witnesses and other law enforcement agencies.

To protect me, the SEU assigned three-man details—one officer from each of the RCMP, the OPP, and the Metro Toronto Police—to each shift. I didn't go to the bathroom without their checking out the room first. If we weren't in a hotel room—and many of our meals were eaten there—I was on the road with SEU investigators, showing them where I had planted bombs, where I had dynamite and blasting caps buried, and where biker hangouts and other crime centres were located.

In early June stories were breaking in Canada and the United States about the plot to murder Helen Nafpliotis in Connecticut and the Volpe murder plot. The stories centred around attempts by the Canadian government to extradite Vincent Melia and Gerald Russo to stand trial for conspiracy to commit murder. One of the FBI agents, John Schiman, testified in federal court in Bridgeport, Connecticut, that the FBI had staged the abduction of Nafpliotis to make it appear as though she'd been kidnapped and murdered. He said he'd worked with me as I gathered evidence on the case and collected money for the planned murder.

"He was suave," Schiman testified. "He knew what he was doing. He was the best source I have ever seen. He knew how to handle underworld figures." As I read the story, I remember thinking, "Yeah, but how do you handle living like this?"

It was so confining that after one month I slipped out of my hotel room one night and went to the Beverly Hills Hotel for a couple of beers with an old friend. I was gone most of that night. I stayed at the home of a friend who worked for a catering company. The next day everyone, including Murphy, came down on me like a ton of bricks for my stupidity.

June 12, 1981, was another day of jangling nerves — a day I wanted to shout and kick and yell about being constantly surrounded by dozens of noticeably nervous plain-clothes men. It was the day I had to appear in county court with Linda Cadwell, my ex-girlfriend, and Alan Stewart to plead guilty to charges of breaking into a home in Toronto in 1979. The court looked like an armed camp. Everyone was checked, and the security people covering me had me so tightly guarded, it would have taken a team of commandos to penetrate the protection and reach me.

The charges against me stemmed from a planned gun theft from a gun collector Stewart had told me about. Stewart had said he had a key to the place, the collector would be gone, and it would be a simple matter for us to get into the house and steal the guns. He had estimated that there were forty to sixty handguns in there, guns I could sell to the Commissos and others. But the collection was gone when we broke in. Stewart didn't have the key, and all we found were five antique guns that couldn't fire bullets.

Sgt. Lyle McCharles of the OPP testified that my life was in danger. "I've received reliable information," he testified, "that a $100,000 contract has been placed on Kirby's life." Crown attorney Howard Morton told Justice Lloyd Graburn that my work as a police operative had resulted "in laying fourteen very serious criminal charges. My submission of sentence is he ought not to receive a jail term. It's not a submission the Crown takes lightly." As I listened, I found myself wondering what Morton would be saying if Murphy hadn't made them come up with the agreement that we had all signed.

Graburn didn't pass sentence that day, but on June 14, noting my previous convictions for assault, drug dealing, and theft, he placed me on probation for two years with the "special condition" that I testify in court when subpoenaed by the Crown. Linda and Stewart got suspended sentences of twelve and eighteen months. At the same time the Commissos were being held without bail by the Ontario Supreme Court on charges of conspiracy to murder Volpe, Scarcella, and Nafpliotis.

But my walking away from my security detail earlier and arguments I'd had with some of the investigators upset and embarrassed some people in the details, who decided to put me in a squeeze play without telling the Crown prosecutors or Murphy. One of them, who is now a friend of mine, told other investigators that "we have to get a hammer to Kirby's head to make him testify."

The hammer they tried to use was Linda Cadwell, who was my girlfriend between 1978 and 1981 and who was being provided protection and secret living quarters. Her whereabouts were a secret to those who wanted to use her to get at me. Somehow, through some finagling with police in charge of her protection, they located her in mid-July. They sent me out with Murphy on a wild goose chase and then interviewed Linda for hours in an attempt to get her to give them some evidence they could use to keep me in line.

When we returned to the hotel, I asked Murphy to call Linda so that I could talk to her, as I often did to make sure she was all right. He placed the call and then put me on the phone. When she told me about the visit by the two investigators and what they had tried to do, I went wild. I turned on Murphy like a cornered tiger and began shouting. "So that's the way you fuckers keep your word!" I shouted. "You're trying to put me in jail, you bastards!"

"What the hell are you talking about?" he roared.

"I'm talking about two of this fuckin' outfit's flunkies going to Linda and trying to get her to testify against me, that's what!" I shouted back. "After all I've done—after all the risks I've taken, some people are still looking to shaft me. Hey, go to hell. Take this whole fuckin' thing and shove it. I'm getting out. I'll take my chances on the street alone."

I thought Murphy was going to go into orbit then and there. For two hours or more he tried to cool me down. I wanted to go out and get the two guys who Linda said had talked to her and take care of them myself in my own way. Luckily Murphy talked me out of that. But I told the detail that I was going to see Linda whether they came with me or not. They came with me and stayed in another room while we had a hell of an argument. I found out she had lied to me about the two police officers trying to make her talk about me. She was nothing but a troublemaker. I finally belted her in the mouth.

Reporters later made it appear that I was in a jealous rage. One tried to have my security guards and the attorney general publicly roasted for not arresting me for violation of probation for hitting Linda. He didn't know the truth, and he didn't try to get at the truth. He just wanted headlines, and he got them when he broke the story in November 1981. Linda never pressed charges. I admit I hit her. But she'd been drinking, and she said I was fooling around with other women, and she said she was going to make life miserable for me. I lost my temper and knocked out one of her teeth and cracked another.

My nerves were razor-thin, and I was walking on the edge. There were nights when I went to bed hoping I wouldn't wake up. There were other nights when I seriously thought about killing myself or getting myself killed by going after some of those I knew wanted to do me. Depression is a constant companion and enemy when you're an informer and a witness. You don't think too highly of yourself. You've cut yourself off from the people you know and the world you've lived in to enter a different world with people who don't respect you, don't like you, even hate your guts. I had nothing in common with any of those on my security details or in the Crown prosecutor's office. I was a means to an end for them, and they were my ticket to survival.

After the Cadwell incident the strings that were binding me were loosened somewhat, and I managed to get along better with many of the men on the details. They were really decent guys doing a tough job, trying to protect a guy who just couldn't handle that kind of confinement. Murphy, meanwhile, never let up on providing me with the best security possible — not just physical protection but also street intelligence. And one of his sources was Paul Volpe.

On July 29 Murphy met with Volpe secretly, and the old man provided him with information about those behind the contract to kill him. It was his belief, and he had ways of getting information, that some former partners of his in real estate both in Toronto and in Atlantic City were behind the hit order. The motive was greed, pure and simple — more than $2 million collected in a sale and millions more that Volpe was laundering through land transactions.

The former partners wanted it all, or so Volpe thought, and they arranged to go to see the right people, offer them a piece of the action, and convince them that with Volpe out of the way, everyone would make more money in Toronto and Atlantic City. But there was a hitch. The partners went with Michele Commisso to see someone in the Buffalo Magaddino mob for approval. The partners, Murphy found out later, had been stopped at the border by immigration. Michele got across to talk to the mob people and apparently got the okay. Volpe's information may have been good, but I had sources who said it was Vincent Cotroni in Montreal who gave the final approval. I'm convinced that information was good.

Volpe was also convinced that with a little pressure from the coppers, one of the former partners would roll over and begin talking. And if he talked, he could bring down a lot of high-level people in organized crime. To this day no one ever went to talk to that guy that I know of, and nothing was ever done to develop Volpe as an informer. In fact, Volpe was never given official RCMP informer status, although he remained Murphy's confidential informant with the code number 0-1943.

"They blew a hell of an opportunity," Murphy said later. "With a little work, Volpe could have been the most important informer in mob history." The attitude of the government, and particularly of the RCMP, was that Volpe was trying to use the RCMP to escape some charges he was facing. The truth is, Volpe was probably looking for a way out. He knew his days were numbered, just like I did, and he was searching for a way out. By turning him down, the knuckleheads who make these decisions blew the biggest source of information on organized crime in Canada. He could also have provided them with a warehouse full of information on the United States, on international mob plots, and on casinos from Haiti and Cuba to Atlantic City and Las Vegas. It's amazing to me how short-sighted and jealous people get in law enforcement. That's why the mobs are always ahead.

Volpe predicted there would be no trial on the murder conspiracies. "The Commissos and their friends are going to plead guilty," he told Murphy. "They don't want this to go to trial."

Murphy said that Volpe was grateful to me for helping save his life. He wanted to help, and to show his good faith, he told Murphy he had heard that there were a lot of bikers in Canada, particularly Toronto, who were hot to kill me. He promised Murphy to do "what I can" to cool off the bikers through his underworld contacts. Murphy said he kept his promise, and many of the bikers who were actively hunting me turned their attention to other things.

As Volpe predicted, the three Commisso brothers and Antonio Romeo plea-bargained with Crown attorneys. Rather than face trials for conspiracy to murder Volpe, Scarcella, and Nafpliotis, the four of them pleaded guilty in return for a guarantee of less than maximum jail terms. The Crown went for the deal because it would eliminate costly trials that they could not be certain would be decided in their favour.

Remo and Cosimo got eight years each, but they were going to face considerably more time in jail on charges relating to other crimes they hired me to commit. The charges in those cases would be based on my recordings of their admissions on the covert tapes as well as recordings I made of others who admitted they had paid the Commissos to hire me to bomb and torch buildings for them. Antonio Romeo and Michele Commisso got just two and a half years because they were more message carriers than actual plotters.

A couple of months passed before Volpe touched my life again.

This time I was technically no longer under Murphy's protective wing, but under that of the SEU and Cpl. Ted Bean of the OPP Nevertheless, the message from Volpe went to Murphy, and it probably saved my life and that of my security detail, including Corporal Bean. On October 6, 1981, believing Murphy was still protecting me, Volpe called Murphy to tell him that the security detail protecting me had been spotted by some members of Satan's Choice.

"They spotted your friend Kirby and his three security guards in Aurora," Volpe told Murphy. "They're going to kill him and the guards."

Murphy was between a rock and a hard place when he got that call. He couldn't tell anyone that his tipster was Volpe, and the people on the security detail would want to know where the information came from in order to judge how reliable it was. Murphy told me in confidence that the bikers had found out that I was staying at the hotel, where I was holed up with security agents, and that they were going to kill all of us.

"We've got to figure out a way to move you and the detail," he said. "And we have to do it without telling anybody that we know who tipped us."

I had no patience for the politics of the moment, and I didn't have to worry about the chain of command the way Murphy did. I called one of the detail supervising sergeants and told him. "The wrong people know I'm here," I said.

He didn't believe me, and he refused to order the detail to move me. "It's just another street rumour," he said. "More bullshit. You stay put."

That ticked me off. I didn't waste any time. I did the only thing I could do at that moment to save our necks. I walked into the security detail's room, picked up the telephone, and called my dad.

"Dad," I said loud enough for everyone to hear me, "I just want you to know where I'm at before something happens. I'm here in Aurora, at the hotel."

The security agents stood there, dumbfounded. "Jesus Christ," one of them yelled, "you've just blown our security!"

"Good," I said. "I'll just take a taxi and get the hell outta here." And that was just what I did. It was the only way for me to get out of the area and get the detail moved in time before something happened, before the bikers came and killed them and me.

I had to figure a way out without blowing Volpe as the source, and that was it. So I took off. I returned to the security detail about a week or more later. They were having fits, and Inspector McIlvenna wanted to have me thrown in jail as a material witness until he was told he didn't have that right unless I failed to answer a subpoena or appear in court, something I never did.

Murphy told his bosses about the Volpe warning and that Volpe had also offered to turn over, no strings attached, information and evidence on an international Korean terrorist organization in Toronto. But they didn't want to hear about it. They told Murphy he couldn't accept any information from Volpe and ordered him to cut off all further communication with him.

Talk about short-sighted people. Anytime you can get information like that from someone of Volpe's stature, you grab it. Volpe could have buried a lot of people. Instead nothing was done, and Volpe was later killed before he could tell what he knew. I guess Murphy's bosses were afraid that Volpe would use the RCMP and that they'd get criticized for dealing with someone like him, but the law in the United States has dealt with bigger guys than that to get testimony in major Mafia cases.

It was maybe a week after Volpe saved my life with his tip that I decided to see him. I told Murphy what I wanted to do.

"Have you lost your mind?" he asked.

"I don't think so," I said. "I want to see him. I want to thank him for what he did."

"You could be killed. You could get your head blown off."

"I'll take that chance."

Without another word I left the place where I was in hiding from the bikers, the mob, and my own security detail and drove off in my car to Fox Hill, the Nobleton home of Paul Volpe.

It was impressive. Behind the giant iron gates at the driveway entrance was an almost palatial home, like that of some English squire or Lord. A castle-like turret with a pointed, circular, domed room was the centrepiece of a giant two-storey home. The house had once belonged to a retired judge from Toronto. I forget what Volpe paid for it, but it was worth hundreds of thousands of dollars then and maybe a million or more now. In the back was a big pool, two tennis courts a little farther back, overhead floodlights, and some guard dogs.

Volpe wasn't home when I arrived, but his wife was, and she answered the door. I showed her my identification and asked to see Volpe. He wasn't home, she said, but he would be back by 5 P.M. I told her I'd come back. I returned on schedule. Volpe was there waiting, and we met, for the first time, at the door. I showed him my driver's licence and assured him that I was by myself and unarmed.

"Come on in," he said with a friendly smile. He was a tall man, maybe a little over six feet, bald, with sad eyes. He wasn't muscular or as strong as I was, but he wasn't in bad shape either. He could probably have handled himself pretty well if he had to, even at his age, which was about fifty-four then. He pointed ahead of me and said, "Come on downstairs where we can talk."

As I followed his directions, we walked through his living room into a kitchen with a long counter and a kitchen table off to the side. Off the kitchen was a staircase leading down to the recreation room on the lower level.

As I walked down the stairs, Volpe's damned dog bit me on the back of the leg, almost sending me sprawling into the rec room. He was a mongrel, part German shepherd, part who knows what, named Caesar. I wanted to kick that bloody mutt in the teeth, but I held my mouth and my foot as Volpe called the dog off and mildly scolded him. I was taken aback by the view of the rear yard through the huge glass windows and doors—the pool, the lush landscaping, the tennis courts. Over to the side of the rec room was a small bar with a cappuccino machine on it.

"Can I get you a cappuccino?" Volpe asked. I shook my head. "How about some food? A steak maybe," he said with a smile, pointing to his nephew, Anthony, whom I'd seen up in the kitchen, cooking.

"No, thank you," I said. "I'm not hungry."

Without another word I opened up by briefcase so he could see it was clean, with no tapes or bugs.

"Look, Paul, I got no tape," I said. "I just came here to thank you for helping me the other day." I opened my jacket so he could see there was nothing hidden there either. "There's nothing—no transmitters, no tapes, no nothing."

He nodded with a broad smile on his face. "Okay, Cecil," he said. "I believe you."

He was warm and friendly and interested. He smoked heavily, holding the cigarettes between two fingers as he drew long pulls of smoke into his lungs and watched the thin, blue smoke curl out into the air in front of him as he exhaled it. I felt like choking every time he took a long puff like that. He had a rather gravelly voice, but he was attentive to what I had to say. I got a feeling of real sincerity when he talked, and his eyes were soft, sometimes a little animated, but never cold as we sat there. There wasn't the slightest hint of an Italian accent when he spoke, and I guess there shouldn't have been, since he was born in Canada.

"Do the cops know you're here?" he asked.

I shook my head. "Nope, just Murphy," I answered. "He's the only one who knew I was coming to see you."

"Okay," he said. "I want your word that you're not going to give me up. I don't need that kind of trouble."

"You've got my word," I said. "Nobody's gonna know we met or talked." And nobody did until after he was killed. Funny, everybody had something bad to say about the poor bastard after he was killed. I can only say good things about the man I met that day. He was a man, and he talked straight — no bullshit.

"I want to thank you for saving my life," I said. "You saved the life of some cops as well, but they don't know it. Probably never will."

We started talking about the case a bit and about the characters involved.

"I can't understand why they [the Commissos] would want to kill me," he said. "You know what jail they are in?"

"Kingston," I said.

He grinned, those sad eyes sort of twinkling as he spoke. "Got a lot of friends in there." He continued smiling and said nothing else about the Commissos — nothing like "I'm gonna get them," or "They're going to have an accident."

"You know, when I found out you had been here, I had you checked out with Chuck," he said. "He really has a high regard for you. He says you're a very capable person."

"The truth is, I don't like Yanover," I said, looking Volpe squarely in the eyes. "I don't trust him, and if I were you, I wouldn't trust him either. He set up one of his friends with my ex-girlfriend."

Volpe waved his hands, brushing aside the discussion. "It's foolish to argue about women, to have hard feelings over women," he said. "They aren't that important."

Volpe turned the subject away from Yanover and toward my future. "Why don't you walk away from testifying and being a police operative?" he asked. "If you want, I can get you a job down in my casino in the islands. You can stay there for a couple of years, work there for me and come back, and I guarantee nobody I deal with is gonna bother you. Of course I can't guarantee the bikers. I have little influence with them."

Volpe didn't say what casino he was talking about or exactly where it was located, and I didn't ask. It was supposed to be in the Bahamas, but he didn't identify it. I knew he and his brother had operated a casino in Haiti at one time and in other parts of the Caribbean and the Mediterranean as well, but I had no way of knowing which casino he was talking about other than that it was somewhere in the Bahamas. I just thanked him and said I'd think about it.

I did ask him if there was some way he could lend me a couple of thousand dollars. "I'll pay it back as soon as I can," I said. "You can go to the bank with that."

"I'll have to talk to my lawyer about it, Cec," he said. "Come back in about a week or so — about 8 A.M."

I gave him a number where he could call and leave a message for me without worrying about the cops. Then I thanked him and promised to see him the following week.

When I returned, we went once again to his rec room, and for a second time that lousy dog of his nipped my ankle. I felt like kicking the fucker through the glass window, but I restrained myself. Volpe wacked him lightly on the fanny and sent him off to another side of the room, where he lay staring at me. I could see in that dog's eyes that I was dead meat if I ever made a move toward Volpe. For some reason that damned dog hated me from the start, and I hated him.

"I haven't been able to talk to my lawyer about that loan yet," he said, "but I will. I'll have an answer for you next week for sure. Incidentally, I told Peter Scarcella about your being at the house. I'm expecting him here later today."

Now I didn't feel too great hearing that. Scarcella, I was convinced, had sold out to the Commissos to save his own skin. They had said as much in taped conversations with me. I thought to myself, "That's not the kind of guy you should trust, Volpe, not at all." I sure as hell didn't trust him, and I didn't want to be around Volpe's house if Scarcella knew I was there.

Just then the telephone rang. It was Scarcella. When Volpe was through talking to him, he turned to me and said, "I told Peter that I had an old friend of his here visiting with me. I told him I wanted him to meet you. It's a shame. Peter said he couldn't come. He has a touch of the flu." There was a strange smirk on his face when he said that. I wanted to say something, but I bit my tongue. Instead I said goodbye and promised to see him again the following week.

Our third meeting took place outside his garage. That fuckin' Caesar was by his side again as I got out of the car, and again he went for my leg. Volpe called him off. "I'm afraid Caesar doesn't like you," Volpe said with a chuckle.

I didn't think it was too funny, but I didn't say anything. "Talk to your lawyer yet?" I asked.

Volpe nodded. "I'm afraid he's advised me not to give you any money while you're still working for the police," he said. "It could cause a lot of problems. I'm sorry, Cec, but I don't want the cops on my back, and they'd be on my back if they knew I was lending you money."

"I understand," I said. "Don't worry about it. Nobody's gonna know we talked. I appreciate what you've done and what you tried to do."

It was months later, in March 1982, that I heard that the Luppino crime family had issued a contract to kill Volpe. Murphy had been tipped, and he had asked his bosses for permission to talk to Volpe, warn him, and see if he could convince him to roll over and become an informer. The RCMP had turned thumbs down on his request. Instead he'd been told not to speak to Volpe or have any further contact with him.

On November 14, 1983, I flew into Toronto International Airport to meet with some security people about a case that was pending. The airport was swarming with cops. At 2:40 P.M. that day the cops had found Volpe's body stuffed in the trunk of his wife's BMW in the Terminal 2 parking garage. He'd been shot in the back of the head.

Who did Volpe in? I can't be positive, but I had good information from a source of mine that Vincent Cotroni had ordered the hit after sending his brother, Frank, to Toronto to meet with a lot of Volpe's friends and enemies.

Frank Cotroni was facing heroin-smuggling charges in Connecticut, interestingly enough, in September 1983, just two short months before Volpe bought it. I was told that he had met with Johnny (Pops) Papalia and an old Sicilian Mafia boss who was wanted by the Italian government on narcotics charges. A good source also told me that a Montreal assassin and friend of Cotroni's was at that meeting. He was supposed to be in Toronto around the time Volpe's body was found. He was arrested on some homicide charges in another case and, I was told, was questioned about the Volpe hit. He refused to talk to the cops about it because the Cotronis had been so close to him, like family.

They had decided at the meeting that Volpe had to go. It was embarrassing to the Calabrian Mafia. Here he'd been set up for a hit in 1981, and two years later he was still walking around, telling people what to do, running gambling in Toronto, making millions in real estate in New Jersey and Ontario, collecting from casinos around the world, and running big loan-shark rackets. It's probably true that he was living in fear behind the floodlights of his home, certain someone would carry out the contract that started when the Commissos tried to have me do the job. But he was still in business, still a boss, and this was embarrassing.

I found it interesting that on December 10, 1983, less than a month after Volpe was knocked off, four guys gunned down Domenic Racco, the son of the old Calabrian don, Michele Racco. Now that couldn't have been done without approval from some Calabrian Mafia bosses, but none of the four who were arrested and convicted in the case ever said who was behind it, and the Commissos were behind bars. Being in jail, of course, never stopped a boss from running his business, and the Commissos were no exception.

One of the last people to see Volpe alive was his good friend Scarcella. He was the guy the Commissos had wanted me to kill but then changed their minds about because he had made a deal with them. Scarcella told the coppers that he'd had coffee with Volpe the morning of November 13, 1983, the last day Volpe was seen alive. Volpe had told his wife that he was going to meet someone at the airport. That's where they found him, at the airport, in the trunk of the car. For anyone to get a crime leader like Volpe in that manner required some planning and the help of someone he trusted. I've always thought I knew who that trusted Volpe friend was who set him up. What I am certain of is that with the killing of Volpe and Racco, the Commisso crime group became one of the most powerful of all the Calabrian groups in Canada and the United States.

CHAPTER
21

RUN, STOOLIE, RUN

When I broke away from my security detail in October 1981, I was frustrated, bored, and upset. I'd be a liar if I said I wasn't worried when I learned that the bikers knew where I was staying with the security men.

I was concerned about my life and the lives of the men protecting me. I knew bikers. I knew them better than any security supervisor at the SEU or the RCMP did. When Volpe told Murphy that the bikers were coming to the hotel in Aurora to kill all of us, I knew that was just what the Satan's Choice would do. They'd have no hesitation about blowing me away and anyone who was with me. Since I couldn't tell the detail who had tipped me, blowing the location was the only choice I felt I had left. I wanted no one killed, least of all myself.

I want to make it clear, in unmistakable terms, that the men who provided me with protection during those tension-packed years that I was a witness were really super guys. They were all different—guys that came and went—and I barely got to know them the way I would have liked to. Not all of them were lovable or even likable, and a few of them didn't like the idea of protecting a criminal like myself, but 99 per cent of them were super guys with a lot of guts. You had to have guts to be on a detail like that.

I think most of them tried their damnedest to make life a little easier for me. They lived in a room next to me, and tension was always present, as was danger. Every move had to be thought out and planned, and wherever we went, whether it was to a court proceeding or to an interview, the men of the security detail preceded me and stood in front of me. If assassins had been waiting and started shooting, many of my protectors, most of them family men, would have fallen first, attempting to save my life.

There were some light moments. When I wanted to go jogging, one or more of them would jog with me, while others followed in special unmarked vehicles. The joggers had a hard time keeping up with me because I was in better shape and used to jogging. I'd often kid them about what lousy shape they were in when they ended the jog, huffing and puffing like old men.

We played cards together and pool — anything to provide a relief from the tension that seemed to consume us in the boredom of waiting, always waiting. One of the team members, a young guy named Byron, was a pool shark. He beat the hell out of anyone he played at pool — me, the detail, anyone who challenged him. He really made the pool cue talk.

At times we left the city to go to a place for a quiet drink. One location I remember vividly and enjoyed the most was a small island about three hundred miles north of Toronto. We spent two weeks there just to relieve the tension and relax. It was a fantastic place to fish, exercise, and just plain talk.

The details were always heavily armed, alert, and damned well trained in the use of all types of firearms. If we decided to go somewhere, they checked it out thoroughly before they would let me go near the place. They would also spend hours talking with me, picking my brain about people who might be looking for me, who might want to kill me. What did they look like? What kind of weapons would they use? Who were their friends? And where were their hangouts? The questions seemed endless, yet they were all posed to provide them with the information to protect me and the details from a surprise assault by assassins.

They had photographs of Ken Goobie, a dozen or more bikers, Calabrian mafiosi, Rounders — every type of criminal who I felt and they felt was a serious threat to my life.

I was convinced during that period — between 1981 and 1983 — that my most serious threat was from bikers, not the Calabrians. There were so damned many bikers all over Canada and in the United States that you never knew when you'd run into them. In August 1981 I was taken to Florida for three weeks for security reasons and to ease the tension. While we were there, I remember worrying the most about running into bikers — Outlaws, Hell's Angels, Pagans — who had connections with biker gangs in Canada. I was certain that pictures of me had been distributed to other gangs by the Satan's Choice and the Vagabonds.

I often told detail members that outlaw bikers were more likely to make a stupid open hit than Calabrian Mafia members, who were more conservative, more careful. The bikers were reckless, prone to be careless, and they didn't and still don't care who else might be killed in trying to get at me. There were a lot of agents, people like Murphy, Byron (the pool shark), Ted Bean, and Lyle McCharles, whose lives were in danger from bikers because they helped and protected me. I know that Murphy was threatened. He had to take precautions not only for himself but also for his family. He had to live on the edge for a long, long time. So did some others.

Bikers are persistent if nothing else. I remember one ex-member of the St. Catharines Outlaws, a guy named Jimmy, who gave me real trouble before I became a witness. He and another guy they called Gypsy had threatened to blow my head off. I caught up with Jimmy in a gym one day and beat the hell out of him. He couldn't open his eyes for a week. In fact, he had to use a seeing-eye dog to get around.

The trouble was over Linda Cadwell. Linda and I had split up for a while. We had an on-again, off-again love affair that was often violent. We split up often and made up often. Anyhow, they tried to make a move on her. I told them to keep away from her. One night they figured the best way to get rid of me was to lie in ambush outside her house with shotguns, waiting for me to come to the door so they could blow me away. I didn't show up, but not because I was tipped. I wasn't. It was only luck that they didn't nail me at the ambush. When I heard about it, I was very concerned.

First I went to the St. Catharines Outlaws and told them that I wanted these two guys. I made it clear I was going to get them. The Outlaws didn't care. Both Jimmy and Gypsy had broken with the gang and were on their own. I'm certain that even if they had still been members, the Outlaws would have helped me get them because I was a road captain and vice-president of Satan's Choice at the time. The St. Catharines Outlaws were all good friends of the Choice and of the Italian mob in Niagara Falls. They bought and sold dope provided by the Italian mob. Heroin was going to insiders for $2,000 an ounce pure. The cops never understood that relationship in the seventies. They couldn't believe that bikers and the Italian mob would work together like that.

With the okay of the Outlaws, I went hunting for Gypsy, but I couldn't get him away from his house. One night, at five in the morning, I went by and let all the air out of two of the tires of his car. I figured I'd get him while he was changing the tires. His wife came out instead, got in the car, and didn't realize she had flat tires until she got halfway down the street. She pulled into a gas station and had them fixed. Later I watched her walk back to the house. Gypsy came out, went to another car, and then to the gas station. He then came walking back and stopped a truck right across the street from me.

"Come on over here!" I shouted. "Come across the street and talk to me like a man."

"No way, Cec," he said. "I'm not coming to you — you come here."

I had a gun. I always had a gun taped to me, but we were in the open. There were too many witnesses. "I'll see you some other time, Gypsy," I said. "Count on it."

Gypsy was about six feet two, weighed about 220 pounds, and towered over me. When I finally cornered him in the gym and tried to wrestle with him, I had a little trouble with him at first. He didn't want to fight. But I broke loose and gave him a hellava beating. He was bloodied, and I got my pleasure beating his face in. I told him if I ever heard him mouthing off about me or making a move on Linda again, I was going to come back and kick his head in.

Linda was a problem for the security detail, mainly because of me. Being shut up with three men or in a room by myself drove me up a wall, and there were times I felt I had to see her, despite our fights. Occasionally they arranged for meetings between Linda and me when we weren't fighting. After she'd leave, we would always pick up and move to a new location. They didn't trust her and for good reason, although for a long time I didn't agree with them. I had to be hit with a hammer quite a few times before I realized I couldn't trust her.

Our relationship came to a head on October 28, 1981, when Linda tried to set me up — tried to have a young kid shoot me. One night she called, half drunk, said she was at a local Toronto bar, and asked me to go to her apartment to make sure her daughter was all right. I told her I'd take a taxi and be there before she was. I went up to her apartment, knocked on the door, and got no answer. I tried the door handle, and the door was open. There was a note on the floor, so I walked in. The note was from someone, I don't know who, but it read, "Your daughter is next door." So I sat there and waited.

It wasn't long before I saw a Chrysler pull up instead of a taxi, and out of the car stepped Ronald Ambrose, who was friendly with Linda and with her former husband. The car was that of lawyer Brian Jones. They came upstairs and rang the buzzer. I wasn't about to answer it. They left. About half an hour later Linda came stumbling up the stairs. She was drunk. She came into the room and for a moment didn't notice me standing there. Finally she saw me. "Where's Lisa?" she asked.

"Next door," I snapped.

She stumbled out of the room to get the kid and put her to bed. As she left, I noticed a forty-ounce bottle of wine on the table. I took it off the table and hid it. When she returned, she noticed it was gone and began screaming at the top of her lungs, "My wine! Where's my bottle of wine?"

"I hid it," I said. "You've had enough for one night."

The phone rang and it was Jones, her lawyer. I grabbed the phone and told him to screw off. A minute later Ambrose phoned. She answered, and all I could hear her say was, "Yeah, come on over." Then she turned to me with a sneer on her face and said, "You know who's coming here? You better take off. He might have a gun."

Ambrose lived in an apartment across the street, and I could see him come running across and through the front door of her apartment building with a rifle. He started ringing the buzzer. I yelled at him, "Look, I saw you coming across with the gun!"

He yelled back, "Open the fuckin' door!"

I didn't answer. I went to the phone, called police, identified myself, and told them there was a man with a rifle standing in the hallway waiting to shoot me.

The cops got there fast, let me tell you. I was going to go out, but I decided I'd wait until I saw the cops there. I looked out the peephole, and there they were, wrestling this guy out in the hall. I opened the door, and suddenly the cops were throwing cuffs on me, telling me I was under arrest. They didn't say what for, but I went along, figuring it was to get everybody under control. The cops swarmed through the apartment, searching it. Linda was going nuts. She saw Ambrose in the hall being held by three cops. She wound up and hit one of the cops. Then she shouted, "Yeah, an' he [pointing at me] raped me!"

I looked at her and started to laugh. "You better come up with something better than that," I said. "You should have said that when they came in the door instead of dreaming it up now." She wanted me so bad she could taste it. She was willing to do anything, say anything, to get me.

One cop had the rifle. He stood there beside me, pulled the bolt open, and the bullet popped out. I looked at him and said, "That fuckin' bastard was gonna shoot me." The cop, who had been looking down the barrel of that gun when Ambrose pointed it at him, was upset. So were the other cops. They took the cuffs off me.

Ambrose was only twenty-four and a punk. But I'd have been out of my mind to go out to meet him without a gun. He was crazy enough to gun me down in the hallway for sure. His brother had been convicted in Nova Scotia for killing two RCMP officers. He'd made them dig their graves first, then shot them.

They charged Ambrose with pointing a loaded rifle at a policeman, and in April 1982 I was forced to testify in the case by his attorney, Michael Caroline. Ambrose's defence was that he'd acted because he thought Linda was in danger, and he believed I was a man above the law because of what the media said about me. Caroline, who later became my lawyer, asked me in court what I would do "if a man like yourself, Cecil Kirby, came at you with a gun." I answered, "I would have gone out and bought a bigger gun." Ambrose still got convicted and sentenced to six months in jail, but not before the newspapers tried to crucify me with the incident.

I never did figure out why one reporter went after me so hard in the press. In October 1981 I gave him an exclusive interview about the role Murphy had played in the Commisso investigation. I pointed out in the story that others were getting credit for work that Murphy should have gotten credit for. I thought the reporter, Peter Moon of the Toronto *Globe and Mail*, had done a good job on the story.

In November Ontario Attorney General Roy McMurtry asked the press to keep a lid on stories about me. The reason was that I had been asked by the Crown and the SEU to carry a body mike to gather additional evidence against businessmen who had hired me through the Commissos to commit arsons, bomb buildings, and extort money. The plan was to nail down more charges against the Commissos and against those who had gone to the Commissos to hire me.

The idea of hitting the streets again, gathering evidence, jolted me out of my depression. My adrenalin was flowing, and the excitement of the hunt gripped me. I was once again working with a team of top investigators, including Cpl. Danielle Bouchard of the OPP and SEU, who was going to pose as my girlfriend. But Murphy wasn't allowed to participate. He'd been transferred and admonished. He was later disciplined for standing by his promises to me in the face of orders to sink me by some of his superiors.

Most of those we approached and taped knew me only as "George." They did not put "George" together with Cecil Kirby, and since the Commissos were all in jail, they were unable to call Cosimo or Remo to check to see if I was still acting on their behalf.

Make no mistake. What we were doing — the investigators, myself, the security people — was dangerous. A slip of the tongue, a chance meeting with the wrong person, could have cost us our lives. And there was always the chance that one of them might have found out that "George" was Cecil or have made a successful effort to talk to Cosimo or Remo in jail about "George." If they had, I would have been dead.

For a while it worked fine, and I recorded admissions by a number of businessmen. Armando DiCapua, Bruno Spizzichino, and Rocco Mastrangelo admitted paying Cosimo to have me blow up their sporting goods store in Guelph. And I recorded admissions by Istvan Szocs, a real estate salesman who had gone to Cosimo in 1978 to get help collecting $15,000 that he'd said Cornwall developer Hugh Fitzpatrick owed him from a 1973 land deal. Szocs had paid me $200 to break Fitzpatrick's arms and legs and threaten his family. I never got to Fitzpatrick to break his bones, but I'd spent two weeks trying. Szocs claimed he never collected the $15,000.

There were other cases, and there could have been more except for the newspapers. For reasons I've never been able to figure out, they broke stories about the immunity and support agreement I had with the Crown and charges from Linda and her attorney that I had beaten her while my security guards stood quietly by in another room doing nothing.

The stories had an even more serious effect. They terminated the undercover investigation I was working on, endangering not only my life but also those of Corporal Bouchard and other investigators on the case. On February 8, 1982, we tried to tape admissions from another Commisso associate. All we got were denials and claims of total innocence. I got the strong feeling at that moment that this guy knew who I was. My role as an undercover agent was over.

The stories created an atmosphere that made it impossible for me to continue my work for the Crown. Metro Toronto Police Staff Insp. Donald Banks said that they carried "distortions of facts" that made my underworld connections "wary and on their guard. He was still making connections until the publicity made it impossible to continue." Banks headed the intelligence squad and had worked closely with the investigators from the time I started working on the Commissos.

McMurtry was furious, and he went public to attack the stories. He said that "irresponsible reporting" had undermined my effectiveness. He pointed out that until I had confessed under immunity, law enforcement in Canada had no evidence against me for the crimes I'd talked to them about. He defended the new agreement that the Crown had drawn up with me that provided me and my family with $1,950 per month in support plus my living and travel expenses. But he refused to disclose the terms of the agreement, and I have also been prohibited from disclosing them. If I disclose more than I've been required to in court, all bets are off — the Crown can walk away from me.

RCMP Chief Supt. Donald Heaton was also upset by the newspaper disclosures and said that police had known about the criminals I'd worked on for twenty years. He said that despite millions of dollars spent on investigations, no one had ever put them in jail. "For the first time ever we had someone [Kirby] on the inside . . . and they [organized-crime figures] were going to jail."

It was over—the street work, the recordings, the moments of exhilaration and anxiety, the excitement. All that remained now were the trials and the boredom.

If I had it to do over, I probably would never have become a witness. I certainly wouldn't recommend that other criminals follow my path. The reason is simple. Aside from the danger, the boredom, and the frustration that a witness faces, there are the threats to his family, the spiralling costs, a life spent constantly on the run without any stability, and the broken promises of the government.

When I first signed an agreement on April 7, 1981, the government promised me immunity from prosecution for past crimes. It also promised to provide physical protection for me and my family during the criminal proceedings, including all the trials. The agreement was revised on November 12, 1981. While it increased my expense allowances from about $700 a month to $1,960 plus $550 for rentals, it was still inadequate.

Reporters and the public read figures like that and say, "Hey, I could live on $32,000 a year–plus very nicely, thank you." Sure you could—if you didn't have to live in hotel rooms, if you weren't required to move almost every week, if you didn't have to eat in restaurants most of the time, and if you didn't have to fly or drive hundreds and thousands of miles in the course of a month. When you are on the run, when you live the life of a nomad not by choice, but by necessity, it's costly. I can't remember a week when I haven't been broke or the end of a month when all I've had left to buy food and other essentials wasn't less than five dollars.

It's a hell of an existence, a hellava way to live. Since those two agreements were signed, there have been a couple of updated agreements—each one narrowing the promises made by earlier agreements, each one making it tougher and tougher to exist.

There have been a lot of broken promises along the way. I've publicly challenged McMurtry for breaking his word. His answer was to deny me the help I wanted and then get bodyguards for his personal protection because he thought I was going to hurt him. That has to be the dumbest thing I've ever heard. I might be mad about the Crown's broken promises, but I'm not stupid enough to go after the Ontario attorney general.

The most important thing I wanted, more than the money I have requested, was a sense of security. I'm supposed to have a documented new identity. But what good is an identity if there is nothing in the history of that identity to show that you existed before 1981? Without a history, without something to show you went to school, without someone to verify that you were employed someplace, it's almost impossible to establish credit or get a job. Who's going to hire a man with no history? Dozens of times I've applied for jobs, and the employer was ready to hire me until I was unable to come up with that history that says you exist, you are, you've worked and lived somewhere and gone to school.

So it's do an odd job here, an odd job there — nothing with security, nothing with a future, nothing that lets you earn a solid salary. You can't establish roots that way. You can't move into a community and try to buy a home if you have no background, no money to put down on a house, no steady job to pay the mortgage and the taxes and all the other bills that a man has to pay.

There should be some job training, something that would prepare me to work in something I haven't done before. I can't drive trucks cross-country with bikers and the Calabrian Mafia hunting me. I was promised job training, but the promises turned out to be empty. The government hasn't made the slightest attempt to train me to earn a living.

I don't want to live from government cheque to government cheque. Too often they let you hang, waiting for that cheque that comes a week, two weeks, a month late. You call, you protest, your attorney does the same, and everyone ignores you. They don't need you any more. They've got their big convictions; now they don't want to know you or live up to their word, their agreements.

Since May 1981 it's been hell on my family, particularly my father. From the beginning, when my name first hit print, he received threatening phone calls. The RCMP put a tap on his line to find out who was making the threats, but they got nowhere. Their answer to the problem was to tell him to sell his house, to move. When he did move, he lost $20,000 on the sale, and the RCMP provided him with only $500 for moving costs. All told, he's had to move nearly a dozen times, and the government's never provided him with more moving costs — just $500 for all those moves. It costs that much and more to move all your belongings to a new location just once.

When I began taping the Commissos, not only did the RCMP never supply a car, but there were also times when I wouldn't have enough money for gas. They didn't give Murphy money, and I didn't get it either. They just insisted that I continue using the car the Commissos were familiar with, my father's Chevrolet. It was only three years old then, practically new, with very little mileage on it. Once the Commisso investigations ended, the car was stripped of its electronic listening devices and returned to my father. There was no attempt to replace it, pay for the maintenance, or paint it a different colour. That caused him problems. One evening two guys with full beards smashed into the rear of his Chevy and tried to force him off the road. They were bikers who had recognized the car and were trying to get at me through him. The car had to be sold later at a loss.

In December 1982 a guy with a high-powered rifle shot up my father's truck at my brother's cottage at Wasaga Beach. The bullet went through the tailgate, a steel box in the back of the truck, and into the cabin, where it hit a steel jack behind the seat. It then cut through the seat and slammed through the glove compartment before finally stopping at the engine fire wall. Police found it was an armour-piercing, .303 rifle slug. An hour before that someone had shot at my uncle's house two or three miles away in Wasaga Beach. The bullet had gone through the front door and whistled over his head while he was sleeping in bed. The papers reported it, the police investigated, but nothing happened. Nobody was ever arrested.

You would think that after the shooting police would have driven up and down the street a couple of times at night or sat out in front of the homes of my brother and my uncle for maybe half an hour. No such luck. Nobody provided protection or even offered to.

In March 1982 my brother, Mark, was arrested for selling a small quantity of marijuana to an undercover detective. Mark shouldn't have been fooling with drugs, but he was all screwed up at the time. He had to fight his way in and out of bars as every biker tried to take him on. I appealed to the judge in the case, County Court Judge Donald Thompson, not to send my kid brother to jail. I told him it could cost the kid his life, that prisoners associated with the bikers or the Calabrian Mafia could kill him in prison. Judge Thompson didn't listen. He said it was up to jail authorities to make sure my brother was safe. Then he sent Mark to jail for ninety days. That Mark survived without harm was a matter of luck. It wasn't because the Crown or the courts took any special precautions for him.

While I was testifying against the Commissos and others, the government didn't provide any protection for my mother or father, and both were constantly subjected to threatening calls. Almost every weekend my mother would get calls from some biker or some biker's broad, threatening her. They were messages to me, really. They were telling me, "Here's trouble for you, informer — and there's more to come. Here's how easy it is to get at your family if we want you." It was hell on both my parents. It still is.

In addition to the threats, there have been endless attempts by bikers and the Commissos to frame me, to discredit me as a witness by attempting to show I was a liar or had committed crimes after signing my agreement. Anthony Speciale is a typical example.

I first met Tony through Ken Goobie. At the time he was on the run for shooting someone. Until I told police about the incident, they weren't aware that Tony was involved in the shooting. He was pretty wild. He'd rather shoot you than fight you, and he always carried a .38 snub-nose revolver on him for protection or murder. I remember one night we all were returning to Toronto from a nearby town when we got stopped in a radar trap. The cop was walking over to our car when Tony, who was sitting in the back, reached for his gun.

"Jesus Christ, Tony," I said, "leave that fuckin' gun right there and don't say a word. Just let the cop give us the ticket, and we'll leave."

He had a real cruel smile on his face, half sneer, half smile, and there was a kind of faraway glint in his eyes. He'd been ready to blow that cop away until I said something.

Tony had a long record. He had gone to jail for assault, car theft, B and E, robbery, and wounding, but in 1978 he hit the heights. He got life imprisonment for killing three people, including a Rounder named Stan Norman. Norman begged for his life, but Tony just shot him through the head. Then he shot Norman's girl, Diane. Norman was shot twice and lay there hearing Tony reload the gun to shoot her again. Somehow she survived to tell her story.

Now I had been with Tony that day just before the killings

started. He was with me waiting for a guy, a courier, whom we were supposed to rob. We waited a few hours, the target never came out, and we left the area. I dropped Tony off at some girl's place in Mississauga. The next day I saw the Sunday paper, and splashed across the front page was the story of Tony and the shootings.

Tony went to jail for the murders. He got life. While he was in jail, he came into contact with Cosimo Commisso. In March 1984, while he was serving time in the same jail with Cosimo, Tony tried to implicate me in the Norman murder. He charged that I was with him when he killed Norman. Luckily I was able to prove that I wasn't, but it was clearly an attempt by Cosimo to destroy me as a witness.

Cosimo had tried that before. In September 1982 he got Richard Cucman to claim that I had ripped him off, taken $140,000 in jewellery that he and Nicolino Pallotta had stolen from the Dolly Jewellers, fenced it, and kept the money for myself. It was a lie, of course. I'd tipped Murphy off about the jewellery and the fact that they'd handled the robbery.

Then there was Satan's Choice biker Joe Ertel of Kitchener. Ertel has a long record of convictions for robbery, assault, trafficking in drugs, and possession of stolen property. With a record like that and a hatred for cops, he still hated me more. He charged that I had murdered another biker named Duke Coons. I was questioned by Crown prosecutors in the case, and I told them I knew nothing about the homicide. I took a lie detector test to prove I had nothing to hide and passed it.

Today I'm still on the run, still looking for a hole I can crawl into and hide and survive in. Canada's a big country, but it may not be big enough. Wherever I've gone, I haven't been able to stay long because I was unable to get a job, unable to obtain credit, and unable to show a history of employment.

For several years the government was concerned. I was important to them in 1981 and through the trials that led to the conviction of more than fourteen criminals. They were people who'd burned down hotels, people who'd wanted to extort money, so-called respectable people who'd wanted other peoples' legs and arms broken. I was important because the government needed me to crack the Calabrian Mafia and put away their leaders, people like the Commisso brothers and Vincent Melia, who's now free after serving only three years of a nine-year jail term for paying to have Helen Nafpliotis killed. I was important because they wanted my intelligence information, my tips—tips that led to major drug busts, to the arrests of gamblers and jewel thieves, to biker crimes, and to Calabrian Mafia plans for murder.

But now all that's over. Prosecutors can no longer make headlines and further their political careers on sensational disclosures from Cecil Kirby. They can no longer win press attention by duelling with prominent defence lawyers who try unsuccessfully to discredit me as a witness. They are content with their press notices; some have new and lucrative jobs outside government that resulted from their "handling" of Cecil Kirby. So what happens to Cecil Kirby is no longer of concern to them. If members of the Outlaws find out where Kirby's living, as they did in 1985, don't bother telling him. He's finished testifying, and it's not our responsibility to keep him alive forever.

In truth, the only ones who care are a few dedicated cops — members and former members of the SEU who, after doing their jobs, were returned to their units with the RCMP, the OPP, or Metro Toronto Police. They've tried to help in many ways. But what they've done, they've done on their own, out of a sense of responsibility and decency.

I don't mind saying one bit that I'm bitter. I'm no angel; I've never pretended to be. I was a hardened criminal. But I've tried to follow a new path, keep within the law. However, the bureaucrats who run this nation don't make it easy. If I survive, it won't be because they helped or kept their word. It'll be because I kept my wits and my instincts keen.

In the end they and the public will be the losers. For while I've kept my word and done all I was asked to do, there won't be any other Cecil Kirbys willing to come forward and deal with governments who fail to keep *their* word. And without witnesses who trust the government as I once did, organized crime, whether it be outlaw bikers, the Mafia, or Chinese triads, will flourish, picking the pockets of Canadian and American citizens alike.

AFTERWORD

From Toronto all the way to Orlando, Florida, Canadians and Americans alike are under seige. They are hostage to a new and increasingly dangerous organized crime intent on intimidation, extortion, drug trafficking, murder, and the infiltration of the consumer marketplace. Its aim — to accumulate wealth.

Organized crime takes many forms: motorcycle gangs larger in membership than Cosa Nostra; Asian gangs with hundreds of thousands of members internationally, from Hong Kong to the Netherlands; a Calabrian Honoured Society that blends insidiously into the cultural mosaic of North American society and Australia as well; Colombians who export death in the form of tons of cocaine; Russian emigrés who murder, steal, cheat, and import and sell doctored oil, while evading hundreds of millions of dollars in fuel taxes; Israeli Mafia hoodlums who traffick in narcotics and dupe insurance companies out of millions; dozens of new and dangerous ethnic gangs that prey on their own people before branching out to victimize society in general; and Cosa Nostra, the criminal enterprise that spans our two nations and infiltrates every fabric of society, corrupting, murdering, and plundering our resources.

It is an awesome, frightening array of criminal organizations that our law enforcement communities and governments must face down and fight with an increasingly limited array of weaponry and an even more limited number of experienced, qualified investigators. Wiretaps, bugs, informers — all are vital to the battle. So are laws such as the Racketeer-Influenced Corrupt Organization statute so successfully used in recent years against Cosa Nostra and other organized crime groups by federal authorities in the United States, a law Canada lacks but its law officers seek.

But the most vital and effective tool of all is the witness against organized crime. He has to be cultivated and nurtured. He has to be carefully used, and, more important, his role as a criminal must be weighed against the value of the evidence he can provide.

Witnesses can sometimes be forced to testify with the threat of a jail sentence or other dire consequences, but in organized-crime cases they generally testify only when the government agrees to a deal. That deal frequently ensures immunity from prosecution for past crimes, a promise of job opportunity and training after testifying, subsistence for the witness and his family while he's testifying, and a new identity.

The United States Congress, in its infinite wisdom, authorized the creation of the Witness Protection Program in 1970. More than six thousand witnesses have passed through that program after testifying for federal and state authorities. Under the control of the United States marshals, it has often been maligned, sometimes with justification, for failing to live up to the promises given to witnesses and for failing to provide the proper protection, identity documentation, and job opportunities for those witnesses.

Canada had a golden opportunity to learn from the mistakes of the Witness Protection Program and provide a more stable future for its witnesses. It failed miserably with Cecil Kirby.

Like him or not, Cecil Kirby made a deal with his government to gather evidence against the kingpins of organized crime in Ontario. And he was successful beyond the wildest dreams of those who cultivated him. Unlike so many witnesses, he was a man of his word. He lived up to the promises he gave to testify. And he went beyond the pale. After charges had been filed against a number of Calabrian crime leaders, he carried a body mike so he could gather more evidence against more criminals.

Without question, the Canadian government saved millions of dollars by using Kirby. He provided them with a wealth of intelligence on outlaw bikers and the Calabrian Mafia and led agents into the world of the Rounders. These are all criminal societies with codes of silence that until Kirby surfaced, law enforcement had been unable to properly penetrate and attack.

Kirby is owed a debt — a debt made payable because of the promises that were made to him when he embarked on his dangerous and shocking adventure. While his subsistence has continued, promises of job training and a solid, documented new identity have not been kept. What is worse, Kirby has been left to his own devices, to survive by his own wits and instincts without the necessary protection, counselling, and guidance for his relocation, re-identification, and job placement.

Incredibly, while working for government agencies, Kirby worked for some months without immunity, without an agreement in writing, without subsistence or expenses. He lived by his wits. He was forced to use the funds collected from criminal conspiracies to pay his bills and feed his family. He was required to use his father's car, and quite often his father paid for the gas used to help the government gather its evidence.

By any standard of law enforcement undercover operations, the penny-pinching practices of the police forces involved was amateurish and patently dangerous. Kirby should have been properly funded and, as a result, never permitted to keep the proceeds of a criminal investigation, as he was in the conspiracy to murder Helen Nafpliotis of Connecticut.

Unless a vigorous and carefully constructed witness program is developed in Canada, law enforcement officers and prosecutors will soon find that witnesses such as Kirby will not become willing weapons against organized crime. Sources of information and intelligence will dry up, and the word will spread in the underworld that the law and those who administer it do not keep their word. Without that trust there can be no effective fight against organized crime in Canada or the United States. And in a world where new organized-crime groups are breeding like rats on the waterfront, this could be a fatal mistake—one that could have profound and immensely costly effects on the public at large.

1

CONVICTIONS AS A RESULT OF KIRBY TESTIMONY

COSIMO COMMISSO
•1981   Conspiracy to murder, three counts (Helen Nafpliotis, Pietro Scarcella, Paul Volpe): eight years each count, concurrent. Counselling to commit murder: two years, concurrent.
•1984 (**March**)   Conspiracy to set fires (Guelph sporting goods store): sixteen months, consecutive to time already being served. Conspiracy to possess stolen cigarettes: six months, concurrent.
•1984 (**April**)   Counsel-to-murder conspiracy, two counts: eight years each count, concurrent, but consecutive to the time already being served. In addition, he received sentences of from three to eight years, concurrent, for charges that included extortion, explosion with intent, arson, counsel to extortion, aggravated assault, and willfully setting fires.

ROCCO REMO COMMISSO
•1981   Conspiracy to murder, two counts (Scarcella, Volpe): eight years each count, concurrent.
•1984 (**March**)   Conspiracy to possess stolen cigarettes: six months, consecutive to the eight years already being served.
•1984 (**April**)   Counsel-to-murder conspiracy: six years, consecutive to the time already being served. In addition, he received sentences of from three to six years, concurrent, for charges that included extortion, arson, explosion with intent, and aggravated assault.

MICHELE COMMISSO
•**1981**   Conspiracy to murder, three counts (Nafpliotis, Scarcella, Volpe): two and a half years each count, concurrent.
•**1983 (April)**   Released under mandatory supervision.
•**1984 (April)**   Planned arson: sentence suspended, two years' probation.

ANTONIO ROCCO ROMEO
•**1981**   Conspiracy to murder (Nafpliotis): two and a half years.

GERARDO RUSSO
•**1981**   Conspiracy to murder (Nafpliotis): two years, ten months.

VINCENZO MELIA
•**1982**   Conspiracy to murder (Nafpliotis): nine years. Currently free on parole.

COSIMO MERCURI
•**1982**   Second-degree murder and arson (Dominion Hotel, Acton): life imprisonment, no consideration for parole for ten years.

MICHAEL McCRYSTAL
•**1982**   Manslaughter (Dominion Hotel, Acton): two years less a day.

ARMANDO DICAPUA
•**1983**   Arson conspiracy (Guelph sporting goods store): two years.

ROCCO MASTRANGELO
•**1984**   Arson conspiracy (Guelph sporting goods store): one year.

BRUNO SPIZZICHINO
•**1984**   Arson conspiracy (Guelph sporting goods store): two years.

NICHOLAS PALLOTTA
•**1982**   Robbery (Dolly Jewellers): two years.

RICHARD CUCMAN
•**1982** Robbery (Dolly Jewellers): three years.

ANTONIO TRIUMBOLI
•**1983** Three years.

ISTVAN SZOCS
•**1983** Attempted extortion: six months.

RICHARD CORBETT
•**1983** Possession of stolen cigarettes: three months.

ARMAND SANGUIGNI
•**1983** Possession of stolen cigarettes: three months.

In addition to the above, Kirby supplied information that led to the arrest and conviction of twenty more people, including disco owner HAROLD ARVIV for the bombing of Arviv's disco; disco manager YVO SAJET for filing a false report with the police in the robbery of the cash boxes from the Hippopotamus disco; and CHARLES (CHUCK) YANOVER for his part in the plot to overthrow the government of Dominica, possession of forty-two pounds of hashish (three people arrested), conspiracy to smuggle gold out of British Guinea (one person arrested), five robberies, two shootings, and information on six unsolved homicides.

2
STRUCTURE OF THE HONOURED SOCIETY

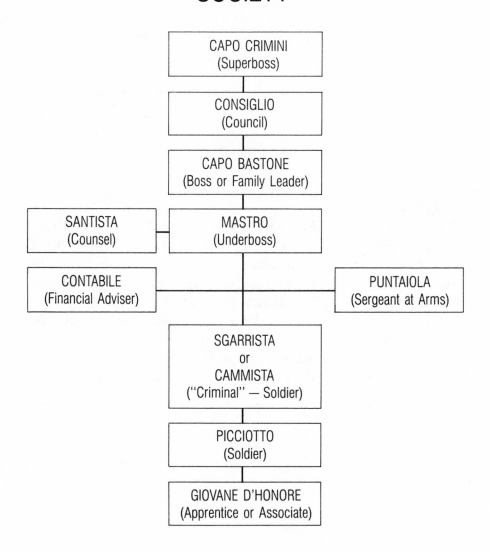

CAPO CRIMINI
(Superboss)

CONSIGLIO
(Council)

CAPO BASTONE
(Boss or Family Leader)

SANTISTA
(Counsel)

MASTRO
(Underboss)

CONTABILE
(Financial Adviser)

PUNTAIOLA
(Sergeant at Arms)

SGARRISTA
or
CAMMISTA
("Criminal" — Soldier)

PICCIOTTO
(Soldier)

GIOVANE D'HONORE
(Apprentice or Associate)

CAPO CRIMINI: The highest-ranking boss in the Honoured Society or Calabrian Mafia. He is the equivalent of a Cosa Nostra boss of bosses, but that title is rarely used. The last-known boss of bosses was the late Don Antonio Macri of Siderno.

CONSIGLIO: The sitting Council or ruling body of the Honoured Society, which includes the most influential bosses of the organization. The *Consiglio* is roughly the equivalent of the Cosa Nostra Commission, with between nine and eleven members.

CAPO BASTONE: Calabrian or Honoured Society boss. It is an archaic term that is generally no longer used, having been supplanted by the shortened title of *Capo*, or "Head." This includes all bosses in each area. There are fifty-four bosses in Calabria, and there were three suspected bosses in Canada, including Cosimo Commisso and the late Mike Racco. A *Capo Bastone* is the equivalent of a Cosa Nostra crime boss, such as Anthony Salerno of the Genovese family or Antonio (Ducks) Corallo of the Lucchese family.

MASTRO: Second-in-command of a Calabrian family. The *Mastro* is similar in stature and responsibilities to the underboss of a Cosa Nostra family. He is the *Capo Bastone*'s right-hand man.

SANTISTA: The family adviser, the equivalent of Cosa Nostra's *consiglieri*. The *Santista* gives counsel and advice if asked to by the *Capo Bastone* or the *Mastro*. He is usually an older man with experience who enjoys the respect of family members at both high and low levels. The name is derived from the Greek word that means "to act as an honourable person."

CONTABILE: There is no equivalent of this position in Cosa Nostra. The *Contabile* is the family's financial adviser and is generally an attorney or accountant. He usually picks up money, gets bail for incarcerated members, and invests money for the *Capo Bastone*. He can be a businessman with legitimate business fronts. He is often in direct communication with the boss and directs communication on important financial matters.

PUNTAIOLA: Roughly the equivalent of a Cosa Nostra *capo decima* or crime captain. The name is an expression that is known to mean "a stick with a nail at the end used to move animals," a prod.

SGARRISTA or CAMMISTA (CAMORRISTA): The equivalent of a higher-than-average soldier in Cosa Nostra. He approaches businesses for extortion purposes and gives orders to associates and *picciotti* who work under him. He is a visible operator of the family.

PICCIOTTO: The worker, the out-front hustler, and the enforcer who plants bombs and beats loan-shark victims. He is the muscle of the Honoured Society and is directly associated with criminal activities. His equivalent in Cosa Nostra is the soldier, the "made guy," the "wise guy."

GIOVANE D'HONORE: A person who wants to become a member of the Honoured Society. In Cosa Nostra he is the trusted associate vying for initiation as a member. He is required to do favours for the organization to prove his loyalty. He must have the right background and the right friends and, before becoming a member, must be sponsored by someone in the Honoured Society. Once accepted, he is initiated, as are new members of Cosa Nostra, in a ritualistic ceremony in which he swears loyalty to the organization and *omerta* (silence) on pain of death.

3
STRUCTURE OF A TYPICAL MOTORCYCLE GANG

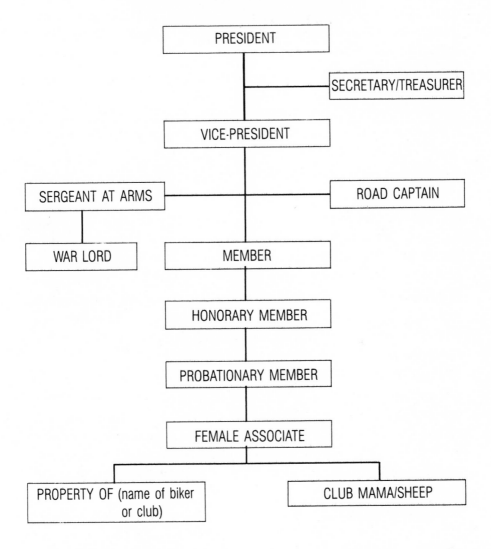

PRESIDENT: The leader of the motorcycle club and the person who makes the final decision about all club business. He rules the club with an iron hand and can overrule any decisions voted on by the club membership.

SECRETARY/TREASURER: Keeps the minutes of all club meetings and collects dues and fines. He pays club bills and any bail for members who are arrested. He is responsible for the names and telephone numbers on the club roster and keeps all the books on club-related business.

VICE-PRESIDENT: Fills in during the president's absence.

SERGEANT AT ARMS: Keeps order during all club meetings and outings and usually rides at the rear of the pack on club runs.

ROAD CAPTAIN: Is in charge of the club during runs and rides at the front of the pack with the president. The club forms in two columns behind them, and no member passes them or leaves the column unless his motorcycle has mechanical problems.

WAR LORD: Carries out the president's orders when the club goes to war with another club. In many instances he keeps the club's arsenal.

MEMBER: A biker who has passed his Striker or probationary period and has been indoctrinated and accepted by members of the outlaw club. He pays dues, carries out orders of club officers, and is entitled to wear the "colours" of the club.

HONORARY MEMBER: Usually a member in good standing for a number of years who then retires from the club. He pays no club dues, wears the club colours, and must attend club funerals.

PROBATIONARY MEMBER: Must be nominated by a club member in good standing and wears an arm band, not the club colours. He does all the menial jobs around the clubhouse and on runs, and he must commit any criminal act deemed necessary by the club. To become a full-fledged member of the club, the membership casts a vote; two dissenting votes can continue the probationary period.

FEMALE ASSOCIATE: There are two types of female associate. The property of a club member is an associate of a member in good standing and can wear the club colours with a rocker. Other club members are not allowed to touch or train her. The club mama or sheep is a woman of loose morals who mingles with club members. She cannot wear the club colours, and she can be used by any club member for sexual purposes.

4

CRIMINAL ACTIVITIES OF OUTLAW MOTORCYCLE GANGS

Murder
Assault
Arson
Rape
Prostitution
International White Slavery
Kidnapping
Massage Parlours
Burglary
Bank Robbery
Bombing
Gambling
Manufacture, Importation, and Distribution of Narcotics
Forger of Government Documents
Theft of Trans-Border Shipments
Trans-Border Transport of Stolen Property
Theft at American Military Installations
Hijacking of Trucks
Extortion and Blackmail
Insurance Fraud
Theft of Motorcycles and Automobiles
Gun Running
Loan-Sharking

5
SIMILARITIES OF ORGANIZATIONAL STRUCTURE

TYPICAL ORGANIZED CRIME FAMILY

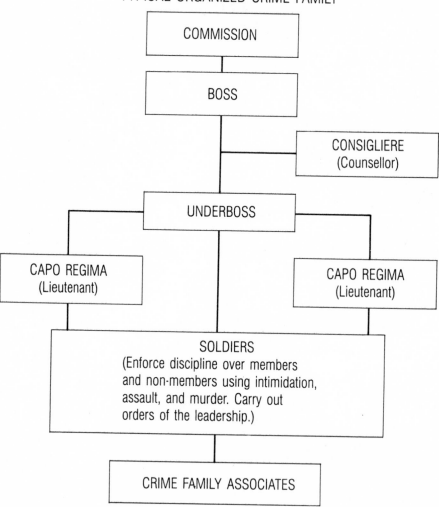

- Corruption of police and public officials.
- Exercise control over specific geographical area or specific criminal activities.
- With and/or through non-member associates and fronts engage in, control, or influence:

LEGITIMATE BUSINESSES:	ILLEGAL ACTIVITIES:
Banking	Alcohol
Bars, Clubs, Casinos	Arson
Food Products	Assault
Garbage and Sanitation	Blackmail
Labour Unions	Bombing
Produce	Corruption
Securities	Extortion
Waterfront Activities	Gambling
Cleaners and Launderers	Hijacking of Trucks
Uniforms, Towels, Hotel Supplies	Intimidation of Witnesses
Real Estate	Labour Racketeering
Restaurants	Loan-Sharking
Entertainment	Murder
Vending Machines	Narcotics
	Prostitution
	Robbery
	Securities Fraud
	Theft

TYPICAL MAJOR MOTORCYCLE GANG CHAPTER

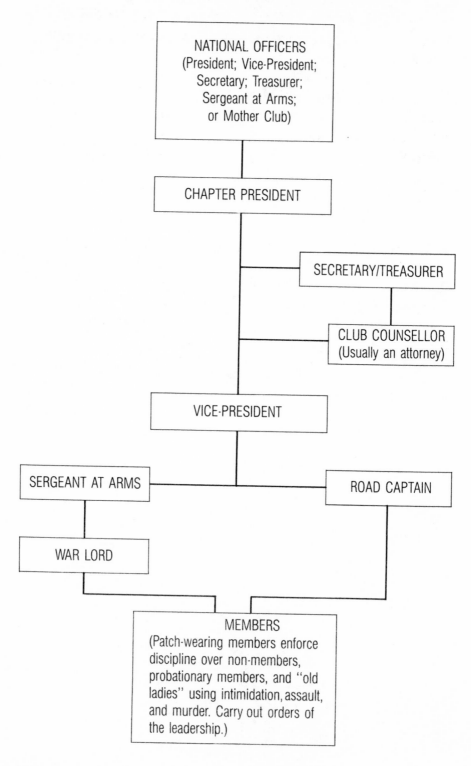

- Corruption of police and public officials.
- Exercise control over specific geographical area or specific criminal activities.
- With and/or through non-member associates and fronts engage in, control, or influence:

LEGITIMATE BUSINESSES:

Amusement Arcades
Antiques
Auto Salvage and Wrecking
Bars and Clubs
Billiard Parlours
Construction
Entertainment
Firearms Dealers
Florist Shops
Food Products and Catering
Independent Trucking
Massage Parlours
Motorcycle Shops
Real Estate
Restaurants
Tattoo Parlours
Trailer Parks
Vending Machines

ILLEGAL ACTIVITIES:

Arson
Assault
Blackmail
Bombing
Corruption
Extortion
Kidnapping
Insurance Fraud
Hijacking of Trucks
Loan-Sharking
Murder
Narcotics Trafficking
Pornography
Prostitution
Rape
Robbery

INDEX